Another Lousy Day in Paradise

and

Dances with Trout

JOHN GIERACH

With a New Introduction by the Author

Illustrated by Glenn Wolff

Simon & Schuster Paperbacks
New York   London   Toronto   Sydney

Simon & Schuster Paperbacks
A Division of Simon & Schuster, Inc.
1230 Avenue of the Americas
New York, NY 10020

First Simon & Schuster trade paperback edition April 2011

SIMON & SCHUSTER PAPERBACKS and colophon are registered
trademarks of Simon & Schuster, Inc.

For information about special discounts for bulk purchases,
please contact Simon & Schuster Special Sales at 1-866-506-1949
or business@simonandschuster.com.

The Simon & Schuster Speakers Bureau can bring authors to
your live event. For more information or to book an event,
contact the Simon & Schuster Speakers Bureau at
1-866-248-3049 or visit our website at www.simonspeakers.com.

Manufactured in the United States of America

10 9 8 7 6 5 4 3 2

Library of Congress Cataloging-in-Publication Data is available.

ISBN: 978-1-4516-2127-3

These titles were previously published individually.

TABLE OF CONTENTS

Dances with Trout

INTRODUCTION

by John Gierach

I may not be the only writer who's through with a book by the time he's finished with it. You can work on a book for what seems like forever, until you've forgotten you ever did anything else. A friend said it sounds like doing homework for a living and she's not far wrong. You spend your days painstakingly writing and rewriting, then reading and rereading what you've written, stopping often to stare at sentences that obviously aren't right without being able to tell what's wrong with them. Maybe another cup of coffee would help, or another long walk.

It's not an unpleasant job—in fact, it's a job I worked long and hard to get and wouldn't trade for anything—but it's awfully time consuming, and a lot of your work rightfully ends up on the cutting room floor. A writer friend says, "You know you're about done with a book when you start putting things back the way they were in the first draft." Another writer suggests never beginning a sentence with, "Suddenly . . ." An editor once told me any book would be improved by simply removing all the adjectives. Which is to say, there are rules of thumb but no shortcuts.

When you do finally let go of it, the manuscript seems perfect down to the last comma, but when it comes back from the copy editor, the profusion of red pencil marks sends you on yet another long walk. (In the course of writing this book you've hiked six hundred miles in three- and four-mile increments. Your brain may be mush, but your thighs are like leaf springs.)

But then when you sit down to go over the thing word by word yet again, you see that, as usual, the copyediting is dead-on nine times out of ten and that tenth time is a judgment call that could go either way. You might put one or two of those back the way they were to create the impression of control, but on the whole you accept the changes gratefully. A copy editor can't turn a bad book into a good one, but he can leave a book exactly the way the author would have written it if he'd done a noticeably better job.

Sometime later the typeset galleys arrive. At this point you're mostly looking for typos, and although the galleys have already been gone over by a professional, you get the final approval. That means anything that slips through now into the finished book will be your fault. Unfortunately, I'm a rotten proofreader, especially when it comes to my own work. By this point in the process I have the book all but memorized. I know what I wrote and that's what I see, regardless of what actually appears on the page.

Even under the best of circumstances, typos are insidious: capable of hiding in plain sight from any number of careful readers. I've found the odd typo in several of my books—and I don't mean in the manuscripts or galleys when there was still time to make the save, but after they were in print. In every case they were so obvious they might as well have been set in bold type, but they'd somehow slipped through anyway. A friend of mine even had a typo on the cover of one of his books. Instead of "time-tested" in the subtitle, it said, "tme tested." No one saw it until the book was printed, shipped, and on the shelves. Then everyone saw it.

In the end, there's the usual satisfaction of finishing a big job and, after all, writing and fishing are the only things I ever really wanted to do and I now write about fishing for a living, so what's not to love? It's just that when all the work is done, the book and I are a little tired of each other and need some time apart. Life being what it is, sometimes that trial separation becomes permanent.

Which is to say, until the publisher decided to do this omnibus edition and asked me to write an introduction, I hadn't cracked either of these books since they were published fourteen and sixteen years ago. Reading them again was like getting a long letter from someone I used to know well, but hadn't heard from in a long time.

As always with my own work, I had to fight the now nearly irresistible urge to edit. I don't mean that I found mistakes or things I didn't like, and it wouldn't matter if I had. (A published book is like the adult son who's finally moved out of your basement. You still love him and always will, but it's time for him to fend for himself.) It's just that other writers' words on paper always seem permanent or even preordained, while my own, through force of habit, strike me as provisional. It could be that, to its author, no work ever seems quite finished. That would explain why The Grateful Dead never played a song the same way twice. Fans who followed them from concert to concert counted on the fact that those guys could never stop tweaking. Of course I mean "tweaking" in the editorial sense.

But by now it was just plain fun to go back and read about my first trip to Labrador in *Another Lousy Day in Paradise*. I've been back to that Canadian province five times since—once to the same fishing camp, four times to other remote parts of the region. It's become one of my favorite places to go, even though it takes me five flights and two grueling days from the nearest airport in Denver before I board a small floatplane and the trip really begins—or maybe because of that. I've made some friends there, I've caught lots of fish and have been stranded for days at a time by bad weather on three different occasions, once in a hotel in Goose Bay, once in a cabin and once in a tent. (Believe it or not, I enjoyed the tent the most.) That essay constitutes my first impression of a place that I've since come to know better and love more. Like many first impressions, it wasn't wrong, just incomplete.

The same goes for Alaska. My first trip there, recounted in *Dances with Trout,* was pleasantly frenetic. Every other day we were on a different river with a different guide, catching rainbows, arctic char, Dolly Varden, sockeye salmon, and grayling, but never staying in one place long enough to lose that sense of perpetual strangeness. I found that I remembered the fishing and most of the people, but I'd completely forgotten about the totally rebuilt De Havilland Beaver floatplane known as The Cream Puff that I used as a symbol of the whole misfit subculture of Alaskan guides and bush pilots. I didn't remember getting quite so literary with that one.

On my next trip to Alaska, I settled down on one river for the duration and fell into a comfortable routine—or as comfortable as you can get while sharing a river with six-hundred-pound bears. It wasn't better or worse, just different, and I got more sleep.

On the other hand, trips to Scotland for Atlantic salmon and Texas for Guadalupe bass were onetime events. I liked both places but, for one reason or another, I never went back to either one. Also, two of the people I fished with on those trips—Bud Priddy in Texas and the writer Scott Waldie in Scotland—have since died, so my recollections of those places are not only self-contained, but bittersweet.

It also occurred to me that I haven't appreciably changed my work habits since writing those two books. For some reason, one of the most common questions I'm asked at book signings is, "Do you take notes on trips?" I do and always have, but only enough to help me remember the nuts and bolts. Beyond that I almost never work on essays on-site to avoid the temptation of trying to arrange an adventure along literary lines. I'm not against that on ethical grounds; I just learned early on that it never works. I may be a professional writer who's always sniffing out a story, but it still seems best just to go fishing for the same reason other people do, which, as near as I can tell, is simple curiosity.

I've also learned that if I go to work on a story too soon after I get home, the first draft usually amounts to a flat recitation of events more or less in order, not unlike the interminable vacation slideshows I was forced to watch as a child. "Here we are getting on the plane." "Here we are in our seats." "Here's Bob going down the aisle to the bathroom . . ." I've always operated on Nick Lyons's dictum that the best fishing stories aren't about fishing, so I want to begin writing before the memories have passed their expiration date but after they've settled and the odd, left-handed stuff has begun to float to the surface.

It also helps to let the residual excitement pass. Aspiring writers often assume that the best stories are those that mean the most to you, but in fact the best ones tend to be those you can be objective about. The emotion may be the heart of the story and you don't want to lose sight of it, but an essay is an attempt at communication and that takes a steadier hand.

Of course I do sometimes wonder what happens to the actual recollections in the course of turning real experiences into essays. It's no secret that memories fade with time, and, for that matter, both psychologists and philosophers tell us there's no guarantee that we're seeing what we think we're seeing even as it happens. But even assuming that the raw material is real, multiple retellings cause some events to take on greater or lesser significance, while others vanish entirely and time expands, contracts, and in some cases ceases to be linear. So in the first draft, the memory becomes the story, while by the final draft, the story has become the memory. The essay still tells the truth, but it's no longer the whole truth and nothing but. If you've done your job right, it's better than that.

—John Gierach

Another Lousy Day in Paradise

The wild geese do not know where they are
but they are not lost.

—JAMES P. CARSE

1

Another Lousy Day in Paradise

A long time ago, my old fishing partner A. K. Best and I decided not to count, weigh or measure our fish, or otherwise keep score, so as to avoid the competitiveness that can creep into fly-fishing if you're not careful. Or maybe we didn't actually sit down and decide; maybe it just happened. Anyway, we've been more or less sticking to that for years now, and although it hasn't exactly made saints of either one of us, it's an outlook we like: the idea that success in fishing is something you have to work out for yourself—pretty much without reference to how the guy in the next boat is doing.

Okay, but then after the first day at Anne Marie Camp in Labrador, we broke down and began keeping records of the brook trout we caught and released. We told ourselves the guides were counting and weighing the fish anyway and it's only polite for outsiders to observe the local custom, but I have to say we got into it. And why not? In a confusing world, you have to have the guts to break your own rules.

A.K. and I have always had soft spots for brook trout —because they're pretty, tough in some ways but delicate in others, and because big ones are so rare—and for years we'd talked about fishing for them in Labrador, which is the spiritual heart, if not the exact geographic center, of the brookies' native range.

So on the premise that life is short, I picked up the phone one day, called Doug Schlink at Angler Adventures in Connecticut and asked him where the best brook trout fishing in Labrador was. He said, "Jack and Lorraine Cooper's camp at Anne Marie Lake."

I'd heard of this place and seen the magazine ads saying the brook trout caught there *averaged* 5½ pounds. I can't exactly say I didn't believe that, but, like some other fishermen I'd talked to, I was a little skeptical. I mean, to survive at all in this civilization of ours you have to assume that advertising is a fabric of lies, and this wouldn't have been the first time either fish size or the benefits of toothpaste were overblown in print.

Then again, wonderful things do exist out there in the world, and if you hope to see some of them you can't just sit at home stewing in your own cynicism, so we decided to go anyway. Doug said that, allowing for the normal vicissitudes of fishing, the claims were pretty much true (he has actually fished at most of the places he books trips to, claiming it's part of his job), and as I said to A.K., "So what if they only average *four* pounds? I could live with that, couldn't you?"

So, just to get this out of the way, of the brook trout I kept track of at Anne Marie, my smallest weighed $2\frac{1}{2}$ pounds, my largest went $7\frac{1}{4}$, most were between 5 and 6 and the average weight was, lo and behold, 5.45 pounds: close enough to constitute truth in advertising.

It still seems a little strange to put it in those terms— sort of like saying that, taken together, Charles Dickens, Mark Twain and Edgar Allan Poe average out to 190 pounds of dead writer—but I guess it does make the point. Judging from the world records that have come out of the area, these are probably the biggest brook trout anywhere.

The Minipi watershed is huge and "roadless," as they say —a word I've always liked the sound of. For that matter, most of Labrador itself is roadless: In something like 120,000 square miles there are just two highways, both gravel. Anne Marie Lake is just under 100 miles by float-plane from the small port and military outpost town of Goose Bay, which is a snug little settlement, even if there isn't much in the way of nightlife.

But of course that doesn't matter. Unless you get stranded there by weather (which does happen), it's just the place where you get off the twin-prop Dash-8, drive down to the dock and get on a de Havilland Twin Otter or one of the other planes I really like: the kind that are probably at least as old as I am, but more dependable.

From Goose Bay, Anne Marie Lake lies to the south, in low, rolling hills thickly forested in black spruce, tamarack, birch and such: archetypal sprawling, cool, damp, dense, sweet-smelling, bug-infested north-woods lake country. There are countless lakes, ponds, puddles and sloughs, most unnamed, many of which are connected by flowing channels that most of us would call trout streams but that are referred to locally as "narrows."

The fishing in the Minipi watershed was discovered by Lee Wulff, exploring in his Super Cub back in 1957, and the camp at Anne Marie Lake was established in the early 1960s by Ray Cooper (no relation to the current owners). From the beginning, mostly due to Wulff's prodding, the rule was fly-fishing only, with a limit of one brook trout per fisherman, per trip. Lee said this was the best brook trout fishing in the world and he thought people should see what a place is like when "God manages the fishery"—a statement I take to be more poetic than theological.

Catch and release with a one-fish limit was a pretty futuristic idea back in the early '60s, when carnage was still pretty much the rule at wilderness camps, and they say the guides squawked louder than the clients. But records going back three decades indicate that the fish are about as big now as they ever were. That's a claim not many camps that have been in operation that long can make.

Without getting too sloppy about it, I have to say the fishing here is a testament to the radical idea of doing the right thing in the first place instead of screwing it up and then trying to fix it later. If there's anything wrong with the way all this was handled it's that, unbelievably, you can't find a Wulff Lake or even a Lee's Narrows on the map. On the other hand, you can still fish Howard's Point with the very Howard for whom it was named.

The guides now at the camp are sold on catch-and-release fishing, and they handle the brookies tenderly. Technically, though you *are* allowed to keep that one fish as a trophy—and some anglers still do that—A.K. and I didn't, nor did anyone else in camp that week, but I can't say the temptation wasn't there. I don't know if the guides actually discourage the practice, because it never really came up, but I can say they don't *en*courage it, even when a fish is clearly trophy sized. The upshot has been, in the previous two seasons only eight brook trout have been killed at the camp, and there's evidence that even the head-hunters are mellowing out a little, beginning to wonder what point they're trying to make.

I talked to a guy several years ago who'd been to Anne Marie and had caught a 6 pounder he'd had stuffed. (He carried photos of the mount in his wallet.) Then he went back the following season and got a $7\frac{1}{2}$ pounder. "I really wanted to kill that fish," he said, "but then I thought, What the hell would I do with the little one?"

I will admit that when I landed my $7\frac{1}{4}$ pounder (I mean a *$7\frac{1}{4}$-pound brook trout*, for Christ's sake) I experienced a moment of weakness. The guide was holding the trout in the net. I looked at him; he looked at me and said, "Nice fish, ey?" I said "Yup," and he released it. It was a fairly close call.

Later, over shore lunch, A.K. said, "You're never gonna mount a fish, are you?"

I said, "I don't know. Maybe not."

I've always held off on stuffing a fish because I knew it would have to be a real milestone: a trout so big, so heroically caught and otherwise so perfect that I'd never get another one anything like it. I went to Labrador for fish like that and caught some, but once there I just couldn't get away from the idea that there are not a whole lot of brook trout there, and that if up to eight anglers a week for an

eleven- or twelve-week season each kept a big fish, there'd
be a real dent in the population after not too many years.

As it is, if you bring five or six of these pigs to the net
in a fourteen-hour day, you're doing as well as can be
expected, better than most, and you can see that only a
greedy shit would want more than that. So sure, it would
be fun to have the brook trout of a lifetime hanging on the
wall for all your fishing friends to drool over, but you'd
have to have no regrets about it, and avoiding regret is
getting harder and harder these days.

Don't get me wrong. I haven't become a pacifist or an
eco-Nazi, it's just that this is one of those delicate natural
balances you always hear about but don't often see in the
flesh. There's more than enough food and adequate
spawning habitat for the brook trout, but there are also
many predators—pike, char, osprey, mink, otters, etc.—to
keep their numbers in check and allow the few survivors
to grow large. Eliminate or even reduce the predator populations and you might get more brook trout, but they'd be
smaller.

To put it in terms of regional history, there was a time
when guides killed pike because they ate the brookies;
now they release them for the same reason.

It also helps that these brook trout can live as long as
ten years, unlike their relatives farther south who rarely
make it to even half that age. You'll sometimes hear that
these Labrador brookies are a separate race, and for all I
know that's true, but a fisheries biologist recently told me
it's just that the same species of fish tend to have longer life
spans as the growing seasons get shorter. The growing
season *is* short in Labrador—it's not that far from the Arctic
Circle—but the waters are so rich that the average growth
rate for brook trout is still about a pound a year.

So when you get a real big one and you're tempted to

kill it for a mount, you have to think about all that. And if the biological realities don't get to you, you can always remind yourself that for what a good taxidermist would charge you to stuff that fish, you could buy a week on the best spring creek in Montana.

One of the great things about fishing with an old friend is that the same things automatically stick in both your minds, so you can pick up the thread of a ten-hour-old conversation without a lengthy preface. Out on the front porch that evening, looking for northern lights, I said to A.K., "Maybe if it had gone *eight* pounds . . ."

When I got home and some friends asked about the trip, they winced a little at the size of the brook trout I described. I even told it tastefully, starting at a modest, less-than-average 5 pounds and working my way up dramatically to 7-plus. But as the fish got bigger, the eyes of some listeners began to narrow. They probably didn't think I was actually lying, just that I'd gotten excited and had guessed high, as fishermen are known to do.

When I got the snapshots back and showed them around, my friends said okay, but then some doubted that I'd caught most of these hogs on size 16 flies. The only thing they seemed to buy without question was that there weren't a whole lot of fish and that that was as it should be. Any angler who's been around can see the logic in that.

The thing about fishing is, at about the point where it begins to take over your life, it becomes a search for quality, not so much from the spoiled or vain delusion that you deserve it, but because, just this once, it seems like it would be fun to learn for yourself what quality is, instead of accepting someone else's definition.

It turns out that a thing of quality is exactly as it should be. It may or may not be what you hoped for, but if it's not, it's your hopes that were flawed, not reality. In a word, it's appropriate—like the fact that the longest sentence in the English language is in a book called *Confessions of an English Opium Eater* by Thomas De Quincey. Of course. Where else would it be?

And, naturally, the biggest brook trout in the world would be few and far between, wouldn't they?

So most of our days in Labrador were spent hunting fish: out in the morning after breakfast, lunch on a sandbar somewhere, back to the camp for supper and then back out on the water until about ten in the evening, later if things were really cooking.

There's a lot of water here, but there are only a relative handful of more or less dependable spots where the brook trout are known to congregate at certain times of year. On any given day you tour a few of those places off in one direction or another, sometimes hitting the same ones at intervals of a couple of hours because, you know, something could have changed—a hatch could have come on.

Now and then, if things were slow, we'd end up blind casting with streamers at the inlets and outlets of narrows where, if fish were there and hungry, there were more or less obvious places for them to be holding. But mostly we cruised in a flat-sterned canoe with an 8-horse outboard, looking for rising fish.

If the trout were working, they were usually around some kind of structure—a rocky point or a bed of lily pads. The guide would roar up in the boat, cutting the motor far out to keep the wake down, and then quietly switching to a paddle. Then we'd all watch for a while, usually without conversation. If fish were rising, boiling, tailing or otherwise showing themselves, we'd cast to them. If not, we'd watch for a while longer, then crank up the outboard and try another spot.

Most days there were several hours of furious fishing and as many more hours of cruising in the canoe with time to relax and look around. This is lovely, green, silent country, and you're far enough into it that you won't meet anyone you didn't have breakfast with that morning. Sometimes I'd sit back and think, I might come to a place like this just for the hell of it, even if there weren't huge brook trout.

That's crap, of course; it's just that when I'm in wild country far from home I tend to feel calmer and more grateful to be alive than I really am. Maybe that's why I do this.

You fall into a routine at a fishing camp, and at a *good* camp you almost begin to feel at home. I liked this place. The four-bedroom cabin, with woodstove, that serves as a lodge is old, clean, comfortable and funky. There are no vaulted ceilings, no two-story picture windows, no fabulous collections of game mounts. (What looks at first like a big, stuffed brookie is actually a painted wood carving.) This is a by-God cabin in the north woods where fishermen stay, built out on an open point to catch the breeze off the lake. If some mosquitos get in at night and there aren't enough bats in the loft to eat them all, those are the breaks.

And the people have that firm grasp on reality I always envy in those who make a living in the real world, whether they guide fishermen or grow corn. Rule one is, Well, I won't get it done sittin' here drinking coffee. Rule two is, The best you can do is the best you can do, so don't panic.

•

They say if you're going to fish for brook trout in Labrador you should bring lots of dry flies and nymphs in lots of different sizes because there are many hatches and they're mostly uncatalogued. A fly-tying kit would be handy, but it would also be a clumsy piece of luggage, considering that the round trip from Denver takes ten separate flights over four days.

The guides are pretty casual about fly patterns—much more so than some of the clients—and that's refreshing. Fly-fishing does get way too scientific at times, although I guess that still beats the phony-macho, pulp-magazine approach I grew up with. Back in the 1950s, this story would have been called, "I Fought Labrador's Killer Trout and Lived!"

It's also a good idea to have some streamers—Muddlers and Mickey Finns are favorites—and some #2 deer-hair lemmings. (Okay, if you're not an absolute purist, a mouse pattern or even a bass bug will do.) We didn't see any lemming action, but I'm told that in years when these little critters' populations are high, the brookies feed on them ravenously. It's best to have a fair number of streamers and mice because, unless you're in the habit of fishing wire leaders for brook trout, you'll lose some of your big flies to pike.

The guides say the hatches of the really big bugs—stoneflies, mayflies and caddis all up to size 2 and 4—are glorious but unpredictable; that during some hatches you'll catch big landlocked arctic char on dry flies; that a snow-shoe hare is called an *ookalik;* that Sasquatches can sometimes be heard howling in the night and so on. They say a lot of things in the course of a week's fishing and, since these guides have been there a long time and seem to know what they're talking about, you listen. Eventually you get a faint but larger picture, even though as a tourist sport you know you'll only ever see thin slices of the local reality.

Friends back home have asked me if the brook trout up there were selective. That's the third question a fisherman asks, after "How many?" and "How big?" In translation it means, "Are they easy?" because, after all, brook trout have the *reputation* for being easy.

The answer, as always, is yes and no. Mostly we tried to match the shape, size, color and action of the bugs the fish were feeding on because that's just how we fish, but the accepted wisdom is, these fish are huge and wild, but they're still brook trout with a brook trout's inherent goofiness. So if what should work, doesn't, you try something else. Hell, try a lemming.

Looking back on it now, most of the trip runs together, as most trips do, while some parts stand out clearly, self-contained.

We saw a few long, lazy multiple hatches lasting half a day or more, stalked a few solitary risers, and one night after dark we sound-fished to huge brookies rising to a spinner fall on a silent, glassy pond between two narrows.

We found a few fish that were very picky (one refused three or four little mayfly dun patterns and finally took an emerger) and a few that would eat a #8 Royal Wulff when there was nothing like a Royal Wulff hatch on the water, or chase a dragged Muddler through a sedate hatch of small mayflies.

One afternoon, a long boat ride and a long portage from camp, we were casting streamers in a lonely stretch of running water. I'd been standing in one spot for almost an hour, running one streamer and then another along a likely looking far bank without a strike, while A.K., fifty yards downstream, had landed two brookies weighing something like 5½ and 6 pounds.

Finally I broke down and yelled, "Okay, what the hell are you using?"

He said, "Size 4 Muddler, of course," as if only an idiot would have failed to deduce the obvious by now.

So I changed flies.

Now, you know how when you've just tied on a new fly and you're standing there with the tippet in your hand and the rod under your arm, you'll just toss the fly on the water at your feet before you start casting? Well, I did that, and a 5-pound brook trout came out from under the rock I was standing on and ate it.

All I could do was pay line out through my fingers until I could get hold of the rod at the ferrule, hand-over-hand my way down to the grip and get the fish on the reel. Once I got things under control and began playing the fish in the conventional manner, I glanced downstream. A.K. was laughing so hard he had to lean on a big boulder to keep from falling in the river. Ray, the guide, was polite enough to just shake his head and grin.

Too bad. I was hoping they hadn't seen it. I did land the fish, though, and I think I handled the whole thing pretty damned well, all things considered.

The weather that week was mostly warm and bright, but we were also treated to a couple days of that maritime rain, wind and cold you can get in the neighborhood of the North Atlantic.

At around ten-thirty at night on the second day of the storm, we were heading back to camp and we had to cross a long, exposed stretch of lake that was boiling up into

2-foot whitecaps. We were in a 16-foot canoe with an 8-horse outboard.

If I'd been driving the boat, we'd have been slapped silly and drenched within half a mile, if not outright swamped and drowned, but our guide for that day—Howard, of Howard's Point fame—slowly rode the swells, gunning the motor gently to slide from one wave to the next, rocking the canoe no more than you'd rock a cradle. There was too much wind and engine noise to yell over, but A.K. turned around in the bow, gave me an amazed look and nodded at Howard by way of saying, "Hell of a boatman." I grinned and nodded back, "Yup, hell of a boatman."

It had been an uncomfortable day of fishing, though somewhat short of actual misery. We'd been wet and chilly since half an hour after breakfast, the coffee at lunch was good and hot, but the sandwiches were soggy. The wind had been biting, but when it calmed to that eerie northwoods silence, the mosquitos materialized, sounding like the whining of a thousand distant dentist's drills. We'd caught some fish. Big ones.

I remember being cold and generally beat up coming back across the lake that night. I wasn't hypothermic, but I was chattering a little, my fingers were numb, and bug bites itched where there was still some feeling. Maybe a mile across the lake, we could see the porch light at the cabin —the only electric light for a hundred miles.

I remember feeling good. Not like Superman or anything, it's just that I was wet and cold in a small canoe on a big lake in a storm a hundred miles from anywhere and I didn't feel fragile or even especially tired. All in all, it was just another lousy day in paradise.

●

So we did well, but there were fish we couldn't catch and some we hooked but couldn't land, which is as it should be. Most days we fished at a pretty leisurely pace, what with the long canoe rides and all, but between the high drama of trying to hook trophy fish and the elation of landing a few, I found it was possible to become emotionally exhausted. By the end of a day I was tired enough that even A.K.'s god-awful snoring didn't keep me awake.

It was glorious fishing, and in six and a half days of it I think I managed not to get too spoiled. Okay, one time I did refer to a 3½-pound brookie as "a little one," but A.K. gave me one of his schoolteacher scowls, and I said, "Yeah, right, what the hell am I saying?"

A week of cosmic fishing never quite seems like enough at the time, but it probably is. I mean, just before you actually start to get used to it, the floatplane comes to take you back to civilization. One morning you're in camp, drinking strong coffee and joking with Helen, the cook. That evening you're in a bar in Halifax, trying to ignore the canned music. You've already made plans to book another week the following year and the conversation has wound down to ten minutes of silence. Then someone says, "Jeez, I didn't think they made brook trout that big!" It's probably best that you left before the newness of it started to wear off.

I guess I should say, the floatplane *usually* comes to take you back. Operations like this often have better on-time records than the major airlines, but this is bush flying, and delays aren't unheard of.

One of the guides told me about a guy who, on what he thought was his last night in camp, drank all his whiskey and gave away all his cigars. Then the weather turned bad and he was stuck there for two more days. To his credit, he didn't ask for his cigars back, but you could tell he wanted to.

And there was this entry in the camp log: "Last day, weather socked in so plane can't come to take us out. Only three fishermen injured in scramble to get back on the water."

We never got around to fishing for the char or pike (both respectable game fish, just not quite as sexy as trophy brook trout), but I did get one northern by accident. We'd anchored the canoe at the head of a narrows, and I was playing a nice brook trout. It was going well, and I nearly had him to the boat when the line thumped once and went dead. This was a spot where I'd already lost several big fish to the jumbled boulders on the bottom, getting back nothing but a frayed leader, so I said, "Shit, I think he's got me in the rocks."

Our Guide, Al, peered over the gunnel and said, "No, a poik's got 'im."

The light was poor, but I could just make it out down there: my big brook trout with a long green thing that could only be a northern pike hanging off it. I carefully hauled the brookie toward the surface, and the pike was either unwilling or unable to let go, so Al netted them together.

It was a mess, but we got them untangled and released both fish. The brookie was stunned, but he wasn't too badly injured, considering. After a little resuscitation, he swam off strongly and I like to think he survived. The trout weighed 6 pounds, the pike, 9½ and—since we were counting such things on this trip—I guess I'll always think of it as 15½ pounds of fish on a #16 dry fly.

On our last night in camp, I was filling out the log book and, bowing to local custom, I recorded that in six and a half days, five fishermen had landed and released fifty brook trout with a total weight of 253 pounds and an average weight of 5.1 pounds. My pike was the only one caught (if you can call it that), and I asked A.K. how he thought I should enter it.

He said, "I guess you'll have to say you got it on live bait."

CHAPTER
2
Rock Bass

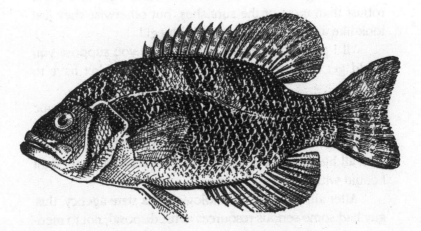

A couple of seasons ago, a fisheries biologist with the Colorado Division of Wildlife asked me if I could get him some rock bass. It just came up by accident in conversation. He was asking me about some of the warm-water ponds I fished—out of professional curiosity, since he's in charge of managing most of them, and also out of the common (though often mistaken) idea that fishing writers know more about this stuff than regular old fishermen. In the course of things, I happened to mention that, in addi-

tion to the largemouth bass and the various kinds of sunfish
I was getting, I sometimes caught rock bass.

He perked up at that, said he'd been trying to get a few
rock bass as specimens, but in all the netting and shocking
surveys he'd done, he hadn't been able to turn any up,
even though he knew there were some around.

The rock bass is a pretty common sunfish, as sunfish
go, but there are so few of them in Colorado they're not
even listed in the fishing regulations, and not every fisherman recognizes them. They're a little fatter and more
robust than most of the sunfishes, but otherwise they just
look like a chunky, dark-colored bluegill.

"If I gave you a jug of Formalin, do you suppose you
could get me a few?" he asked. "They wouldn't have to
be big."

I said sure, I could do that. The guy had helped me
out with tips and information a few times, and I guess I
was flattered that he couldn't get a couple of little rock bass
with all his scientific collection techniques, but he thought
I could with a fly rod.

After all, as an official biologist for a state agency, this
guy had some serious resources at his disposal, not to mention a federal permit that—although I don't remember the
exact wording—allowed him to catch, trap, snare, shoot or
otherwise take any species by any means at any time, period, no exceptions.

He showed it to me once. Considering that it was the
cosmic fishing and hunting license, it was a small, decep-
tively modest-looking document.

I said, "I know a couple of guys who could use one of
those."

"I'll just bet you do," he replied.

So I picked up the 5-gallon plastic pickle jar of Formalin—a solution of formaldehyde, methanol and water used

to store specimens temporarily—and got the short lecture on how to use it.

"Now you want to put them in here alive," he said, "so they pump the stuff through their systems before they die, but you probably don't want to *watch* that. And don't get any of it on you."

I did know of a couple of ponds that had some rock bass, and I even knew where in the ponds to look, not that that was much of a trick. For reasons of their own, these fish like riprap banks—stone rubble and large rocks— hence their name.

This was no big deal—just a small, return favor for a nice guy—but, driving home with that jug of gunk in the bed of the pickup, I really enjoyed being someone you could ask to locate and identify a certain obscure little sunfish. When it comes right down to it, I think that's the secret ambition of every fly fisher: just to be someone who knows the territory.

When I moved out here to the Rocky Mountains, almost exactly a quarter of a century ago now, I didn't do it entirely for the fly-fishing, although that was part of it. A larger part, I think, was the idea of learning the place and making myself at home here. It wasn't until later that I fully realized how much fly-fishing had to do with that.

Sure, I could have stayed in the Midwest and learned to be at home *there*, but I think I saw things in the heartland going in the wrong direction, so I came out West to start over. After all, that's what dissatisfied Americans have been doing for the last two hundred years, never mind that if you come West now you'll meet the eastward migration of Californians who've sold their surfboards and are now trying to retrace their steps.

I did want to learn how to fly fish, but there were other considerations—most of which I've all but forgotten by now—and because of them I rattled around Colorado for a while, working odd jobs, living in odd places with odd people, and finally ended up on the outskirts of a small, foothills town on the East Slope, a stone's throw from what, in the grand scheme of things, you'd have to describe as a fair to middling little trout creek.

Besides the creek, there's a lot of other fishing nearby, and if none of it is downright fabulous, there's at least a good variety.

And this is also a great jumping-off place. Within a day's drive of here are maybe a quarter of the best trout streams and rivers in the West. Add a second day on the road and you're probably in range of over half. More water than a guy could adequately fish in a lifetime.

Hell, I still haven't even fished all of the 300-some miles of the nearest local drainage—although I'm still working on it—and even after all this time, I could probably make a longer list of places in the region I'd like to fish than of places I *have* fished. But I still feel like I know the area pretty well.

For instance, it took me a few trips to get my friend his elusive rock bass, but I did finally manage it. He'd said all he wanted were little ones and that, actually, little ones were all he'd ever seen. So I pickled five dinks and one nice big one, just because I thought he'd appreciate that. Under "location" on the form he gave me, I wrote "Nameless pond in Boulder County." To his credit, he never asked me to be more specific.

I've lived in the same old house since 1977, but of course it's not quite as sleepy and quiet here as it was when I moved in eighteen years ago. That little town down the road has grown out to meet me, and although I'm officially still in the county, the town limit now lies up against my property line, which strikes me as a little too close for comfort. They keep asking me to annex and I keep saying, "If I'd wanted to live in town, I'd have bought a house in town in the first place."

Okay, that's a technicality, but it seems important because where you live in relation to a town is a lot like where you place yourself in society in general. That is, you don't have to be completely outside of it, but you should stay close enough to the edge to be able to see out.

If a handful of people have their way, the town will grow more and faster than it has already, against the wishes of almost everyone who lives here, but then it's always possible that certain greedy developers and politicians *won't* have their way. That does happen, you know.

Since I've lived here I've been involved in an effort that killed one development, another that just recently mounted a referendum and reversed a 40-acre annexation for a monster housing project, and also an ongoing movement to put a little water back into the creek for the trout, although the jury is still out on that last one.

Not long ago a town official pointed out that I was, after all, just a county resident and accused me of being an "outside agitator" in the town's affairs, an epithet I haven't heard since the 1960s. Luckily I had the presence of mind to say, "Right. What's your point?"

Any grass-roots political effort is so easily derailed by money, influence, arrogance and bureaucracy on the opposing side and by laziness, rage, egotism and cloying attempts to "achieve solidarity" within your own ranks that it's almost not worth doing. But then if you stay in one place long enough, you become part of the community—

like it or not—and eventually you have to pitch in, especially when the things that are going wrong where you are now are the same ones you had to escape from twenty-some years ago.

But politics is ugly, and it won't be long before you find yourself up a spiritual box canyon: You began with the best intentions, only to end up as ruthless as a paid assassin because that's what you have to do to win. So you have to wonder, Are those the only two choices: complete bastard or helpless victim? There are those who'll tell you not to let it get personal, but the dirtiest secret in politics is that it *is* personal.

And then there are those eerie reversals. One day someone asks you to annex into the town again, but this time it's not so they can gouge you for hook-up fees and taxes but so they can run you for mayor. You think, My God, are these people fools, or are things really that desperate?

Naturally, all of this can cut deeply into your fishing time.

Still, it *is* sometimes possible to achieve one single small thing that could make a difference, at least for the time being. When it comes right down to it, I hate politics as much as I love writing and fishing, but in all three of those endeavors it's possible to momentarily achieve the kind of clarity and precision you'll never see in your day-to-day life.

So I guess I've reached stage three in the long, slow process of becoming a bona fide local. Stage one was when no one knew or much cared who I was, and that went on for a long time, as it often does in small towns.

Stage two came when something clicked and people started speaking to me, usually asking how the fishing was.

Stage three came when I got involved in local politics

(always on the pro-environment, anti-growth side, of course) and now, in some circles, I am known as "that son of a bitch Gierach."

I don't mind that. I figure, if you think you're right and you're making enemies of people you think are wrong, you're doing okay. And anyway, it's sort of a family tradition. If you go to a certain small town in Wisconsin and ask for that son of a bitch Gierach, you'll get directions to my uncle Al's place.

I've written some stories about the little creek here (sometimes trying to disguise its name and location, though not always successfully), and when I met a man who'd read some of them, he said he was disappointed when he finally saw and fished the thing. Interesting. I thought I'd described it pretty accurately, right down to the gas station next door to the house, the cement plant on the stream and the small trout you catch.

I like it, even though the trout aren't that big and parts of it aren't entirely picturesque. That's because I've come to believe that life isn't, can't be and probably shouldn't be perfect, and that you'll be a lot happier if you live as much the way you want to as possible, while at the same time not having to cross every *t* and dot every *i*. But then I suppose some romanticism inevitably creeps in when you're talking about your favorite trout stream.

Then too, some of those stories go back a few years, and although you don't always notice when you're right in the middle of it, things do change.

The first Good Old Days parade I saw here consisted of a flatbed truck full of drunks from the Sundance Saloon with a hand-painted banner reading LIFE IN THE FAST LANE, a handful of guys in buckskins from the local black-powder gun club and the Pet Parade: a woman leading a golden retriever bitch that was clearly nursing, and four kids, each carrying a puppy.

They formed up in one block of Main Street and marched down the other block in front of an audience of twenty or thirty people. It was so much fun they went around the block and did it again. Then everyone went home except the drunks, who went back to the saloon.

Now, Good Old Days has a craft fair, flea market, carnival rides (cheap, little ones that don't look very safe), third-rate rock bands, loud cars, drunken fistfights and other elements of the full catastrophe. The city fathers and mothers are real proud of it, but a number of us make it a point to be out of town fishing the weekend it happens.

For a while the little sign you passed as you came into town said HOWDY, FOKS, but they changed it. I think someone realized it would only be funny if it was clear that the spelling error was intentional.

More to the point, down here on the lower stretch of the creek, there's more traffic than there used to be, more noise, more people fishing and so on. Don't get me wrong. It's still the Rocky Mountains and, compared to much of the country, it's pretty idyllic. But, still, it just ain't quite the same.

When I break down and complain about that (I try not to, but I'm only human), people sometimes ask me why I don't just move someplace where there are fewer people and better fishing. "In your line of work," a friend pointed out, "you could live anywhere. All you need is a phone and a mailbox and a generator for the word processor."

I do think about it sometimes. In the course of twenty years spent writing about fly-fishing, I've been to some neat places where—at first glance at least—it looks like a guy could live a quiet, pretty much undisturbed life with lots of space, few human neighbors, fish and game right out the back door and so on. It can be tempting, especially when you're experiencing that nervous, anything-could-happen freedom you feel when you're far from home.

Parts of western Montana are also not what they once were, but there are still some backwaters the movie stars haven't discovered yet. Wyoming, Utah, Idaho and, for that matter, parts of Colorado still have little one-horse, one-café, one-gas-station burgs that are near decent trout water but still nicely off the beaten path.

I really liked the Texas hill country north of San Antonio, with its rolling, forested hills, acres of wildflowers, polite people and lonesome limestone rivers full of bass and panfish, but then I was there in April, and I'm told the summers are kind of grim.

On the farther edge (unlikely, I suppose, but still sort of tantalizing) there's, let's say, King Salmon, Alaska, where there are fish the size of small canoes, or Goose Bay, Labrador, where one could spend time with some of the biggest brook trout in the world. Or, for less-terrifying winters, how about the bull trout and west-slope cutthroats around Fernie, British Columbia?

There's an interesting pattern here. All the places I'm thinking of have good fishing, but they don't have fly shops yet. I dearly love a good fly shop, but the presence of a new one is a symptom of growing popularity and all the nostalgic heartaches that come with it.

But then I keep coming back to the episode with the rock bass and all the other bits and pieces that would fit into the same category: things I know about now only because I've been kicking around here for twenty-five years, and I mean kicking around in a way I probably wouldn't do in a new place because I'd be in my late forties instead of my early twenties when I got there.

Not that I'm exactly a doddering old fool, but if you're in middle age yourself you know what I mean, and if you're in your twenties, trust me. If nothing else, you get a little smarter, take fewer risks, pace yourself better and run up fewer mountains just to see what the view is like.

Then again, you ran up some of those mountains once, so you already *know* what the view is like. Age doesn't necessarily bring wisdom, but you do build up a backlog of useful experience.

There are great fishing spots I know about and still go to, the likes of which I might not find in new country. And when I do go, I know—or at least have some ideas—about the best season, time of day, the weather, where to start, where to end up at dusk, approaches, tactics, fly patterns and I don't know what all else.

Sure, most of this is stuff that would work on any similar water, but I know from fishing similar water in other places that there's a subtle, intuitive, bioregional angle to it. A stream in British Columbia can be exactly like a stream here in northern Colorado in almost every way you can put your finger on, but I still fish the home water better. And it doesn't feel frozen in time the way a new stream can to a tourist who fishes it only once. If the home water is better or worse than it was ten years ago, I know that, and sometimes I can even tell you why.

Now, I'm not claiming to be such a great fisherman. In fact, that's probably the point. Without being a Dave Whitlock, Lefty Kreh, Joan Wulff or Dave Hughes, to name a few, and without knowing all that much about casting or entomology, I still do okay because I have a comfortable old familiarity with the place that fills in the large gaps in my skill with . . . Well, I don't know what exactly, but something just as useful.

I didn't even have to work at it in the way I usually understand that word. Sure, I've expended, and continue to expend, a lot of time and effort, and I do sometimes get deeply philosophical about it or claim I have to do it because it's my job, but I also love every minute of it.

My girlfriend Susan thinks it's interesting that, although most of my friends and I are fairly serious travelers, when we're *not* traveling we tend to be homebodies: apparently happy to kick around in a 20- or 30-mile radius of home, hang around the house and haunt the local cafés. There's always a little wanderlust in evidence, she says, but there's also a kind of satisfaction.

In the last year, two friends have told me they envied my sense of community. Both of these guys have spent the same years I've lived here moving restlessly from place to place, leaving behind pages in my address book with dozens of crossed out P.O. boxes and phone numbers. One of them, after a day's visit, said, "You know, I bet you've waved at or said hello to thirty people today."

A nice detail: one I wouldn't have noticed on my own. Luckily, on that particular day no one from the pro-growth side gave me the finger.

Now that I think about it, I also know who's a good carpenter, fly tier, rod maker, auto mechanic and gunsmith; who'll return a favor and who won't; which café makes the best coffee and where I might even be able to get a free cup now and then: the same sorts of things I know about the fishing.

So maybe I don't move because I'm lazy. Or maybe by now I enjoy the familiarity of it all as much as anything else, and I'm afraid it would take me the rest of my life to get back to the same thing somewhere else—or that I'd never get it back at all.

And anyway, if I did move it would probably take my new neighbors a decade or more to recognize me, take me in and then finally realize I'm an outside agitator and a son of a bitch.

3

Folk Art

*E*d Engle, Steve Peterson, Larry Pogreba and I had bought a day on a pay-to-fish private spring creek in Montana, one of the famous ones in the Paradise Valley, near

Livingston. This is the kind of treat we'll sometimes decide
to give ourselves for no other reason than that we're going
to be in that part of Montana anyway and can all afford the
rod fees at the same time.

I can't speak for Steve and Larry because they'd been
off on their own somewhere, but Ed and I were only a few
days into the trip and were just beginning to run up against
a little sleep deprivation. Nothing serious yet—no need to
declare a camp day to sleep in, have a big breakfast, wash
out some socks and then doze under a tree with a book
until noon. Still, a little minor road burn always creeps in,
even on those trips where you promise each other you'll
take it easy this time.

We'd all met at a campground on the Yellowstone
River the night before. I don't remember where Steve and
Larry were coming from, but they pulled in well after dark
and woke us up.

Before that, just about the time Ed and I were turning
in, a few pickup loads of cowboys had pulled in nearby
and launched into what we used to call a "woodsy." That's
a spur-of-the-moment party where a bunch of people drive
out into the country to build a huge fire, drink beer, yell,
discharge firearms into the air and so on. In some parts of
the world this is considered a valid and harmless form of
therapy, and, having been a participant in a few, I can
vouch for that. A woodsy can be aggravating as hell if
you're not actually taking part in it—and sometimes you
can't help but wonder where some of those stray rounds
are landing—but if you were young once, you let it go,
stuff in some ear plugs and try to sleep through it.

I did drift off finally—the way you can if you're tired
enough, even though someone in the next room is watching a loud war movie on TV—but I couldn't have been out
for more than an hour when Steve and Larry pulled in,

flashing a spotlight through the pale blue wall of my tent and bolting me awake, thinking I was about to either relive a scene from *Deliverance* or get busted by the local sheriff for God knows what.

So then, of course, we had to help set up Larry's elaborate, homemade fold-out camper, hear about their trip so far, tell about some highlights from ours and so on, all just happy to see each other. After all, when two parties of fishermen on separate driving trips plan to meet at a certain campground on a certain evening, it can begin to seem like a pretty unlikely rendezvous. Two courses, each several days and hundreds of miles long, have to converge at a single spot at a single time, cheating the combined forces of breakdowns, accidents, emergency detours and just plain getting lost on strange roads in the dark.

When someone *doesn't* show up—and that's been known to happen—you have to think, This could be serious. It's fishing, after all, and you don't just change your mind. When Larry is one of the people involved, you can always say, "Well, he probably got distracted by a junkyard or a farm auction," but then in the back of your mind you also have to think, Jeez, I hope they're not dead.

So when they finally did come dragging in at something like three in the morning, there were a few camp chores and a little celebration. By breakfast, we'd all had maybe two or three fitful hours of sleep, tops, and we hit the spring creek wired on coffee and a little edgy, which is actually not a bad state to be in for some meticulous dry fly fishing.

This was somewhere around the first week of June. The Pale Morning Dun mayflies were starting to come off pretty well, but the hatch wasn't in full swing yet, so there weren't as many fisherpersons on the water as there could have been, just one couple besides the four of us.

The morning was ideal for dry fly fishing—chilly, still and overcast, with a light drizzle coming and going—but by early afternoon the cold front had piled up and stalled against the Gallatin Range. It had turned colder and started to rain seriously, so we'd retired to the fishermen's hut for a lunch and weather break.

You pay to fish a spring creek for the big trout and great hatches, not for amenities, but this fisherman's hut is a nice, European touch. It's not fancy, but it's dry and, once you get a fire together, it's warm, too.

We had a good blaze going in the cast-iron stove and a pot of coffee on when half of the couple we were sharing the creek with—the woman—walked in. The hatch had gone off, but presumably the man was still out there grimly nymphing in the rain.

Ed and I were wolfing sandwiches, talking loudly with our mouths full and otherwise not exhibiting the best table manners, while Steve and Larry were standing by the stove, waders down around their ankles, toasting their backsides. Steve's long johns were faded red, Larry's had once been white and both had some pretty substantial holes in them. (After all, you don't wear the dress long johns on a fishing trip.) There was nothing actually obscene about it, but, you know, there were nonetheless gaping holes in the underwear, revealing hairy male anatomy.

We were engaged in a spirited discussion about carp. The day before, Steve and Larry had spent the afternoon hooking big carp on flies off a high bridge somewhere. It was the only way they could get a good drift over the fish, they said, but there was no way they could land them, so they just played them for a while and then broke them off.

Ed wanted to know why they didn't climb down from

the bridge and play the fish from the bank. Steve said they'd thought of that, but the bridge was too high and the bank was too steep.

"I guess I wasn't into risking my life to land a carp," Larry added.

"Why not?" Ed asked.

I wanted to know what flies they were using, what kind of drift and how the fish were taking. Violently? Lazily? Fly-fishing for carp is an obscure business, so any new information is welcome.

"They were really cool carp," Steve said. "I bet some of 'em went 20, 25 pounds."

"Yeah, easy," Larry said. Then he turned to the woman, who'd been standing there in the open doorway, rainwater dripping from her hat, and said, "Hi."

"Hi," she answered with the uncertainty of someone who has accidentally wandered into the wrong neighborhood. Then she found a chair in the corner, picked up an old fishing magazine and began paging through it.

"You wanna turnip?" Steve asked her, holding out a big, sickly white tuber.

Steve doesn't eat turnips as a joke or to make a point about macrobiotics, he actually likes them, and on this trip he had a whole large cooler full of them, which he had lugged into the hut.

"These are good, strong ones," he told the woman. "They make your lips tingle."

"No thank you," she said, a little coldly, I thought.

We asked her how she'd done that morning, what flies they'd been using, where they were from and such, but after a few terse, one-word answers we realized she was trying to ignore us and decided the most polite thing to do was return the favor.

That was okay with me. I've always thought courtesy

was overrated, and that if you don't feel like talking to people you don't like, you shouldn't have to.

Maybe she was tired or bored or just uncomfortable crammed into a small hut with four strange men. Or maybe she thought that when you paid a $50-a-day rod fee on a fancy spring creek you could expect to meet a better class of people and be offered elk pâté instead of raw turnips; hear more talk about dry flies and brown trout and less about carp. I guess it's even possible that Larry had made a bad first impression when they'd met earlier in the day.

It had been a fine morning, as I said. The hatch wasn't especially heavy, but it was long and steady; there were enough flies on the water to get the trout good and interested, and the cool, damp weather kept the duns on the surface for a long time before their wings dried and they could fly off.

The fish were your typical catch-and-release spring creek trout: browns and rainbows as plump and healthy as hothouse tomatoes and no pushovers. They were rising to the little duns with the casual, unhurried confidence of fish who have it good, know it and think they deserve it. Sometimes they'd spook at a bad cast, but they were just as likely to calmly sink down a foot or two in the clear water and sulk, clearly more annoyed than frightened.

They'd refuse a poorly drifted fly and, even though it was still early in the season, many of them seemed suspicious of the little post-wing thorax duns that are the standard pattern for this hatch. By standard I mean it's the fly you automatically start with, although the one you eventually catch fish on (assuming you do catch some) can be something else entirely.

This whole business of the perfect fly presented flawlessly to rising trout is why you go to some trouble and expense to fish a great spring creek. You're trying to have the courage of your convictions. As a fly fisher you're supposed to love a challenge—love it so much that you'll pay for it, even with hundreds of miles of free public water in the neighborhood. If you're a competent fisherman having a decent day, you can usually manage a few big trout. On a bad day you can at least know that getting skunked on a spring creek puts you in the same class with some of the world's best fly casters (whether they'll admit that or not).

Ed, Steve and I were doing okay, catching some fish on light rods and small dry flies, as one is expected to do on water like this, and Larry was doing what he likes to do, which is to go about it all wrong but catch fish anyway.

Well, maybe "all wrong" isn't exactly what I mean. In fact, Larry is what you'd have to call a great fly fisherman of the old Rocky Mountain school. He's up on all the current, technical stuff, but at heart he's a practical, instinctive angler who through much of his life has fly fished as much for food as for sport. I've noticed that guys like that have a kind of goofy, predatory edge we pure-sport types usually lack.

And he's also one of those born experimenters: He taught himself about blacksmithing and metallurgy and now hand-forges Damascus-steel knives, he makes guitars, builds cabins, raises game birds, repairs and sometimes redesigns automobiles and so on. He does so many things well that those of us who know him are seldom surprised anymore, although we're still sometimes amazed.

For instance, Larry once built a car from the ground up: the only Pogrebamobile in existence. At first glance it

looks like a cross between a silver dune buggy and a for-
mula racer. It has a chrome trout hood ornament and goes
very fast, although Larry is always trying to make it go a
little faster yet.

He believes that a broken item that's imaginatively
patched has a lot more style than a new one and also,
apparently, that things can always be done another way.

If guys like this could afford to fool around with space
travel, we'd have cities on Mars and warp drive by now.

More to the point, when Larry finds that trout can be
caught on, say, a size 18 Pale Morning Dun thorax dry fly,
he immediately wonders what *else* they might be caught
on. A Royal Wulff? A streamer? A bigger streamer? What
about a fluorescent pink rubber squid left over from a trip
to Belize?

He seems especially eager to try things like this on
catch-and-release water. I mean, if you have to put the fish
back anyway, why not try something strange just to see
what happens, in the spirit of vernacular pure science?

By now this approach to things has evolved into something like an art form. Larry has some interesting ideas
about art as life and vice versa, but I won't try to go into
them in any detail here. Suffice it to say that he's been
known to accumulate ridiculous fly patterns not only because he knows he can catch fish on them, but because he
likes the statement that will make.

Before I met Larry I'd never fished with anyone who
had this degree of playful curiosity. Almost every other fly
fisher I've known (and me too, for that matter) just wanted
to figure out what the fish were taking, arrive at something
like the correct pattern and then catch as many as possible.
If you tied the fly yourself, so much the better, but even
picking the right one out of a bin down at the fly shop is

something you can take credit for. You can say, "It just kinda jumped out at me."

Either way, the more fish you catch, the more convincing the proof that the fly and the tactic you settled on were the right and proper ones.

I've come to think of this as the place-tab-A-into-slot-B school of fly-fishing, and there's nothing wrong with it, but Larry seems more interested in locating the edges of the envelope than in just catching a lot of fish in the accepted manner. It's fascinating to watch—and you'd be amazed at how often the rubber squid works.

So that morning, using a rod many would say is way too heavy for a little spring creek, Larry was fishing a large, bright yellow Pistol Pete through a perfect, delicate mayfly hatch and catching more and bigger fish than anyone else.

A Pistol Pete, by the way, is a Woolly Worm with a brass propeller on its nose, a kind of rig that's out of style now, but that you'll find mentioned in old fishing books in which the authors talked about catching your limit and included recipes. I've never seen one in a fly shop, but you can find them in many hardware stores, usually right next to the worm cooler.

I appreciate people who fish like that, because they help keep me honest. I know myself too well, and I have to admit that if I'd fallen in with the wrong company at the wrong time, I'd probably have become a snob myself. As it is, I have this thing for fine tackle and this tendency to think flies that float are somehow morally superior to ones that sink. But having a friend like Larry—with his torn bluejeans; battered, oil-stained baseball cap and "Dracula Sucks" T-shirt—reminds me that all snobbery is defensive and that, as important as fishing seems, the most important thing about it is, it's just fishing.

Of course there are some anglers who don't see it that way.

Around midmorning I was casting to a pod of four or five good-sized trout when I spotted Larry working his way downstream. (Larry seldom pounds a single lie for long. He prefers to cover water, looking for the fish that will bite rather than fooling around with the ones that won't.) In a hundred yards or so I saw him land four trout, each 20 inches or better.

Then he ran into the couple. They were fishing close together, apparently consulting often and in great detail about insects and fly patterns. Larry had gotten out of the water and was walking around them on shore so as to give them plenty of room, but the man waved and they stopped to talk. I was too far away to hear the conversation, but I could tell how it went by the body language.

The man asked, "What are you using?" expecting to hear about something like a cul de canard, half-spent, crippled Pale Morning Dun emerger with one wing folded into the trailing nymphal husk.

Larry held up his fly and said, "Size 8 Pistol Pete."

The man's face went blank—I mean, a thing like that isn't supposed to work on a spring creek, is it? And even if it does, isn't it, well, unacceptable?

Larry, sensing weakness, explained that you could get Pistol Petes at the feed store in town, that they only cost 75 cents and that they held up a lot better than them little mayfly patterns.

That's only a guess because, as I said, I was too far away to hear, but I do know Larry and I'd seen him do this kind of thing before.

The couple seemed dumbfounded—possibly even a

little scandalized—and I've seen *that* before, too. Maybe
I'm just getting old, but it seems like a lot of fly fishers these
days have lost the capacity for delight and the ability to kid
around.

One thing I *could* tell—even at that range—was that
the woman was staring hard at Larry's T-shirt, which fea-
tures Dracula biting the neck of a near-naked woman
whose bare ass is padded to produce a startling 3-D effect.
It's in pretty bad taste, I guess, unless after careful consider-
ation you've determined that a certain kind of bad taste
qualifies as folk art.

CHAPTER

4

Solitude

*I*t's surprising how seldom I fish alone, considering how much I enjoy it. Well, okay, in the sense that fly-fishing isn't a team sport and it's not competitive, you *always* fish alone, even when you're casting from the same boat with another fisherman and a guide, but you know what I mean. I mean by myself, without arrangements or conversation, without even seeing another human, if I'm lucky.

That's not to say I don't like fishing with other people. Nine times out of ten it's the folks more than the fish that define the character of a trip, and among my fly-fishing friends there are some who define character in distinctive ways.

As unfair as it is to sum people up in a phrase or two, I'll say that Steve fishes hard without being obnoxious about it and continues to wear neon colors no matter what anyone says; Ed approaches fish and water with a weird kind of detached curiosity and seems to be on a perpetual guide's day off; Mike Price delights in going to notoriously difficult rivers during highly technical hatches and catching fish on a Royal Coachman; Mike Clark is usually just happy to be casting—instead of painstakingly *making*—bamboo fly rods; A.K. is a good-natured purist who thinks everything that happens on a fishing trip amounts to poetic justice and so on.

If pressed, I think all those guys would agree that fly-fishing eventually causes you to look into your own soul, but I'm probably the only one among us who would actually say something like that with a straight face. When I try too hard to be profound, none of these guys are shy about telling me to cram it, but I don't think any of them realize what a great service that is.

A trip with any one of these people has a distinct flavor —without being predictable—and a trip with any combination of them can turn out like a good Brunswick stew made from high-quality leftovers.

And then there are the strangers: people you bump into on the water in those offhand encounters that can make your day, piss you off or mean nothing at all. There was a man I used to run into on the South Platte River all the time. I never knew his name, but I always thought of him as The Gentleman. We never spoke, we'd just nod or wave and otherwise give each other plenty of room, neither of us wanting to intrude on the other's solitude or have ours intruded upon. I saw him maybe a dozen times a season for about two years and I haven't seen him since. He was a young guy, so maybe he just moved away.

And there's that first-date sensation you get meeting a guide you've never fished with before; you size each other up, each wondering if the other has a clue, both knowing you'll find out soon enough. And there's the sense of reunion when you hook up with a guide you *have* fished with before and you're doing it again because he was so good the last time. You remember what a fine job he did. He remembers that you tipped okay and didn't fall out of the boat.

Friends of friends can be interesting, too. Sometimes they're great, but just as often they're lushes, whiners, fish hogs or fascists and you end up asking the friend who brought them, "Now, this guy is actually an old *pal* of yours, is that right?"

Sometimes people you think you know can also turn out to be strangers of a sort. Have you ever gone fishing for the first time with someone you've known forever in more polite circumstances and found yourself adjusting your opinion of them one way or the other? Have you ever had someone pitch a deal on a bass pond or try to sell you real estate during a Red Quill hatch?

I sometimes even fish with an old-guard Reagan Republican—on his private water, of course. It's always fun, although I think there are times when we both view these trips as acts of charity.

But when it comes right down to it, I guess I have to admit I'm not all that fond of people in general—if nothing else, there are too damned many of them—although the occasional good ones are so delightful they do sometimes seem to make up for all the schmucks.

Still, there are times when I want to get away from the whole species for a while. A New Age type I know once pointedly told me that what we don't like about other people are usually the same things we don't like about ourselves. Okay, fine, but a guy can still take a break, can't he?

I do most of my solitary fishing near home. Sometimes I'll drive out to a bluegill pond or a local lake for a few hours: someplace where I may well run into someone I know, and that's usually okay. It's usually even okay if we end up fishing together for the afternoon and then meet at some joint for supper. In the long run, fishermen are better company than most. If nothing else, most of them don't feel obliged to fill up normal moments of silence with meaningless chatter.

But if I really want to be alone, I'll take a day and do one of the small mountain trout streams up in the national forest or wilderness area: streams that require a fair amount of four-wheeling, and then some walking, to reach stretches where the fish aren't that big anyway and where, consequently, it really is rare to run into anyone.

Naturally, I take the normal precaution of having someone know roughly where I went, or at least of tacking a note on my front door, so that in the unlikely event I break a leg and need to be rescued it won't take someone two weeks to figure that out.

I try to be mindful of my motivation when I go off alone. I mean, if you're weary, sick but still ambulatory, fed up, overworked, angry, frustrated, heartbroken, need to think things over or need to *stop* thinking things over for a while, you should definitely go fishing, and you should probably go alone so you don't bother anyone. But then fishing, like most other simple human pleasures, is better when it's done out of love than when it's used as a painkiller.

Of course things aren't always simple. I've gone fishing alone a few times because it was either that or resort to violence, and as it turned out, fishing was usually the better choice. It's not that I'm exactly opposed to the idea of revenge, but, as the old Italian saying goes, it's a dish best served cold. If I'm still pissed after a day of fishing, I know I should start planning to do something about it.

It's not likely for a solitary trip to end in a great epiphany or anything, it's just that I think the way you fish when you're alone is the way you really fish: your own personal style, uninfluenced by crowds, guides or friends, and it's interesting to plug back into that now and then. Solitude is educational and it *can* be satisfying. For instance, I've lived alone off and on for better than half my adult life and have found myself to be decent company.

Apparently, my true calling is to fish dry flies with a bamboo rod, even to the point of leaving the nymph box at home, because that's what I do when I'm by myself. Of course the trout in these little pocket-water, freestone streams do rise freely whether there's a hatch on or not, but carrying nothing but dry flies still makes me feel pretty stylish.

The rod I've been using lately doesn't hurt, either. It's a little 7½-foot, 5-weight F. E. Thomas Special bamboo, circa 1940, that casts a short line beautifully. Normally a rod like this could be considered too good to bang around on a rough stream, but this one has been refinished and one tip is down an inch, which moves it neatly from the museum piece into the nice old fishin' pole category.

I wear hip waders because it's rare to wade more than knee-deep in these little creeks, but I usually do a lot of walking, and the old boot-foot jobs I used to use have been known to get uncomfortable and even raise blisters. So now I have a pair of those neoprene hippers that take a lace-up wading shoe. They're a little more of a production to get into and out of, but they fit better, and footwear is the hiker's most valuable tool.

Otherwise I travel as lightly as possible, but I still carry a sheath knife, waterproof matchbox, water purification tablets and an empty canteen (to keep the weight down), coffeepot, tin cup and a few other odds and ends, including a simple lunch.

Once in a great while I bring the sandwich home at the end of the day, having dined instead on raspberries, wild mushrooms and a brace of small brook trout roasted on a stick. That's one of the great meals of all time, but it does take some effort to put together.

Even if I just wolf down the sandwich and a piece of fruit, I almost always find a pretty spot and take an elaborate coffee break, if only because I carried the coffeepot a couple of miles and am, by God, gonna use it. I own a small, lightweight backpack stove, but on trips like this I prefer an open spruce fire with the coffeepot suspended over it on a stick. I've long since graduated from the old wood, canvas and steel school of woodcraft I knew as a kid, where you cleared brush, dug drainage ditches, felled trees for a lean-to and otherwise conquered the wilderness, but I do still like a little fire.

After coffee, I put the pot in a plastic bag before stashing it in the day pack. That keeps the soot from the fire off of all the other stuff. Not that it would matter much, but in the woods, unlike at home, I like to be neat and efficient.

I think I walk more, cast less, spend more time distracted and take longer breaks when I'm alone, but I can't be absolutely sure of that. Trying to remember it now, from a desk chair, it seems like I'm less aware of my own pace when I'm alone, so maybe that's the difference. When I've been out with partners or guides, I can tell you in no uncertain terms if it was lazy or frantic or somewhere in between.

I think I also see more when I'm alone, although, again, I don't know if that's an accurate recollection or not. It seems like there's more scenery, weather, wildlife and birdsong in my head at the end of a solitary day, but maybe that's just because that space isn't filled up with conversation and other people's fish. My memory isn't exactly poor, but it does seem to have a limited capacity.

But I suppose it's really the fishing that sets the pace, as always. If the trout aren't rising, I'll cruise, working the good-looking water with a Royal Wulff or a hopper, or maybe something slightly more exotic, like a Roy Palm–style crane fly.

The trout in these little streams are usually curious, aggressive and just plain hungry, so any number of dry flies will work, but I'll still fool around with patterns until I find the one that, on that particular day, really rattles their cages. It's funny what that turns out to be sometimes.

If the trout *are* rising, my natural tendency is to try to match what the trout are eating, because that's how we do it now, but up there it's likely to be one of those sparse, mixed, multiple hatch/spinner fall deals where a #14 Wulff will work as well as anything else and be a lot easier to see.

Ed says that's what he likes about freestone streams, as opposed to the classier tailwaters and spring creeks. They're pretty much nontechnical, and all that stuff from the old fly-fishing books still works.

•

One of the best things about being alone is that if you put down a big fish (a big fish here would be a foot long or more—but not much more) you can stop and rest the water if you feel like it, or even leave it and come back in an hour.

I can remember when it was a standard item of courtesy among fly fishers to let someone rest a pool. ("Resting the water is the same as fishing it," my friend Koke Winter once said in that way he has that leaves no room for discussion. "In fact, it's the mark of a competent angler.") But now, at least on a lot of crowded rivers, there'll be another guy in your spot before you even find a comfortable rock to sit on, so your only two choices are to keep casting where you are or move on.

Well, there's a third choice, which is to try to give the guy a lesson in streamside etiquette, but that's a touchy business. My problem is, if I'm worked up enough to actually get into it, I'll begin with something like, "Listen here, you ignorant shit. . . ," which is usually not productive.

I suppose people rush spots like that out of a sense of self-defense, because there are those who'll grab a good hole and camp on it all day, or even try to crowd you out when you start catching fish. I've been on rivers where a real gentleman would end up standing on the bank all day.

At its best, courtesy is like a chess game. At worst, it's like too many hungry rats in a small cage. Having a whole stream to yourself for a day means that, for once, you don't even have to think about it. Plus, you can talk to yourself, pee where you like, scratch where it itches, laugh at particularly amusing rocks, yell at birds and otherwise relax in a profound way.

I don't know if I really see more clearly, cast better, miss fewer strikes and play fish with greater finesse when

I'm alone or not. I guess it doesn't matter, because that's how I remember it, and there are no witnesses.

The last time I was out alone I had a great day. The stretch of creek I was fishing had a nice mix of browns and brookies, and there were all kinds of bugs around, from #10 or #12 Green Drakes and Yellow Caddis down to some little Blue Dun mayflies. I'd spent half the morning switching patterns and finally settled on a #14 Flavilinea mayfly with dun hackle and white goat-hair wings.

I caught lots of trout, most small, but a few up around 12 inches and one chubby brown that might have gone 14. I was having so much fun that by four o'clock I hadn't stopped for coffee yet.

I was just thinking about that—looking for a comfortable spot for a twig fire—when I came on a long stretch of jumbled pocket water that ran out of the sunlight into a tunnel of overhanging spruce and willow. It was dark and steep in there, with what looked like some deep pools, and silhouetted against the sunlit trees at the far end I could see caddis and mayflies in the air. Okay, I thought, coffee later.

I got up on the slope a little, into the more open forest, and hiked down to the bottom end of this stretch so I could fish it upstream. The bank was an unwalkable tangle of trunks and brush, so I got into the water, and I'd been right, the pools *were* deep. This was actually a step beyond pocket water, but not quite a cascade. It was more of a chute, where the water tumbled over and around boulders into small, stair-stepping, braided pools.

Dry fly drifts and back casts were both tricky in there, but if I could drop a fly into the bubbly white water at the head of a plunge, a trout would hammer it as soon as it drifted into a clear current.

Moving from one pool to the next was a matter of scrambling over boulders and deadfalls while wearing hip boots and a pack, which I've never seen anyone do gracefully. I probably wasn't as careful with the old cane rod as some collector friends would have liked, but I think I was as careful as the late Mr. Thomas would have expected, seeing as how there were fish to be caught.

And then a neat thing happened. I flipped a cast to the head of a plunge pool and watched it bob down in the current. It was such a pretty drift that when the fly went completely out of sight behind a big rock, I just let it go, and while it was back there I got this feeling that I should set the hook, so I did. And of course there was a fish on.

I don't know if it was luck or clairvoyance, but it was pretty cool, even though it only turned out to be a 7-inch brookie.

Oddly enough, my first reaction was to look around to see if anyone was watching. I knew I was alone—I'd gone to great pains to be—but I guess I wished someone had been there to see it.

5

Splake

Last year Mike Clark and I went fishing for splake in a little mountain lake in Colorado's Arapaho National Forest. It was a simple case of fly fisher's curiosity: We learned that these fish had been quietly planted there a few years before by the Division of Wildlife (without fanfare or a press release), and since neither of us had ever caught one and the lake was only a few hours' drive from home, we figured we'd better check it out.

A splake is a hybrid fish made by crossing a brook trout with a lake trout: the kind of thing people do because they can, and because they just can't leave well enough alone. These fish were first produced in the 1870s by the legendary New York fish culturist Seth Green, but they didn't start to become popular until the 1940s, when they were experimentally planted in British Columbia. In Canada, a brookie is sometimes called a speckled trout. The name "splake" comes from the *sp* in "speckled" tacked onto the *lake* in "lake trout." It's not a very pretty name, but I guess it could have been worse.

The brook trout X lake trout hybrid is not one that occurs in nature like, say, the cutthroat X rainbow, known as a cuttbow, but once produced artificially the splake is an unusual hybrid because it can and does spawn success- fully. Splake—horny little devils, apparently—will mate with each other and they'll also backcross, breeding with either lake trout or brook trout.

Ask a fisheries biologist about this and he may wander off into the relative viability of the eggs from a splake X splake cross versus those of the original lake trout X brook trout mating or the varied appearance of the young re- sulting from the (splake X brook trout) X brook trout cross and so on.

You'll listen patiently because, after all, you *did* ask, but the upshot is, after a few generations in wild water with pure-strain fish, the splakes' genetics can get a little muddy. I want to picture that as the wild genes trying to reassert themselves, but there may be more poetry than science to that.

As some fisheries managers see it, a splake has at least two advantages as a sport fish: It has a faster initial growth rate than a lake trout—which means it gets to catchable size quicker—and in most waters it tends to be larger at maturity than a brook trout.

According to Jim Satterfield, the biologist responsible for stocking splake where Mike and I fished for them, these critters can also be used to control runaway populations of stunted brook trout. Splake will feed on insects, crustaceans and such, but they also share the lake trouts' aggressiveness and taste for small fish.

"Putting splake into a brook trout lake is a lot like putting bass into a bluegill pond," Satterfield said. "The idea is to achieve the proper predator/prey balance."

Sure, perfect balances can't always be achieved by stocking (and they don't always happen in nature, either), but Satterfield said that under ideal conditions some of the once small, stunted brook trout in a little high-altitude lake with a short growing season could get to be 16 inches long, and the larger splake might weigh in at 3 or 4 pounds. All of which sounds pretty good, at least on paper.

The thing is, I've always had some nagging misgivings about designer fish. It's nothing I can lay out in a coherent argument, it just seems like there are enough *real* fish around that you shouldn't have to cross white bass with striped bass to get wipers or fertilize the eggs of northern pike with the milt of muskellunge (or is it the other way around?) to get tiger muskies. If that kind of thing was supposed to happen, it would have happened on its own. Since it didn't, maybe there's a reason.

Some fisheries managers like these artificial hybrids because most of the fish are sterile, so populations can be controlled with great precision and, with only one age class in the water at a time, they can be grown to large size quickly, like cattle in a feedlot. If they're stocked properly, the biologists say, they won't push any other fish out of their deserved niches, and, as a friend of mine once pointed out, "Some of these impoundment fisheries are so artificial they might as *well* be full of cowalskis." (Just in case you haven't heard that old joke, a cowalski is a coho/walleye/muskie hybrid that doesn't know how to swim.)

Still, I can't completely shake the suspicion that the engineering of unnatural creatures is a selfishly vain business—not unlike having high-priced fertility clinics in a society that's already overpopulated—and maybe even a little dangerous in a 1950s horror movie sort of way. If you watched those things religiously, as I did as a kid, you'll know that monstrosities sooner or later turn on their creators in awful and unpredictable ways. I can't say what might happen with these peculiar fish, but I can picture that obligatory scene in *The Wiper That Ate Denver*, where the earnest young fly fisherman says to the wild-eyed fisheries biologist, "You crossed a *what* with a *what?* My God man, are you *mad?!*"

On the other hand, I've been trying to fight my natural tendency to be a tight-lipped prude about anything new and, for the record, I'm not one of those who wants to see nothing but indigenous fish in their native waters. After all, here in Colorado we have maybe twenty-some species of game fish (the actual number depends on how eclectic your tastes are), and all but the cutthroat trout and whitefish were introduced. I love it here and I sometimes pine for the old days, but I wonder how happy I'd have been catching whitefish, squawfish, chubs, suckers and the occasional cutt.

I've never quite gotten around to trying for the local tiger muskies, even though I'm told they get huge and can be caught on standard pike flies. A guy I know who *has* caught them says they grow bigger than northerns, but lack the famous reticence of muskies, so you can actually hook one now and then.

I did once go after wipers in what I thought was a nice, open-minded sort of way. I couldn't find any and, instead, ended up catching some good-sized rainbow trout on damselflies, which was kind of a relief.

Those trout had been in the water for a few years, but, like the wipers, they were also hatchery fish with questionable pedigrees living in a lake that had once been a low spot in a pasture. Still, under the right conditions the rainbows could spawn. Now that I think about it, maybe that's all it is. Maybe I just can't relate to a fish that doesn't have a sex life.

So anyway, Mike and I strapped my canoe on top of the pickup and ground our way up to the splake lake on a series of steep, rocky four-wheel-drive roads. It was a chilly day with a dense fog settled in at about 7,000 feet, so when we found the lake it gave the impression of stretching to the horizon, even though it was set in a small cirque and only covered about 30 or 40 acres.

There was some evidence of people having been there —old fire pits, a few faded beer cans—but it was mid-week, and there was no one else on the road and no one at the lake.

We launched the canoe after hanging a bright orange rain slicker on the canoe rack so we could find the truck again in the fog. What we could see of the lake's surface was dull, glassy and vacant looking—like a mirror reflecting another mirror—and there were some scattered rises here and there, the kind of lazy swirls fish make when they're eating bugs that are just sitting there being easy targets.

All we could see on the water were a few size 18 or so midges, so we started with #18 Royal Wulffs with the same size Hare's Ear soft hackles on short droppers; the kind of standard, businesslike high-lake rig you'd use for, say, brook trout or cutthroats—not exact, but usually close enough.

Mike caught the first fish—maybe a 7 or 8 incher—and we both had a look at it.

Satterfield had coached us a little on identification. He said that at first glance a splake looks an awful lot like a brookie—and there would still probably be some brookies in there—but on closer examination you'll notice that the wormlike markings on the back of the splake are larger, the snout is more elongated, the white fin margins aren't as prominent and, although a splake may have an orange cast to the belly like a brook trout, the red spots on the body are missing. The initial effect is subliminal. You think, This is a sickly-looking brook trout, without quite being able to put your finger on why.

But the real diagnostic mark is the tail. The tail of a brook trout is nearly flat (they call them squaretails in the East), while the tail of a splake is noticeably forked. This lake carries a limit of two splake 14 inches or better and, fine anatomical points aside, that's how the Wildlife officers tell the difference. So if it has a forked tail, the fish had better be 14 inches long, and you'd better not have more than two of them.

There had once been a sign posted at the lake with the regulations on it, along with a little essay on splake and brook trout, but some fun-loving locals had chained it up to a jeep and dragged it off. I guess I don't understand that. It seems to me a poacher with real guts would break the rules while leaving them posted. Stealing the sign so you can claim ignorance if you get caught is more of a lawyer's trick.

We looked the fish over quickly—in less time than it just took to tell about it, I think—and then let it go. It had clearly been a small splake, and I asked Mike, "Well, what do you think of them?"

"I don't know," he said, "I guess they're pretty cool. What d'*you* think?"

"Well," I said, "it was definitely a fish."

All in all, it was a normal kind of mountain-lake day. We drifted around in the canoe, casting to occasionally rising fish, catching a few and just enjoying the scene.

I'm almost always pleased just to be in a canoe— especially *my* canoe, which I'm very fond of—and the lake was especially gorgeous that day. If we were close to shore, jumbled granite boulders or dark stands of spruce would loom and dissolve as the thick fog shifted, and I felt like part of a Sung Dynasty Chinese watercolor. Out in more open water the fog was just a disorienting gray dome with no horizon, where the rings of rises seemed to float in the air and ranges were deceptive. The rises were closer than they appeared, and it was easy to cast too far.

Between us, we caught maybe twenty splake up to about a foot long, on small flies and light bamboo rods. They stayed near the surface to fight, unlike lake trout, which want to dive for the bottom when they feel the hook. Then we tried some streamers and weighted nymphs, hoping for bigger fish, but didn't get so much as a bump. Satterfield had told us that a recent netting survey showed there were some keepers in there, as well as a handful of splake up around 17 or 18 inches.

Somewhere in there I landed a real brook trout. It was the smallest fish of the day, but beautiful, and I said to Mike, "Look at this."

"All right," he said, "that's nice."

Just a few days before, we'd gone to another lake nearby where we'd caught and released a mess of 16-inch lake trout taken on dry flies. (Before lakers turn to a fish diet, belly out and sink toward the bottom, they act just like cutthroats.) So in less than a week we had, in effect, caught pure lake trout, pure brookies and their improbable off-spring. I couldn't help feeling that the real fish were more, I don't know . . . authentic, I guess—the products of mil-lions of years of evolution instead of one afternoon at the hatchery.

That's not to say the splake weren't fun. I mean, they were troutlike fish eating flies in a pretty mountain lake: the kind of thing that's perfectly okay unless you think too much. I *do* think too much at times, but I tend to do it at home. On the water, I'm usually able to just fish and be happy.

That's part of a conscious effort I've been making. I think you have to have your ideals and even speak up for them, but it's probably a good idea to pick your fights so you're not fighting *all* the time, and otherwise try to get along in the world as it is. (And if you also want to bury some ammunition and canned goods in the backyard just in case, okay.)

If pressed, I can picture a world where the wild critters are all gone, and if we fish at all we'll be after big, dumb, test-tube creations that look and act a lot like domestic turkeys. It might be okay if you don't remember what it used to be like, but the loss will be very real.

You have to do what you can to keep that and other horrors from happening, but at the same time too much lusting after perfection will make you nuts, in which case your own life is ruined and you're no help to your cause. You must avoid becoming that guy you read about in the papers now and then. When he was finally carted off to an institution, the Health Department found that he'd been living with sixty cats and several raccoons without the benefit of litter boxes and had saved all his newspapers since 1953. His baseball cap was lined with tin foil to ward off alien radio signals, and he was mumbling something about mutant fish trying to control his mind.

We never did crack that 14-inch limit on the splake—even after going back and trying again a week later—and I really want to do that because I'd like to eat one, which I would do without a second thought. If I continue fishing for splake, I'll probably release them as matter-of-factly as I do almost everything else, but for some reason I first want to see if they taste the way they fight, that is, more like a brookie than a lake trout.

That's one advantage, I guess. In a world where killing and eating a wild trout can pose a gut-wrenching dilemma, a designer fish has about the same moral weight as a hotdog.

6

Lost Rod

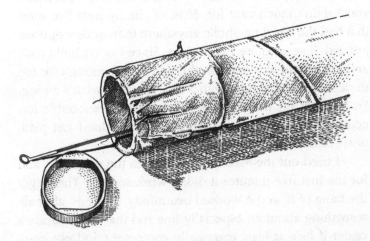

Not long ago I lost a bamboo fly rod, or, to call a spade a spade, I had a rod stolen. The maker, George Maurer of Kutztown, Pennsylvania, shipped it to me on a Monday. The following Monday (a day or two longer than it should have taken) the empty shipping tube arrived on my front porch in Colorado. It took a few seconds to sink in, but, sure enough, one end of the tube had been opened neatly with a sharp knife and there was nothing inside. It wasn't a mistake and it wasn't a joke. Maurer's sense of humor is a little odd, but he wouldn't do something like that.

I called him just to make sure. He thought *I* was kidding.

Naturally, it was a great rod: an 8-foot, 5-weight bamboo with a lovely, powerful but sensitive, semiparabolic action. I know how it would have cast because I'd tried out the prototype a few months before, both around home and on a trip to Montana.

Actually, it had the kind of casting action I'd have told you I didn't much care for. Most of the fly rods I've tried that had the word parabolic anywhere in their descriptions just didn't seem quite right to me. Since I don't build rods and am not an authority on them, it's hard enough for me to describe what's *right* with a rod, let alone what's wrong. So let's just say there are certain perfectly respectable rod actions that are too demanding for me or that I just plain don't understand.

I tried out the Maurer prototype in the driveway, and for the first five minutes it didn't work so well. Then I got the hang of it, and it worked beautifully. There is, after all, something about an especially fine rod that will educate a caster if he's at least marginally competent and not completely brain dead.

I had a thing for this rod because it had spoken to me, and because the one that had been in the now-empty shipping tube was serial number 001 of a model George calls The Trout Bum, an allusion to some old fishing book.

So I stood on the porch, looking down into the empty tube, and after those few initial moments of disbelief, my first rational thought was, This was bound to happen.

I mean it. For more than twenty years now I've been shipping fly rods back and forth to be repaired or refinished, buying and selling them through the mail and lugging them around in cars and on airplanes, and in all that time I'd never lost one. And I know it happens, I've heard all the horror stories. Now and then it would occur to me that I was living on borrowed time, but what do you do with information like that? When you're lucky, all you can do is accept it graciously and forge ahead.

Now I don't mean to say I'm careless. I'm as careful as I can be with my rods, but it's real life and there are perils.

Along with most of the other fishermen I know, I've left spare rods in unattended vehicles for long periods of time; vehicles parked, sometimes for days on end, in secluded spots, where a villain could take all the time and make all the noise he wanted to breaking in.

Sure, I've considered the risk, but you've gotta have a spare, right? And it should be a good rod, too, because if you end up needing it you don't want to spend the rest of the trip fishing with a club. That would only make you feel worse about the one you broke.

In fact, the only time I ever broke a rod on the water was on one of the rare days when I *hadn't* brought a spare. I felt like an idiot. One of the guys I was with had an extra rod, but I don't want to tell you what I had to go through to get it from him. I've often wondered why so many of my friends have a cruel streak. He said, "Now be careful with it," which he thought was pretty damn funny.

I never used to worry too much about spare rods because my old pickup—a Ford so elderly it had been dropped from the Blue Book—always looked like the least likely vehicle in any parking lot to have anything valuable in it: the perfect camouflage. Now I have a new truck—or, I should say, a newer old truck—that actually looks pretty spiffy. Right after I got it I passed a friend on a county road.

I honked and waved, but he just gave me a blank look. Later he said, "Oh, that was you. I thought some yuppie stole your hat."

If the stories you hear can be believed—and there's no reason why they can't—more rods are lost on commercial airlines than anywhere else. Sometimes your luggage just vanishes temporarily, only to turn up a day or two later. The airline is usually happy to drop it off at the hotel for you, but that doesn't help people like us because we're not *at* the hotel. We're two more flights and a boat ride away, trying like hell to borrow a rod.

Another thing that can happen is, you arrive in British Columbia or wherever with empty rod cases. That's the standard trick, they say: steal the rods and send the cases on to their destination to cover your tracks. They say you should open your rod tubes and check inside every time you get your hands on them. That's probably a good idea, but, honestly, how useful would it be to know, when your flight leaves in ten minutes, that your four favorite fly rods are now in the possession of an anonymous slimy bastard somewhere in, say, Vancouver?

The only way to be absolutely sure is to take your rods on board with you. This is problematic with those long, two-piece-rod cases, but I have managed it a time or two, usually on short flights from Denver to Montana. The trick is to insist to everyone right up to the supervisor that the rods absolutely must stay with you, constantly pointing out that rod cases are no longer than a topcoat and that there is a closet on every commercial jet tall enough to hang a topcoat in, right?

All you have to do is get someone to admit, "Well, yes,

I suppose that's true . . ." and then keep pushing, avoiding rudeness if possible, but not forgetting that you're the customer, without whom this android who's currently busting your chops wouldn't even have a job.

Once someone breaks down and says okay, use their name at every roadblock: "Ms. So-and-so upstairs said it would be all right." As long as it was someone else's decision, they'll usually let you through.

But all this takes superhuman persistence, and you have to be a good whiner, so I can't *always* make it work.

The only time an airline ever lost my rods, it happened on the return trip. They showed up a day later, and a guy from United Airlines drove the 50 miles or so from Denver to deliver them to my door and apologize for the inconvenience. It had even been an understandable screwup.

I remember dashing to the United counter in Vancouver with my partner, just minutes before our plane left, and panting, "Our Wilderness Airlines flight was late."

The guy said, "What else is new?"

He also said we might have to live with the fact that our duffels and rod cases would take a later flight to Denver. I didn't like the sound of that, but there didn't seem to be anything to do about it. We could have waited for a later flight ourselves, but then our stuff could have arrived ahead of us.

Sure enough, we got into Denver at about two in the morning and learned that our luggage was probably in either Vancouver or Seattle. The woman at the baggage counter said they'd deliver it to us as soon as it came in.

That seemed okay to me, but my partner was cursing, pacing, sputtering something about suing the airline and kicking those pastel-colored plastic chairs. It was late at night and the airport was nearly empty. The sound of chairs being kicked echoed down the vacant corridors. In the far distance a guy pushing a broom stopped and looked to see what all the commotion was about.

"Look," I said, "this is a drag, but why don't we just get in your car, go home and get some sleep?"

"We can't do that," he said.

"Why not?"

"Because my car keys are in my goddamn duffel bag, that's why!"

When I went to Alaska, I tried something some friends had told me about. I shipped a trunk full of gear and a pad-locked case full of rods to a friend's house in Anchorage—second-day express, heavily insured. That was expensive, but I liked it. My friend called before I left to say that my stuff was safe in his garage, so all I had to do was breeze through the airport with a newspaper under my arm, not worrying about how I was going to catch fish if my gear went to Tibet. I could direct all my attention to the possibility of dying in a horrible plane crash.

So I've been careful and I do insure the rods now, even though that bothers me, because when you insure something you're betting against yourself, which probably isn't healthy. Still, it's a way of negotiating the paradox of wanting to own fine fishing tackle but *not* wanting to be ruled by material possessions. The best solution seems to be to buy the best stuff I can afford (or not afford, as the case may be) and then use it hard and otherwise put it in harm's way with a fatalistic shrug.

And okay, insure the stuff, too, although that may not

necessarily mean what you think it means. As the insurance agent said, "People think I sell security, but I don't. There *is* no security."

For a while I carried the biggest, sturdiest rod case I could find. It was made of some kind of high-impact plastic, padded inside with foam, with a good, solid handle, four latches and two hasps for padlocks. It held as many as five standard rod tubes, plus a couple of reels.

If you thought about it for a minute, you'd have realized it was too long and skinny to be a gun case, but it did have that look about it, and I spent a lot of time explaining to baggage and security types that it held rods instead of firearms.

I lugged this thing to Scotland and back one summer and I was thinking of stopping in London to get a can of spray paint so I could write FLY RODS—NOT GUNS down both sides of it.

In Boston on the return trip, I dragged myself up to the baggage counter and flopped the case on the scale. I'd been up for twenty-some hours, and the strong coffee they serve on Virgin Atlantic was beginning to wear off. The woman behind the counter looked as bad as I did: tired and harried, as though she'd been on duty for three days straight. She looked at the case and asked, "Is that shotguns?"

"No, fly rods," I said.

"Are they loaded?" she asked.

"No," I said truthfully, "they are not loaded."

"Okay," she said, "have a nice flight."

I didn't catch a salmon on that trip, but I flew I don't know how many thousands of miles on seven separate flights through three countries and twelve time zones and still had my rods when I got home. It was a small but meaningful victory.

I once actually spent a week on the phone calling every airline I was ever likely to take, plus the FAA in Washington, D.C., trying to find out how short a rod case I'd have to have to be able to carry the rods on board any commercial flight. You'd think that would be carved in marble somewhere (hence the call to Washington) but it's not. Every airline makes its own baggage regulations, and, judging from the people I talked to, the actual rules are either unknown or none of your business, which means there's probably no absolute guarantee against hearing those dreaded words, "You're gonna have to check that."

The best I could do was learn that a 36-inch case will fit in the overhead bins on the *majority* of commercial planes. That translates into, at a bare minimum, a brace of three-piece, 8-foot rods. Of course most of the big airliners travel between major cities, and a fisherman's destination is usually as far from a city as he can get.

I'll admit to being a tackle freak, but I wasn't anxious to replace all my favorite two-piece rods with new three-piece models. If I was going on a trip, I figured I was headed for a place where the fishing is pretty good, so naturally I wanted to use my best rods. I thoroughly enjoy good fishing tackle until the moment I have to check it as luggage. Then I wish I used garage-sale fiberglass rods and plastic reels.

But I did finally break down—when it comes to fly rods, I *always* break down—and I figured the only way to avoid pining away for my favorite two-piece sticks on a trip was to get equally fine three-piece rods. So I had Mike

Clark build me an 8 foot, 6/7 weight with darkly flamed cane and a little detachable, 2-inch fighting butt. Then, within weeks, I got a lovely old Leonard Model 50-H with a Coke-bottle grip and intermediate wraps that had been flawlessly restored by John Bradford in Fort Worth, Texas. They're both such sweet rods I couldn't tell you which is the backup.

I already had some lighter, 4- and 5-weight three-piece rods, but I still had to get a stubby little hard case with a carrying strap that would hold no fewer than four rods in their bags.

It was a shocking example of what a friend calls "retail therapy," but I've found that if you have a certain kind of inner peace (and no kids) you can buy things you want but can't afford and feel okay about it.

So I've been careful and lucky, as I said, and it was probably inevitable that I would lose a rod sooner or later, if only because it's rare to have so much fun without paying some kind of dues. That fly rod that disappeared somewhere between Pennsylvania and Colorado was insured, and George Maurer made me another one—Trout Bum serial number 001-A—so I suppose it turned out okay.

I was a little put out that the company that shipped it, against my objections, insisted on declaring it "lost" instead of "stolen." I pointed out that the shipping tube had been sliced open neatly and that we were talking about a 50-inch brown anodized aluminum tube with a brass cap, not the kind of thing that disappears by rolling under a desk.

I do have the Gierach family temper, but in cooler moments I can usually manage to become philosophical. Things like this happen; it could have been worse, and so on.

Then again, it's a moral universe and some people just don't deserve to be forgiven. Like, for instance, Adolf Hitler, Saddam Hussein and the son of a bitch who stole my rod.

CHAPTER
7

Fly-Caster's Elbow

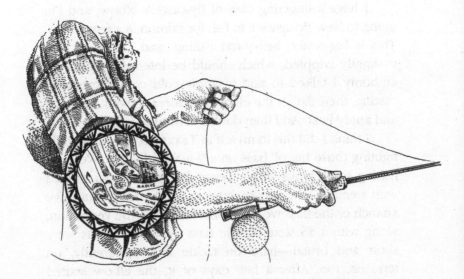

I'm sitting at my desk with the front door open so I can hear the hissing of the camp stove out in the yard. It's running on a nearly empty can of propane left over from the last camping trip, and when the hissing stops, it'll be time to go screw in a fresh one and re-light the low flame under the pot.

I'm slowly boiling the head of a blue grouse to get the skull for my modest skull collection, and this has to be done outside because it stinks with some authority. You'd think it would smell something like grouse stock for soup, but it doesn't. Probably something to do with the feathers.

It's a bright, crisp fall day in Colorado—the kind that makes visitors want to chuck everything and move here—and I'm typing with a big ice pack Ace-bandaged halfway down my right arm. The plastic bag I put the ice in is leaking slightly, so there's a small puddle of water on the floor next to the desk.

I have a lingering case of fly-caster's elbow, and I'm going to New Brunswick to fish for salmon in a few weeks. This is big-water, heavy-rod fishing, and I'm going into it slightly crippled, which should be interesting. The last authority I talked to said to apply cold compresses after casting, then slather the elbow and forearm with arnica oil and apply heat. And then do the wrist exercises.

I think I did this to myself in Texas back in April while fighting those big ol' bass on a 9-weight fly rod. We were fishing some tanks (that's Texan for "ponds") so choked with weeds that when you hooked a fish you couldn't give an inch or the bass would be lost forever in the vegetation, along with a $5 store-bought bass fly. So the fights were short and brutal—hard on tackle and, apparently, on tendons, too. After a few days of it, the elbow started throbbing.

I ignored it, which is usually the best thing to do with aches and pains. I finished the Texas trip and fished through the month of May around home, telling myself I wasn't getting old or anything; that, in fact, young, nimble athletes in their twenties get injured all the time, so much so that you need a medical degree to fully understand the sports page.

By the time Ed and I did a tour of some rivers in Montana in June, the elbow was sore enough that I couldn't straighten it out quickly with that slight but powerful snap you need for long casts. I compensated by stopping the forward cast a little short, hauling the line a little harder than normal with my left hand and lowering the rod tip by dropping my shoulder.

It worked great.

Actually, it worked surprisingly well, considering.

Actually, it hardly worked at all and, in a sport where form is appreciated, it looked like hell, too. But I caught some fish.

So when I got home I went to a doctor, which was a daring and desperate move. I have nothing against the established medical profession except that when you visit an M.D. there's always the chance you'll come home broke and/or dead.

The doc told me that casting a fly rod and swinging a tennis racket were both unnatural motions that could easily cause this kind of tendon injury. Something to do with the distribution of the load and the sudden starts and stops. He's probably right about tennis, but fly casting? Unnatural? I'd already decided the guy was a quack before he told me to "curtail my activities for a while"—in the middle of fishing season.

I thought of saying, "Look, I'm an outdoor writer. If I 'curtail my activities,' I won't be able to pay you," but I thought of that after I got home, which was too late.

I tried to learn how to fly-cast left-handed, which is something I should be able to do since I was left-handed until I was about six years old. I got polio then, and my left side was paralyzed for a while. By necessity, I did everything right-handed, and when I came out of it, I had *become* right-handed, although no one noticed until I went back to school and turned in a writing assignment that was backwards. I mean it was written from right to left with all the letters neatly reversed so you could read it in a mirror.

They thought I was just screwing around until one of my teachers tried it and realized it was pretty difficult to pull off. I was a joker, but I was also known to be lazy, and she didn't think I'd work that hard just for a laugh. She had me write something while she watched. She asked my folks, "Wasn't he left-handed before?" They both talked to some doctors, and so on. Then she actually apologized for yelling at me.

I eventually did learn to write legibly, although for years any time I printed something, a few random letters would always be facing the wrong way.

That was a little over forty years ago, but I thought there must still be some old neural pathways left that would let me cast with my left hand. It was pretty awkward at first, but after a little practice I got to where I could make a decent, short-range cast left-handed. But that was about it. I couldn't do anything fancy and couldn't get any distance because, although I could make the left hand and arm cast, I couldn't make the right hand haul the line.

I guess it had been too long; I just couldn't make the brain switch back to the left side again. On a lawn, where I could think about it, I could cast okay left-handed, but on the water, with the thoughtlessness caused by fish and current, I just put the damned rod in my right hand and gutted it out.

I limped through a few more weeks of trout fishing and then consulted Dr. Pao, an acupuncturist, on the advice of a friend who said, "I've seen people limp in there and dance out." I'd never been to an acupuncturist, but it wasn't because of the witch-doctor paranoia some Americans have about them. The fact is, they were curing people (or at least doing them no harm) back when our guys were still bleeding their patients with leeches.

The woman at the front desk said, "First time, huh? Are you nervous?"

"No!" I said.

"Good," she said. "It not hurt as much if you're relaxed."

"That's helpful," I said.

When I met the doctor, I said, "It's tendinitis."

" 'Tendinitis' just a label," Pao said. "This is your very own sore elbow. How did you do this? Tennis?"

He pulled and twisted my arm until we had determined exactly where it hurt and how much, which by then was a lot. Then he stuck pins in it, toasted it with a burning bundle of herbs that looked like a cigar and smelled like a boiling grouse head, and he gave me some herbs to drink three times a day that tasted like . . . I don't know. There's no comparison. The principle in operation here was pretty obvious: If you have the guts to drink this stuff repeatedly, you have the inner strength to cure yourself.

I didn't quite dance out the door of the place, but it helped a lot. Two weeks later I was almost completely well —just an odd twinge in the elbow now and then—but then I went to Scotland for salmon and then to Alaska for salmon, trout, char and grayling and managed to spring the elbow again. And you thought being an outdoor writer was all fun.

Fly-caster's elbow is a terrible malady because you can't get any sympathy. People say things like, "You hurt your elbow fishing? I haven't been fishing in two months." Those who do fish a lot indirectly question your manhood, pointedly saying things like, "Well, I never hurt *my* elbow . . ." And of course techno-freaks preen: "If you'd use modern graphite rods instead of those old bamboos, that wouldn't happen."

Friends trying to be helpful sometimes can't resist attempts at humor: "I knew a guy who got that. Had to give up fishing. Finally lost the arm." That's the kind of thing you say to stop someone from whining. I didn't think I was whining, but sometimes I might have been and just didn't remember doing it.

Then again, A.K., who's a professional fly tier, once got tendonitis from tying too many flies too fast for too long, and people felt sorry for *him*.

So I grudgingly curtailed my activities a little bit, sticking with lighter fly rods, narrower streams and using the canoe on lakes to avoid long casts. It didn't get any worse, and it might actually have gotten a little better.

Then I went to a great brook trout lake where fish were rising like crazy, but the wind was blowing too hard to float the canoe. I made long casts into the wind all day, caught lots of trout and had a pretty sore elbow by the time I got home.

Then grouse season opened and I found that I had a little trouble smartly mounting the shotgun, which is why there's only one grouse head boiling out in the yard. I was going to make another skull mount for Ed, but at least I have an excuse for missing that second bird.

Okay, so maybe this isn't the kind of thing that forces you to confront your mortality or anything, but it does get you to thinking about basic mechanics.

I went to a therapist who used ultrasound, massage and herbal ointments (but no needles) and gave me a tennis elbow brace: a device that fits below the elbow on the forearm to hold the tendon in place.

The thing had a familiar look to it—simultaneously sterile and mechanical—and when I got home I peeked into that bottom dresser drawer in the bedroom where I keep all my old Ace bandages, heating pads and plastic vials, each containing a few leftover painkillers. Plus, of course, the knee, wrist and ankle braces, some of which date back to the days when they used metal for the stiffeners instead of hard plastic.

For some reason it was comforting to be reminded that I've been banging up my joints since I was about eighteen, both at work and at play. I saved the stuff thinking I might need it again sometime, although I somehow always manage to injure something new, which naturally requires a different gadget. It won't be much longer before I have the equipment to immobilize every part of my body that's supposed to bend.

So, now that I think about it, I guess I've always had this tendency to push a little too hard in most ways, pulling in my horns only after I got hurt. That's why I have a few scars and sore spots—physical and otherwise—which are probably a fair price to pay to learn how things work. That's also why Dad used to say I was reckless. Maybe I was, but after years of testing I've developed a pretty good sense of where the boundaries are. Naturally, they're a little farther out than you might think.

The elbow is actually much better now, considering that the real cure would have been to take a year off from fishing. The ice packs, ointments and exercises help, the brace lets me keep on casting, and there's only one more big fishing trip this season. Then there will be some smaller ones, then it'll be winter and maybe I *can* actually curtail my activities for a while. Maybe I'll get a bunch of flies tied. A.K. told me you can tie flies with tendonitis as long as you prop your elbow up on a stack of books.

I haven't been fishing in eight days now, but I tried casting the salmon rod this morning and the elbow was fine —really—just a slight twinge. The rod is a 9½-foot, 8-weight bamboo with a 5-inch fighting butt, and I suppose a lighter one would be better, but I've already spent the price of a graphite salmon rod on doctors, and I don't care that much for graphite anyway.

So the old rod will do and so will the old elbow. The last doctor said it's not even serious enough for drugs now, which is just as well. I'd hate to catch a huge salmon in New Brunswick, only to have my friends say, "Yeah, but I hear he was on steroids."

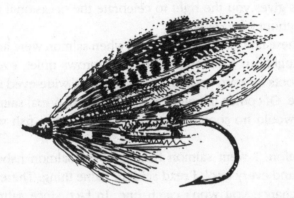

I guess I decided to try fly-fishing for Atlantic salmon out of a feeling of envy. From a distance it doesn't seem to make much sense—fishing for a fish that's not supposed to bite and, sure enough, usually doesn't—but the people who do it swear by it, and that makes you wonder what *they* know that *you* don't.

Apparently, it's an acquired taste, which is something I understand. For instance, like most young men in America at the time, I learned to like beer in my late teens, but if I think back far enough, I can remember a time when it tasted so awful I thought, So this is one of the great pleasures of adulthood. Jeez . . . On the other hand—and maybe more to the point—I never did get into caviar because I couldn't afford the breaking-in period.

I've been Atlantic salmon fishing twice now and I've learned this much: Salmon fishers brag more loudly about their many failures than about their few successes, not only because there are more of them, but because it's believed that enduring failure builds character. But then they also greet success as if they deserved it based on the flip side of the same premise. Namely, that living graciously with your defeats gives you the right to celebrate the occasional victory without false modesty.

These fantastic stories of days when salmon were actually caught are wonderful. The lodge grows quiet, everyone scoots forward on their chairs to listen, wide-eyed and gullible. Of course the guy's telling the truth. A real salmon fisher would no sooner lie about this than snag fish with a jig.

Before I went salmon fishing, every salmon fisher I know and every book I read said the same thing: There's a good chance you won't catch one. In fact, since salmon don't eat when they run out of the sea and into the rivers to spawn, catching one is almost an accident. Almost. There *is* a reason why the odd salmon will bite a certain fly on a certain day, it's just that no one seems to know what that reason is.

That doesn't stop the big volumes from coming, though. One thing I've noticed about fly-fishing writers is, the less sure they are of their subject, the fatter their books get.

I *have* been told by some old-timers that, although catching an Atlantic salmon on a fly has always been a ticklish business, it wasn't always as unlikely as it is now. That's because there used to be lots more fish, so even though it was still maybe only one salmon in a hundred that was dumb enough or confused enough to bite a fly, the odds were a hell of a lot better.

One guy I talked to went so far as to say that at a lot of the places where you fish for salmon now—sometimes paying a hell of a lot of money for the privilege—there just aren't any fish, or at least not enough to be worth the effort. He seemed to be implying that, in some cases at least, all that stuff about the Mystery and the Experience, although once true enough, was now more like a scam.

All I know for sure is, the few Atlantic salmon fishers I'm acquainted with like it a lot and do now and then catch some fish, but they get a little vague when you question them carefully about the actual quality of the fishing, while the majority of my friends see it as the sport of kings and—since they're not kings and don't want to be—they pretty much ignore it.

So I went to the Beauly River in Scotland and got skunked. I had the rhetoric of the sport firmly in mind, but I still couldn't believe it. ("Oh, believe it," said one of the ghillies.) Of course I'd heard this described. You go somewhere far away—preferably to a river with ghillies and castles along its banks—cast methodically for six days with pretty flies and then go home. If you don't have stories like that, you're not a real salmon fisher.

Thank God, four out of the five of us on the Beauly that week went fishless, and the other guy got only one. That's one of the undeniable characteristics of fishing: getting skunked is less painful the more company you have. I did begin to understand why traditional Atlantic salmon flies are so complicated, though. On about the fourth fishless day you begin to think, maybe if I had more stuff on my hook . . .

That was in June. In October of the same year I was at the Nepisiguit River Camp in New Brunswick for the short, four-day week that closes the season there. I was the odd guy in a party of six, most of whom were much older and all of whom had a lot more salmon fishing under their belts.

Many salmon fishers are older folks, at least in part because it can be an expensive sport and it's mostly older people who can afford it. Maybe there's also something about maturity that breeds the necessary patience. Or is it fatalism? Anyway, there's some wisdom to be picked up here, and at the age of forty-something, with some blond hair still left in my beard, I could be referred to as "the young, skinny guy."

Some of these men had fished together for a long time and had some procedures worked out among them. For instance, one of the guys had bad legs and couldn't wade, so a couple of his friends, and maybe a guide, would haul him out to a good spot, prop him against a rock and leave him to fish. When it was time for him to move or relieve himself, they'd haul him back to shore—without any wise-cracks.

When I was introduced to the man known as the Doc, he shook my hand and said, "You look like a flaming, bearded liberal."

"That's correct," I said, "and you strike me as one of those square-jawed conservatives."

"Well," he said, "let's just stick to fishing, then."

Which we did for a change. I do have some political opinions, and I'm usually not shy about sharing them, but getting into an ideological brawl in a fishing camp is like having an affair with a married woman in a small town: It can be worth the trouble, but there are still lots of reasons to avoid it.

I found these guys—the Doc included—to be generous; more generous, I have to say, than your average Rocky Mountain trout fishermen. They coached me as well as they could, considering that the ultimate secret to success is pretty much unknown. There are smaller, more mundane secrets, however.

For instance, in the spring the salmons' mouths are soft, so you don't want to strike when you get a hit. Just the drag of the line against the reel, they say, is enough to sink the hook. But by September and October, the salmons' mouths have grown as hard as dry wall—yet another of the amazing changes these fish go through—so "you want to *hammer* them." You also want to sharpen your hooks to needle points. They said the problem in the fall is that many more fish are hooked than landed and, as always, damned few are hooked.

There were at least two items of tackle these guys all had in common: *very* good reels (including several Bogdans) and professional-quality hook hones.

Fly selection, as usual, was open to discussion, but the preferred local theory called for streamers. Ken Gray, owner of the lodge, explained this in some detail. It seems that in the fall, when the hen salmon are getting ready to spawn, the male fish get particularly aggressive toward the parr. Salmon parr are only a few inches long at best, but they can still fertilize eggs, so the males like to chase them out of the pools. Knowing this, you fish a streamer to imitate a little fish, and if that doesn't work, you try something else, and then something else, and then come back to the streamer again because something (who knows what?) might have changed in the last hour or so.

Ken was different from the Scottish ghillies in any number of ways. Most notably, he seemed to think Atlantic salmon could actually be caught, even by me. He's also the fourth generation of his family to live and fish on that stretch of the Nepisiguit, so his knowledge of it is now almost genetic.

Fall is supposed to be a good time. There are plenty of salmon in the river (at least by modern standards), the water is cool but not too cold, skies are often overcast and sometimes there's enough rain to raise the river a little and get the fish moving. No one can tell you exactly why a salmon bites—*if* he bites—but experience has at least shown what the best conditions are.

The group at the camp the week before had had it all —clouds, rain, rising water—and they'd caught fish. I forget how many now, but it was an enviable number. There were lots more strikes than fish landed, and you could actually look that up in the camp log book. I think salmon fishers count strikes if only to be counting *something*.

Naturally, by the time we arrived the sky had turned bright blue and the water had dropped and cleared and cooled considerably. Everyone agreed that it didn't look good, although, of course, one never really knows.

In four days, fishing the camp's private pools as well as some public water upstream, one guy got blanked, the rest of us each landed a couple of grilse, and one guy also landed a salmon of about 17 pounds, all pretty much against the odds.

One morning I had a salmon on long enough to get him on the reel before the fly came loose. The hook had been sharpened to surgical specifications, and I'd set up hard, though apparently not hard enough. Ken, who'd watched the whole thing from a high bank, said the fish would have gone about 15 pounds. This was generally considered to be not bad—though less than great—Atlantic salmon fishing.

•

The distinction between a grilse and a salmon is something I'm still getting used to. In one sense, a grilse is just a small salmon, a fish around 25 inches in length that's spent one winter feeding at sea. A salmon is the same fish after two or more winters at sea, but those subsequent winters make all the difference.

To a trout fisherman, a 25-inch grilse weighing several pounds is a hell of a nice fish, and even on a stout, 8-weight rod, a big one will really take you for a ride. Okay, but if it survives and returns the following year, it'll be a by-God salmon weighing 10 or 12 pounds. If it survives even more seasons (the probability declines severely with time) it'll weigh maybe 25 or 30 pounds, and then maybe 40, and so on.

What this means to a duffer like me is, you can catch all the grilse you want and be happy as a clam, but you haven't caught a salmon until you've caught a salmon.

I liked it. I even sort of liked it in Scotland in a masochistic sort of way, and when I said that out loud, someone replied, "Ah, you poor lad." But of course New Brunswick was better. I haven't acquired the rarefied sensibilities of the true Atlantic salmon angler, but I do understand that catching fish is preferable to not catching fish.

After two trips and a few fish, I'm beginning to get a vague idea of where salmon lie in a stream, and the fact that they bite best in cloudy weather with certain water temperatures makes them a little more like big trout and therefore more recognizable.

Before you actually do it, Atlantic salmon fishing

seems terribly classy, elite, even snobbish, and that worried me a little. I don't have any business being a snob and I don't think anyone else does, either. But then when you're out there on the water you find that it's just fishing. You know, eat breakfast, string up a rod and wade into the river. You have to learn to live with the unlikelihood of catching anything, but that's really pretty easy: You simply think, This is how it is. It's not like I could be doing it better.

Well, you actually *could* be doing it better, but maybe it wouldn't make a difference.

I've even begun to like some fly patterns better than others for reasons other than that they're just pretty. Like the Herb Johnson Special. I had six or seven strikes and actually landed a fish on that fly—the regional full-dress streamer pattern, with a silver tinsel tag; silver-ribbed black wool body; long, white bucktail throat under a shorter blue hackle; mixed natural, yellow and purple bucktail wing and jungle cock eyes.

In the weeks before that trip I'd pored through some books looking for local patterns and had found only one: the Nepisiguit Gray. It's a handsome, traditional salmon wet-fly pattern, a little on the drab side with its grizzly hackle, gray wool body and bronze mallard wing, but it still has the regulation tip, tag, butt, golden pheasant tail and such—all those bangles that seem unnecessary, even as you're faithfully reproducing the pattern exactly as it's described in the book. I mean, if it didn't mean something, they wouldn't go to all this trouble, would they?

I tied up a handful of them, but when I showed them to one of the guides he said they were nice, but the pattern hadn't actually been fished there "in about a hundred years." Pointing to the other side of the fly box where the streamers I'd just bought were laid out—the Montreals,

Undertakers and good old Herb Johnson Specials—he said, "These are what you'll be using."

So I'm slowly learning, although some important questions still remain. For instance, who is Herb Johnson?

If you ever decide to do this, you *must* read a book on the Atlantic salmon's life cycle first. I won't try to rush through it here because, in human terms, there's just too much starvation, hardship and what you'd have to call heroism to cram into a few paragraphs. But I think you have to know about it because then, although you really want to catch a fish and you try as hard as you can to do it, there will be a small part of you that's happy to see them get away.

I think that's where that gesture comes from; the one Canadian salmon guides do so well when you miss a strike or when a fish throws the hook. It's a lopsided shrug that I take to mean, "Life is ironic, ey?"

Grayling

*H*ave you ever noticed that grayling always get listed last? Below silver, sockeye and king salmon, rainbow trout and char in Alaska; under lake trout and pike in the Northwest Territories; as an afterthought on the Big Hole River in Montana; as a footnote to the high mountain lakes of Utah, Wyoming and Colorado. I don't know how many full-color brochures I've read that say something to the effect that "if there's nothing else happening, you can always fool around with the grayling."

When Ed came back from a fly-fishing trip to Austria a few years ago, I asked him how grayling were viewed over

there, hoping for a little Central European enlightenment.
"They think they're a trash fish," he said. "Face it, grayling
are a neat fish that nobody likes."

Well maybe, but there are exceptions. For instance, I
like grayling—always have—and I've met plenty of other
fishermen who do too, although perhaps not enough to
constitute a real movement.

Mike Schmetzer, a man I met in Alaska a few years
ago, likes grayling a lot and seeks them out, but then he's
an unusual case because he likes to fish with dry flies and
bamboo rods. Nothing against Alaskan fly-fishing—it's a
lot of fun, especially if you like bears—but you have to
admit that most of it is not what you'd call delicate. Many
of the Alaskan fly fishers I met used 8- and 9-weight rods
and carried their 7 pounds of split shot on the hip opposite
their .44 Magnums so they wouldn't walk lopsided.

More to the point, maybe if you catch enough king
salmon the size of small antelope or silvers that smoke your
high-tech reels, you begin to lose interest in pretty little
$2\frac{1}{2}$-pound grayling.

A.K. and our mutual friend Koke Winter also like grayling, although I've never known either of them to go far
out of their way to catch them.

Once we were floating the Madison River in Montana
in Koke's antique aluminum johnboat, the one that looks
like it was used as cover in a gunfight. It was late in the day
and we were down in the channels above Ennis Lake when
A.K. hooked a fish, played it for a few seconds with a
puzzled look on his face and said, "You know, I think this
is a grayling."

"No it's not," Koke said, leaning on the oars and gazing downstream.

"Well," A.K. said, "actually, I think it is."

"You've caught a whitefish," Koke said.

A.K. netted the fish and held it 3 inches from Koke's nose. Koke said, "Son of a bitch! That's a grayling!" and pulled hard for shore.

That's what you do, of course, because grayling are a schooling fish. Where there's one, there's more. Casting from the bank, we caught grayling until well after dark, admiring each one in the failing light and saying things like, "Koke, there's something wrong with this whitefish. Look at this big fin."

Getting into those fish was such a milestone that now, when trying to remember when something happened in Montana, we mark it as so many years before or after we caught all those grayling on the Madison. But when we tell the story, most listeners say, "Oh . . . But did you get any *trout?*"

The first grayling I ever caught were in some remote, pretty mountain lakes and beaver ponds in the Colorado Rockies. We've had small populations of grayling here since they were first introduced way back in 1899. The biologists say they do okay at high altitudes, where the water doesn't get too warm for them, but they've never really caught on with local fishermen, many of whom still think they're some kind of sucker.

It's hard to believe anyone actually makes that mistake. A grayling is a quick, roughly trout-shaped fish with a deeply forked tail and a mouth right in the front of the face where it should be. Of course the distinguishing feature is the tall dorsal fin that looks like an ornate sail. This fin is used in mating displays, so it's larger on the males, but it's still plenty big on the females.

I've caught grayling in several lakes and ponds in Colorado, the Madison and Big Hole Rivers in Montana,

stretches of the Kazan and First Island Rivers in the Northwest Territories and the Agulowak in Alaska. In my color
slides the fish are anywhere from iridescent grayish silver
to bluish purple to bronze, always with those sparse V- or
check-shaped black spots clustered toward the front of the
body. The larger, oval spots on the dorsal fin are blue to
bluish green, and the fin margin is anywhere from pale
blue to a delicate pink. The tail, pectoral and anal fins are
usually a dusky bluish yellow, and the pelvic fins have
cream or pink stripes.

Anyone who honestly thinks this is a sucker shouldn't
be trusted with sharp objects like fish hooks.

Grayling do school up in both lakes and streams, so
although they're not always a snap to locate, once you've
found them, you've found them, at least for a while. In
flowing water they like pools and the slack water on the
insides of bends. In lakes they cruise, often very close to
shore, especially in the mornings and evenings.

It can be misleading to characterize an entire species
of fish, but the ones I've caught do live up to the traditional
profile. For one thing, they're "aggressive to the surface,"
as they say. That is, they'll often rise nicely to dry flies even
when there are no bugs on the water. I have fond memories of big grayling on the Kazan River rocketing up
through 4 feet of miraculously clear water to grab an Elk
Hair Caddis, and of smaller ones in Colorado lakes swimming 3 feet out of their way to take a #16 Adams.

Then again, they'll sometimes get into what seems like
a playful or curious mood and inspect, follow, swirl at and
otherwise mess with three or four different fly patterns
before deciding to take one. As Al McClane said, "You may
come face to face with a grayling and be ignored; yet it will
study every fly as though trying to help you find the right
one."

Standard, boilerplate grayling lore says these fish prefer small, dark flies. That's true enough in my limited experience, and they do have smaller mouths than trout, so maybe they've evolved with a taste for little bugs. Still, you have to wonder how they'd act during a heavy Brown Drake or stonefly hatch.

The old story about grayling being hard to hook because they have soft mouths is flat wrong, but they do have the odd tendency to roll on a dry fly, coming half out of the water next to it and taking it on the way down. That makes most of us strike too soon, either missing the fish entirely or hooking it poorly. In typical human style, we like to think that's the fish's fault.

When fishing for grayling you come to understand the need for a slight but very real hesitation on the strike, which requires a sense of timing and nerves of steel.

Grayling are found in parts of Montana—where they're native—and they've been introduced into some mountain lakes in Wyoming, Utah and Colorado, where they form what guidebooks and biologists like to call "token populations." The once-native grayling of Michigan are now gone. The heart of the grayling's range is in Alaska and northern Canada, especially the Yukon and Northwest Territories where, all things being equal, they grow to their best size.

I guess one should mention that they're often the smallest game fish found in their home waters. A grayling approaching 3 pounds is big enough to mount, and the all-tackle world record is just shy of 6. But then they're also beautiful and real patsies for a dry fly and, after all, size isn't everything, right?

Scientists once thought there were three distinct species: the arctic, Montana and the extinct Michigan grayling.

Now it's believed that there is only one species in North America: the arctic grayling, *Thymallus arcticus.* Or at least that's how things stood the last time I did any reading on the subject.

For the record, grayling are delicious, but then the only ones I've ever eaten were at shore lunches, fresh by a matter of minutes in a situation where a stale granola bar tastes like venison coventry. Also for the record, I'm told they don't freeze well. One of the sad realities of fishing is, you cannot reproduce an authentic shore lunch at home, even if you prop the screen doors open so the mosquitos can get in.

I once had a grayling shore lunch on a stream that, as near as I can tell, had never been fished before. A friend and I were fishing from a camp in the Northwest Territories, and one night as we were going over a map of the area I pointed to a small stream a few miles up the lake from camp and asked the head guide what the fishing was like there. He said he didn't know because no one had ever fished it.

"No one?"

"Well, no white people, anyway, and probably no Indians, either, because they fish from boats with nets and that thing isn't even navigable."

None of the guides wanted to take us there. They said it would be a pain in the ass and, they assured us, the fish wouldn't be very big. But my partner and I weren't about to pass up a chance at virgin water, so we begged, then insisted and finally pulled out all the stops and hinted at an enormous tip.

That was some grand bullshitting on my part, because

at the time I had a plane ticket home and about twenty bucks Canadian to my name, so my share of the actual tip at the end of the trip wasn't what it should have been.

I'm not bragging about that. Actually, I'm pretty ashamed of it because it wasn't a cute little fisherman's fib but a real lie about money to a fellow working stiff. I only bring it up to illustrate how desperate I was to be the first fisherman to cast a dry fly on an absolutely unfished stream. I was almost nauseous from the potential romance of it.

The next morning we motored over to the creek mouth, towing a canoe that we then alternately portaged and paddled a few miles up the stream. There was a pod of grayling in every pool, and our guide was delighted to see that the best fish we caught went about a pound and a half, or at least a pound lighter than the grayling we'd been catching in the nearby Kazan River.

He couldn't understand why we were having so much fun. These guides were already puzzled that we'd spend so much time catching grayling on dry flies when we could have been dredging for 30-plus pound lake trout with jigs and Flatfish. When we started slapping each other on the back over *little* grayling, they probably reached the same conclusion that most fishing guides eventually come to: that the clients themselves are nuts, but there's nothing wrong with their money.

Interestingly enough, these perfectly wild fish were a bit leader shy—as all grayling are said to be—and they would eat small dark dry flies, but not big light ones. Then again, sometimes we'd wade into a pool and the fish would swim over like tame ducks to inspect our boots.

Actually, we didn't have a "shore" lunch. The banks of that stream were so thick in tangled willows and mosquitos that we set up the camp stove on a few dry rocks in the middle of the stream and ate sitting in the water: baked beans, thick slices of homemade bread, lukewarm beer and grayling killed and cleaned *after* the grease was melted in the pan.

Best meal I ever had. I used to think that hunger was the best sauce, but now I know there's a better one: the knowledge that you have just fished where no one has fished before.

According to the map, that little stream ran on for a few more miles to where it drained out of a chain of small lakes that our guide said had also never been fished. "No way to run a boat up in there, and all the lakes are too small to land a floatplane on," he said. His best guess was that the small lakes would be full of pike, while the slack water in the flowing channels between them would be packed with grayling. But then, of course, who knew? Chances were slim that anyone had ever set foot there, let alone cast a fly or stretched a net.

That's when I experienced one of those rare moments of perfect clarity: a simple realization of exactly where I was. I was sitting in the middle of a small, unknown grayling stream looking at a waterproof map that covered 3500-some square miles of lakes, ponds, marshes and streams— a tiny chunk of the Northwest Territories' 1,352,000 square miles, most of which are covered by water, but seldom *enough* water in one place to either take a boat across or land a floatplane, and not enough land to walk more than a couple of miles in any one direction. From the camp we were staying at, you could crank up the outboard and motor 70 miles up and down Snowbird Lake and, if you had the guts and the time, several hundred miles down the Kazan to Hudson Bay, but in terms of total area, that's nothing.

As a perpetual tourist fisherman you can spend your

life stumbling past fundamental truths that, because of the single-mindedness of fishing and the brevity of your stay, you can never quite get a handle on. But when you do accidentally grasp one, it's amazing how neatly everything slips into place.

I waved my hand over the map and said to the guide, "You mean to say *most* of this has never been fished?"

"Hell," he said, "damn near *none* of it's been fished."

10

The Kindness of Strangers

*I*t had been a busy summer so far: lots of fishing (which I sometimes say is my job) with a little bit of frantic writing (which really *is* my job) wedged in between. When I got back from twelve days in Alaska, I found that I was still mentally exhausted from the work, but also refreshed and invigorated from the fishing, which left me sort of stuck in neutral: weary, but not exactly ready to rest.

I guess there was a little sleep deprivation in there, too. Summer days in Alaska are so long you can end up fishing for eighteen hours and sleeping four or five. You don't actually feel tired, but after a week or so you start walking into trees and forgetting your friends' names.

Anyway, that's how I was feeling—pleasantly bushed and a little disoriented—when A.K. called to see if I wanted to go over to the Frying Pan River. I said I should stay home and work, but he didn't want to know what I *should* do, he wanted to know if I was going fishing. I thought for a minute and said, "Yeah, okay."

You have to understand that this is the annual trip; a tradition. Every season, sometime in late July or early August, the Green Drake and Pale Morning Dun mayfly hatches overlap perfectly on the Pan, and A.K., Ed and I have been hitting that—or at least trying to—for quite a few years now.

We always set up a comfortable camp at Roy Palm's place—whatever bird dogs he has around at the moment move in with us as camp mascots—and we fish hard, but also manage to relax a little, too. After all, the Pale Morning Duns and Green Drakes keep banker's hours, so there's no reason to be on the water at dawn, and a leisurely breakfast in fishing camp—drinking a third cup of coffee while scratching a retriever behind the ears—is pleasant if only because it's so rare.

I've fished the Pan long enough now to have seen it change some. The hatches are a little different than they were a dozen years ago—heavier here, lighter there—and I've seen fish sizes and numbers go up and down, though never so far down that it wasn't still a great stream.

But the biggest change has been a kind of gentrification. There are more houses along the river now, and most of the new ones are palatial numbers (rumored to have cost millions) with commanding views, lots of glass and, in the foreground, along the river, NO FISHING signs.

This is something I hate to see on general principles, and the first question that comes to mind when I come upon one of these huge, overbearing monstrosities of a house is, Who the hell do those people think they are? If it turns out that there's an afterlife, the owners of these things are going to have to account for having taken up a lot more than their fair share of room.

Then again, it *is* good for the environment, as holders of private water are always quick to point out. "A trout stream is better off being fished by a select few than being hammered by the mob," they say. As a dues-paying member of the mob, I've never liked the sanctimonious sound of that, and those who use it as an argument don't seem to realize how flimsy it sounds. As a friend of mine says, "If I'll never get to fish it, why the hell should I care how good it is?"

On the other hand, the three of us have fished the Frying Pan long enough to have some loose connections over there, so we can occasionally get on some of that private water. Sometimes we're invited out of the blue, so we don't even have to suck up. We do it when the chance comes along because, well, who wouldn't? But it sometimes makes me feel funny.

On this last trip, A.K. and I got on an especially good private stretch. Ed had already left, and it was my last day there—I really did have to get some work done—but A.K. would be staying on for a few more days to camp and fish by himself, which he likes to do. I knew he'd call me when he got back, just to let me know how great it had been after I left.

We drove up to our benefactor's house, past a sign that read, NO FISHING, DON'T EVEN ASK, and got a couple of big orange buttons to wear on our vests so that whoever needed to know (hired thugs? snipers?) could tell at a distance that we were legitimate guests of one of the landowners controlling that stretch of river.

I don't know if it was the haughty language of the sign or the big, gaudy buttons, but although the fishing was good with a Green Drake dry fly and an emerger on a short dropper, I didn't feel quite right about being there. This is not a new feeling for me, and it's never a simple or even a predictable one. It just pops up now and then to bother me. To be honest, though, it often conveniently bothers me on the drive home, after I've caught a bunch of big, private fish.

But not always. Sometimes when I'm fishing private water I see it as what it probably is—an example of the kindness of strangers—and I just enjoy it. When I pay a rod fee, I usually experience the righteousness of the capitalist: Maybe the fishing is better than on public water and maybe it's not, but by God I purchased the right to be there.

But then there are other times when I feel . . . well, if not actually guilty, then at least embarrassed, hoping no one I know sees me fishing behind the Keep Out sign or recognizes my truck parked up at the Big House. Sometimes I'll try to think of what I'm doing as a populist raid on the ruling class: After all, it may be a private stretch of river, but these are still the People's trout. Other times I'll amuse myself by planning to fish the place *without* permission: figuring out how one could best sneak in, stick some fish and slip back out without getting caught.

For the record, I haven't poached or trespassed since I was a foolish boy, but I find an odd sort of comfort in the idea that I haven't forgotten how to do it. On that stretch of the Frying Pan it would be easy. Anyplace that makes such things could copy that big, campaign-sized button you have to pin on your vest. There are enough landowners involved that anyone who saw you would assume you were a guest of someone else. You'd fish out in the open, standing erect, and wave happily at anyone who happened to pass by. By the time they realized their mistake, you'd be long gone. You could probably only get away with it once, but if you were doing it just to prove a point, once would be enough.

But, as I said, I'm not a poacher. These are just entertaining mind games in the same league with, say, sexual fantasies.

I can't tell you exactly where the embarrassment I feel on private water comes from, but it's real enough that it comes from somewhere. Maybe it's because I spent so many years gazing longingly at private water I thought I'd never get on and alternately hating and envying the people I saw fishing there. I was doing that in my twenties when, typically, one's sense of idealism takes shape. As you grow older you get either more realistic or more cynical (two shades of the same color), but that perfection you once saw sometimes comes back to haunt you.

I know it's not a perfect world, but if it was there'd be enough good water for everyone and all of it would be public; open to the mob, that is, because the water and the fish would be considered the property only of God and the People. If the fishing wasn't good for everyone who wanted to wet a line, then the fishing would not be considered good for anyone.

But of course the mob wouldn't *be* a mob, they'd be a loose society of sporting ladies and gentlemen, each with good manners and the environmental conscience of a saint, so there'd be no vandalism, no garbage and only the occasional fish kept as needed for food.

Naturally, there would be lots of water and so few people (courteous people, at that) that crowds would never be a problem.

In this Utopia there might not be such a thing as money, but even if there was, it wouldn't be used to buy privilege or to close land and water, so there'd be no hard feelings, no class warfare.

Where was I? Oh yeah, back in the real world where the number of anglers is growing while the amount of fishable public water shrinks, and where, just that year, I'd fished a private trout club in Colorado, some private bass tanks in south Texas, private spring creeks in Montana, a private salmon river in Scotland and so on. After all, as I keep telling myself, it's my job.

Okay, but then I know how my luck runs. Anytime I start thinking I'm actually getting close to some kind of inside track, something happens to remind me that I am, as always, just another guy standing on a stranger's front porch with his hat in his hand.

My friend Jack called me once and said he'd wangled permission to fish a spring creek that he (and the precious few others who have fished it) tell me is easily the best trout stream in Colorado and probably one of the best in the country. And there's no aesthetic sidestepping here. It's the best, they say, in terms of numbers of large trout that can be caught on dry flies between about mid-April and the end of June, and then again in late summer and fall.

So Jack and I were scheduled to fish this thing, and it

hadn't been an easy matter; at least not for Jack. I was just along for the ride, having done nothing more than pick up my phone when he called.

To get on the stream, you have to not only know the owner but also somehow get on his good side, which I'm told isn't a snap and can't be done with money. Then you have to negotiate with the old guy who sold the place to the current owner a few years ago, but who still lives there raising his horses, caretaking the stream and, of course, fishing.

The old man is in his eighties and, like all old cowboys, he is bent, gnarled and gimpy from being kicked by and thrown off of large animals all his life, but I'm told he's still a great fly caster.

We were supposed to fish there on Thursday, but we stopped in Wednesday just to say hello to the old man and let him know we were in the area.

"How's the stream look?" Jack asked.

"Not good," the old man said.

He told us the flow was down and he was afraid his fish might be getting stressed. He wasn't sure we should fish it.

We all went over to have a look at the stream, and Jack and I both thought it had a good head of water in it. There were five or six trout rising in the first pool we came to, and at least two of them looked very large.

I said, "It doesn't look bad to me," and the old man said, "Yeah, now that I look at it, I guess it'll be okay."

"Okay," Jack said, "we'll see you in the morning."

That was about one o'clock in the afternoon, and we spent the rest of the day fishing another nearby creek that was also said to be very good. Jack said it was a little low, too—though not dangerously so for the fish.

The famous Mother's Day caddis hatch we'd hoped to

hit wasn't quite on yet (there were a few caddis flies in the air, but no rising fish), so we worked weighted nymphs in some of the deeper holes.

It was the kind of fishing I say I like best: dramatic and a little bit painstaking, so that every fish caught stands out as its own small victory. We worked the stream for about five hours, and I landed four trout. The smallest was 19 inches.

The next morning we drove back to the fabled creek where, Jack said, I should be ready to achieve Nirvana. "Even on a mediocre day," he said, "it's like nothing you've ever seen before."

We were putting on our waders in the driveway when the old man hobbled out. He said that the owner had come by yesterday to look at the stream and had decided it was in fact too low and we shouldn't fish it. Sorry.

Jack, who is well known for his wisecracks, was speechless. I, just along for the ride, as I said, was now just along for the ride home.

That's how it is with private water. You fish—or not —at the whim of the owner, and I accept that because somewhere in my straight line of radical populist leanings there's a snarl of respect for private land. It would have been nice if the guy had changed his mind before we made the five-hour drive and stayed overnight, but those, as they say, are the breaks.

I guess I was a little pissed when we were turned away, but by the time I was driving up the last stretch of highway toward home I'd convinced myself it was probably for the best. I mean, if I fished the finest trout stream in Colorado now, everything else would be downhill, and I'm too young for that.

Does that sound a little hollow? Well, so be it. That's my story and I'm sticking to it.

•

Not long after that, A.K. and I were doing a book signing at a fly shop in Denver. A young guy came in, bought a book and said he was taking the whole summer off to fly fish before he went back to school to do some graduate work.

He was clean cut and well dressed, so I took a wild guess and said, "Law school, right?"

He said, "Uh, well, yeah," looking around a little guiltily.

I said, "Don't worry about it. In ten years you'll own a nice little spring creek somewhere and A.K. and I will be knocking on your door asking to fish it."

He smiled. He probably thought I was kidding.

That was all last season. This year, Steve and Larry and I suddenly have a little piece of private water of our own. It's a small bass and bluegill pond, and it doesn't seem very elitist to us if only because it was a gift. One day the woman who owns it said casually, "You know, if you guys want to stock and manage my pond, you can have it to fish in." No lease, no money changing hands, no strings, just the rare logic of generosity: I own a little pond, I know some fishermen who seem like nice enough guys, why not put the two together?

This is a plain, small stock pond, just big enough to be more than a puddle, just deep enough for fish to winter over, with year-round water from a spring, a small island and cattails on the uphill bank. It's not beautiful, but it's handsome in a homespun, practical way, and it's a ten-minute drive from my house, two dirt roads from the highway.

The pond bottom is a little on the featureless side, so the first thing we did was make five big bundles of brush to sink at the deep end for cover. Then we stocked it with 8-inch bass and lots of fathead minnows. At this writing we're in the process of transplanting crawdads, frogs and a variety of warm-water insect nymphs from surrounding ponds and lakes. We want as natural a fishery as we can get while still stocking three thousand fatheads as fish food.

For a while we considered getting a shipment of hybrid bluegills from a hatchery in Georgia—a kind of designer panfish with a high growth rate that don't over-populate and stunt because they're sterile—but in the end we decided on plain old, garden-variety, sexually active sunfish.

The pond will take a few seasons to develop, but in time it should be okay and it *could* be great. The hardest part will be not fishing it for a while so the fish can settle in and start to grow up.

Once the woman who owns it said she thought it was kind of sad that these fish only existed to be caught. I said, "Look, it's also kind of sad that as far as the government is concerned, *we* only exist to fight the wars, pay the taxes and believe the lies." I'm sure that made her feel better. Anyway, she never mentioned it again.

We will take our friends to the pond once it's up and running—we've already agreed on that—and I think we'll be generous about who our friends are, but even if the woman who owns the place would stand for it, we won't put up a sign reading, BASS POND—OPEN TO THE PUBLIC—EVERYONE WELCOME.

The pond won't have to be posted because it's out of sight of the road, and the driveway, though long, clearly *is* a driveway, complete with mailbox. There's usually someone around, and if not, anyone who just wandered in there would have to deal with Khan.

Khan (or Khan the Magnificent, as I like to think of him) is a large, black, impressive Great Dane. He was taken in a few years ago as a sick, hungry stray, and the theory is he was mistreated as a pup, because he doesn't like men.

The first time we all went out to the pond, it took Khan about ten minutes to decide to let us out of the car, and then there was a moment when we didn't think he'd let us back in.

A few days later we came back with the five bundles of brush, a box of large-size Milk Bone dog biscuits and Steve's young son, Julian. It's men Khan doesn't care for. Children and women are okay. So while Steve, Larry and I tied up the bundles with nylon cord and weighted them with rocks, Julian fed Khan the whole box of treats.

Since all dogs are basically whores, the deal was struck. Now when we drive up to the pond and Khan comes roaring out like the Hound of the Baskervilles, all we have to do is roll the window down a crack and slip him a Milk Bone. You can almost see the light go on as he remembers: Oh yeah, I don't like men *in general*, but I'll make an exception for men with dog biscuits. So Khan is now our buddy, proving once again that everyone has his price.

CHAPTER

11

Blue-winged Olives

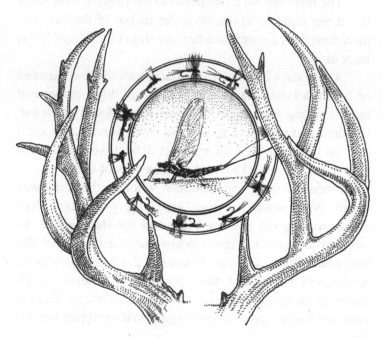

*T*here are some things in life that seem unfair. Don't worry, I won't go down the entire list, but consider that here in Colorado deer season comes right in the middle of the best Blue-winged Olive mayfly hatch of the year. Some friends and I usually hunt deer in the second of the three regular rifle seasons, the long one during which the weather almost always turns wonderfully wet and cold.

There's good tracking snow then, but it's also classic Blue-winged Olive weather.

For the last few years we've hunted up in the headwaters of one of the state's best trout streams. In the tailwater stretch down below the dam that week, the #18 Olives are boiling out of the riffles, big rainbow and brown trout are eating them, and the colder and wetter it is, the better the fishing gets. I wouldn't say the trout are exactly easy even on the best days, but they feed well and you can catch them.

This is the latest predictable hatch on this river and some people fish it, but the weather is often foul, so most of the fair-weather fly fishers are gone, and many of those who also go after deer, elk and/or grouse are out hunting. The crowd that remains is relatively small and it's comprised of the kind of people you don't mind running into on the water, even if there are still a few more of them than you'd like.

In other words, it's just about perfect, and this is all happening forty-five minutes downstream by pickup truck from the cabin we hunt out of.

The first year we hunted up there, I took along the fly-fishing gear. You know what I was thinking: I'll bag my deer in the first day or two of the season and then fish for a week while the venison hangs out in the shed to age properly. It'll be the cosmic cast and blast trip: big fat mule deer, big fat trout on dry flies, a warm cabin with a fireplace and a bed with sheets to come back to at night, and no telephone.

Well, there actually *is* a phone within walking distance of the cabin, but I don't tell people about it. This is one of those rare situations where you can control reality. Just say, "I can't be reached," and sure enough, you can't be reached.

So that first season I packed the fishing stuff: vest, waders, every fly I owned in size 16 or smaller, plus a fly-tying kit in case two hundred-some flies wasn't enough, and three or four light fly rods. As A.K. says, "You pack the rod you're going to use, plus a couple of others you *won't* use."

I had a spare rifle, too, and lots of ammunition—the one bullet I'd use, plus a couple more boxes. I try to pack sensibly and efficiently for trips, but somehow my pickup always looks like I'm off to spend a couple of years exploring a new continent.

Most years, A.K. goes fishing during that middle deer season. He approves of hunting—any professional fly tier who buys bucktails by the crate would have to—but he doesn't do it anymore. Maybe he would if the timing of the season wasn't so inconvenient for a dry-fly fisherman. When we both get back there's the usual comparison of notes. He'll say, "Well, did you get your deer?" and I'll say, "Yeah, did you get your trout?"

Then he'll tell me all about it. The hatch he fished was invariably the best he's ever seen—the longest with the most bugs and the biggest trout—the implication being that every year I miss it, it gets a little better.

The autumn Blue-winged Olive hatch can be a long one around here, so I do get to fish it a few times before deer season and at least once or twice afterwards on a couple of different rivers. But, according to A.K., the absolute, orgasmic height of it comes during that one week to ten days when I'm out in the woods with the .30-06.

I've often thought of compiling a Plain English/Messing With Your Head dictionary as a public service. It should be written down somewhere that "We're sorry" really means "Actually, we're not sorry at all," that "To help us serve you better . . ." translates as "Pay us and then do the work yourself," and that "The fishing was the best I've ever seen" only means "You weren't there."

The Blue-winged Olive is my favorite mayfly if only because I've fished the hatch so often and for so long. I think it was the first mayfly I identified (or had identified for me) and I know it was the first dry-fly pattern I got into after deciding that maybe a guy should have something besides an Adams in five sizes.

These bugs are found on almost all of the streams I fish in Colorado—not to mention some more exotic spots —and they're multibrooded, so there's usually both a spring and a fall emergence. The autumn hatch always seems better to me, but that may just be because it's more poignant: the last of the mayflies, then midges and then winter. Around home the Olive hatches give things a nice, cyclical flavor, and stumbling on the flies *away* from home makes something click so hard it's almost a physical sensation. I think, Okay, I'm probably gonna catch some trout now.

And there's also a feeling of permanence to it. I've caught trout on Blue-winged Olive hatches in psychological conditions ranging from cocksure insolence to emotional wreckage; through two wives, a number of girlfriends, several presidential administrations, dozens of jobs and hundreds of crises that seemed absolutely pivotal at the time, but most of which I can barely remember now. Life hurtles forward, but in an unsure world that one mayfly hatch is as familiar as my own eye color or shoe size.

A.K. and I have come close to blows a couple of times over the exact color of this fly, as well as, in a more general sense, whether or not getting the color perfectly right helps you catch more fish. I say copying the shade of grayish olive *precisely* isn't necessary, but I do use A.K.'s carefully worked-out colors now on the premise that if it doesn't matter, it can't hurt, either—and I suppose, to avoid having to listen to the lecture again on those days when he catches more fish than I do.

I carry lots of flies for the Olive hatch: two or three nymphs, a couple of emergers and no less than four patterns for the dun. My best is a parachute with a dyed quill body and split hen-hackle wings: a slightly fancier variation of A.K.'s good old Olive Dun. It's a killer, but it takes a little longer to tie than most and it's not all that durable, so I usually save the pattern for tough trout in slow water.

I also carry the spinners: #18 and #20 Red Quill and chocolate-colored dubbed body jobs, some with feather wings and some with poly yarn. Most of the entomologists say the Blue-winged Olive spinner isn't important, which is true most of the time. But then every few years there's that hour and a half when it *is* important. It's not the few extra trout that makes tying the flies worth the trouble, it's that feeling of being deeply hip.

There are fishermen around—the few true experts— who understand lots of different hatches on lots of rivers. I've always wondered how it would feel to reek of wisdom like that, and I think I can get an inkling of it with the Blue-winged Olives. I probably don't know as much as I think I do, but, if nothing else, I have this profound feeling of recognition. When the flies are on the water, I honestly know what to do, and then what to do if that doesn't work and so on. I can also watch the weather at certain times of year, decide that the hatch must be coming off on a river a hundred miles from home, drive down there, and sometimes it is. When it isn't, I can only assume the bugs are sick.

So I brought along the fishing stuff that first season we hunted deer high up on the famous trout stream, and it was something of a disaster. The first day I hunted quickly and impatiently, which of course is insane, because deer hunting is one of those endeavors where hurrying is worse than useless. Over the next few days I managed to slow down to something like the proper pace, but I was still anxious and distracted. I knew the deer would be up on the ridges, but I kept finding myself down along the river. It does hold some trout, but up that high at that time of year you won't see them rising. I looked anyway.

One day I decided the hunting was bad and I should just go catch some trout, but by the time I'd walked back to the cabin I realized the hunting wasn't bad, I was just hunting badly, so I went back out. Poor state of mind. Running in circles, literally and figuratively. Unable to focus on the here and now because of . . . Well, there's no other word for it but greed. I wanted it all so badly I wasn't gonna get anything.

I felt a little better the next day when one of the guys in the party actually walked over to the phone and checked in with his office. The rest of us talked about throwing him out, but it was his cabin.

To make a long story short, I never got fishing and I didn't get a deer. When I got home I called A.K., who'd spent several days on the South Platte River that week.

"How was the Olive hatch?" I asked.

"Oh God," A.K. said, "you shoulda seen it!"

(I thought, Yeah, as it turned out, I shoulda.)

Then he asked, "Did you get your deer?"

"Uh, no, not this year."

"Too bad," he said.

The lesson here was one of those complicated ones involving things like respect for the game, inner peace, avarice and concentration. The fact is, we modern Americans seldom get it right. We live entirely too well in some ways and not nearly well enough in others. We either want more than we need or settle for less than we deserve, and we never seem to understand what we're doing wrong at the time.

Last year I must have done it right. In the two weeks before deer season I fished the Blue-winged Olives half a dozen times, mostly with A.K. The fishing was great, and at least one of those days was what you'd have to call perfect: cloudy, cool, lots of bugs and more big trout than anyone has a right to expect. You know, one of those rare times when you walk away from rising fish, thinking, How many do you have to catch before you've proved your point?

Then I went deer hunting and, on the third day, made a shot comparable to the longest, prettiest cast you ever pulled off. There was that inevitable moment of sadness and elation, and then the hard work, but I thought, this is a better reason than most to not go fishing. I hadn't brought so much as a single fly rod, so after that I spent some time looking for blue grouse and helping haul out two more deer.

Later in the week I even spent an hour or so sitting on a stump with the shotgun in my lap, mulling over nothing in particular. The deer season isn't the last event of the year or anything, but it's still the kind of milestone that should be observed by a good hour of stump sitting. I remember thinking, There's still a lot to do, but there doesn't seem to be anything to do *right now*.

When I got back I called A.K.

"Get your deer?" he asked.

"Yeah," I said. "How was the hatch?"

"Oh, man," he said. "It was amazing. I mean, it was . . ."

"Tell the truth," I said, "was it better than that day two weeks ago, you know, when I caught the big rainbow and then the big brown on the next cast and you were so busy catching fish you didn't even want to take pictures?"

"Well," he said, "I don't know if it was *better*, but it was that good."

CHAPTER

12

The Buck

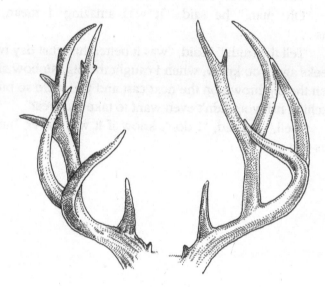

*B*efore last deer season, I'd have told you I haven't cared much about antlers for the last ten or fifteen years. I don't mean I'm not impressed by a great rack or by the hunting skill it often takes to collect one, it's just that in recent seasons I've evolved into a meat hunter and, as every doe stalker has said at least once in his life, you can't eat horns.

This isn't a big philosophical position or anything, it's just the way I've come to think about it. I can't say I hunt for food alone, but I also won't kill something I'm not going to eat, and that has slowly and steadily led me away from trophies—or at least I thought it had.

This last season, Ed, DeWitt Daggett and I hunted the same rugged piece of national forest on Colorado's West Slope that we've been going to for a number of years now. It's a great place: There's game in the woods, but not enough to qualify it as one of the state's more fashionable big-game units, and large parts of it are either too steep, too rocky or too littered with deadfall to get around in easily. Consequently, the area isn't usually crowded and it *is* usually undersubscribed, which means that if you apply for a drawing license, you'll almost surely get it.

And we have the use of a neat little cabin over there, too, complete with a fireplace, easy chairs, warm, dry beds and, of course, some huge local antlers from the old days mounted on the wall. It's nothing fancy, but after a day in the woods it seems downright luxurious and the whole setup just couldn't be better.

We'd all drawn the same tags for the rifle season in late October, licenses that allow you to take either a buck or a doe in the first three days of the season, or just a doe thereafter. It's sort of a weird arrangement—but one the Wildlife Commission apparently thinks is for the best—and for a hunter like me it amounts to a regular old doe tag.

Now this turned out to be a year when there were fewer deer around than in recent seasons. The official explanation was that Colorado had had five unusually mild winters, during which the deer herds grew large, followed by a more or less normal one that pared down the populations in some areas. It wasn't a catastrophe—in fact, it's how the population cycle works—it's just that we'd gotten spoiled, and now things were a little more normal than we were used to.

Anyway, we hunted hard on opening day—each of us going to places where we'd done well in years past—without seeing any deer or even all that much in the way of sign. But we didn't lose heart, and I guess that's one of the reasons I get along with these guys so well: We all want success, but we also believe that you have to go where the hunt takes you and accept whatever lessons it offers.

I mean, if you're paying attention, it's actually possible to learn more by *not* getting a deer than by, say, shooting one in the first hour of legal light on opening day, as I did the season before. The only things I learned from that were how to accept dumb luck gracefully and how to kill a week in deer camp.

So we began to study the maps, pack bigger lunches and range into places we'd never gone before, which meant longer, steeper walks and the likelihood of gut-busting drags if we got something, but okay, fair enough.

On the morning of the fourth day I was on top of a high, steep, quartzite ridge. I'd hunted around the base of this thing for the last few years but had never before thought of climbing it. Or, rather, I'd thought of it, but I hadn't considered actually *doing* it. There's a difference.

DeWitt had been up there the day before and had seen what he excitedly described as an enormous buck with possibly the biggest rack he'd ever seen on a mule deer. The buck was already bounding when DeWitt saw it, and although he got a pretty good look at it, he didn't feel he had a makeable shot, so he didn't fire.

Of course the little three-day buck season was over

when I started up there, but I figured if there was a buck there might also be some does, and anyway, the approaching likelihood of getting skunked gave me whatever it was I needed to grunt up there. I don't think it was desperation exactly, more like the resolve to give it a good, honest try so that if in the end I really didn't get one I could feel okay about it.

It was a long, hard, uphill slog, but it didn't hurt quite as much as I thought it would, which was a nice little surprise. And it was beautiful up there. This is a long, Roman-nose-shaped ridge that runs east and west and falls off to the north—into the valley carved by one of the state's best trout streams—in a series of forested benches, punctuated by two sheer rock cliffs and a ragged scree slope. Real geologic poetry. It's mostly scattered pine and spruce near the top, shading into patches of aspen down the slope a ways. There's lots of deadfall and virtually nothing you could call level ground. The woods there had the feel of a place where humans seldom go, although I can't swear that's true.

Anyway, there was a lot of deer sign up there compared to the places I'd been hunting for the last few days. There were fresh tracks and droppings and recently used beds, as well as a whole system of wide, apparently heavily used game trails.

I worked my way on up the ridge until I came to a little saddle that separated the formation I was on from a longer ridge pointing up toward the Continental Divide. DeWitt had described this the night before after he calmed down about the big buck. He'd come in from the other side —a longer route than the one I'd used, but no easier—and he said he was glad he'd made the hike, because it put the topography of the area together for him in a new way. For me, too. From his description, I knew that if I kept on heading west along that spine, things would begin to look familiar inside of 2 miles.

I hadn't exactly hunted on the way up, I'd just walked, trying to make the best time I could. I think that was the correct tactic, because the wind was at my back and no amount of stealth could do anything about the stink of human wafting out in front of me. And anyway, what I really wanted to hunt were those benches, so I went out the ridge, dropped down the north slope a little and hunted back with the wind in my face.

I thought I was still hunting well—stepping slowly and quietly, stopping every few paces to pick the woods apart piece by piece—but then I flushed a doe that had been lying on a bed no more than 30 or 40 yards in front of me. We danced around in some thick brush for a few minutes, but she evaporated before I could get a shot.

I felt bad because I'd blundered into what could have been an easy standing shot. Then I felt good because I'd gotten so close before the doe heard me and because I'd finally seen a deer after three days of hunting. (I'd had a raghorn bull elk in range the day before, but I didn't have an elk license.) I sat on a log long enough to calm down and eat a few handfuls of trail mix, and then hunted on out along the benches.

About a half mile farther on, as I was working my way down toward a narrow bench, I spotted the cream-colored butt of a deer lying on the far side of a couple of young pines. This time the animal hadn't seen or heard me. It was curled up asleep in the pine duff, so I couldn't see its head.

I began working around above the animal, hoping to see the head (and hoping it was a big doe) but I didn't get more than a dozen agonizingly careful steps before I realized I could easily blow this by being too eager. I could almost hear my father saying, in his most impatient tone of voice, "Goddamn it, a good hunter is *patient.*"

So I sat down where I was, with a good view of the deer's back and chest, but with its reclining head behind a tangle of brush, and waited. How long I waited I couldn't say. It seemed like an hour, so it was probably less than fifteen minutes.

During that time, I'd slowly raised the rifle twice to look at the deer through the scope, trying to get a peek at its head; and the third time I did that there was a ripple of muscle along the back and, sure enough, the head came up, along with a huge set of antlers that I think I'd been seeing all along but had mistaken for part of a dead tree.

At first—sitting there waiting—I'd thought the deer looked too big, but then I decided it was closer than I'd thought it was. That wouldn't be unusual, since I've never been good at judging ranges, even close ones. But now I understood what I was looking at: easily the biggest buck mule deer I'd ever seen, probably 300 pounds, maybe more. The side of the rack I could see clearly had five points, heavy prongs, and the beams at the skull looked as big around as my wrists.

I know, in a story like this it's supposed to be the biggest buck the writer ever saw, but this one really was, honest.

He was, in a word, magnificent, a trophy for sure, maybe even one for the books and, now that I had the perspective in hand, a clear, easy shot at maybe 70 or 80 yards. He didn't seem especially alert and he was looking off down the slope away from me, so I don't think he knew I was there. I believe he'd just awakened naturally from his nap.

I wish I could say there was a moment of moral confusion, but in fact the plan came to me easily and in one seamless piece. All I had to do was punch my license for the day before, when the buck season was still on. It would be an entirely plausible story that I'd shot the buck late yesterday when it was still legal, left it hanging overnight and was only now getting it out. The day was chilly and threatening snow. By the time I got Ed and DeWitt and we'd dragged the carcass out, it would have cooled convincingly. My partners would know what I'd done, but otherwise it was the perfect crime.

It's interesting how badly I wanted that buck, being, after all, a guy who claims not to care much about antlers.

I had the rifle to my shoulder already, and the crosshairs just naturally placed themselves on the heart/lung shot. I'd been sitting there quietly long enough for my breathing to be normal and for my heart rate to have slowed some. I clicked off the safety. The rifle felt alive and friendly, the way a rifle feels the instant before a flawless shot, and I had sin and larceny in my heart.

But of course if I had shot, you wouldn't be reading this, would you? I held the crosshairs on until they started to wobble, then I lowered the rifle, shouted something obscene and watched the buck spring to its feet and thunder off down the slope. When DeWitt was describing this animal—it had to be the same one—he said he thought he felt the ground shake as it bounded off. I had assumed he was using a little poetic license, but then I thought I felt it, too.

I stood up, took a few steps, slipped on a teetery rock and fell down hard, bruising a knee slightly and putting an inch-long gash in the stock of my rifle that I suppose will always remind me of that buck. I don't know if my legs were shaky from adrenaline or just from sitting so long in the cold.

Since then I've occasionally wondered why I didn't shoot. It doesn't haunt me or anything, it's just something I think about every once in a while. It would be nice to say I knew I'd never be able to look at those antlers without feeling a stab of guilt, or that I didn't want to involve my two old friends in a dirty little secret, or that I just knew it was wrong and instinctively did the right thing. Or maybe I just suspected that I hadn't quite thought of everything and that I'd end up getting caught. I don't remember any of that running through my mind at the crucial moment though, so I guess I'll never know for sure.

Then again, maybe what I should be wondering about is why I almost *did* shoot.

That night I told Ed and DeWitt the whole sordid story. They sympathized, said they understood the temptation, but they didn't come right out and say they'd have come as close as I did to actually doing the deed. In fact, I thought Ed gave me sort of a funny look, as if, after all these years, he realized he didn't know me quite as well as he thought he did.

They also didn't point out the obvious: that in a normal deer season you're likely to get that one opportunity that fits your skills and limitations like a glove. If you make the shot, that's your deer; if you don't make it, that *would have been* your deer. And when it was the buck of a lifetime and you're not much of a buck hunter, the karmic implications are staggering.

"Well, anyway," I said, "I know where I'm going next year on opening day."

DeWitt said, "Yeah," then thought a minute and added, "you know, the time is gonna come when we're too old to run up hills like that anymore."

"Sure," I said, "but as long as we can, I think we should keep running up there, right?"

CHAPTER

13

Carp

I do fly fish for carp and I'm not here to apologize for it, which is how a lot of these stories begin. (That there *have* been other stories should tell you something, but never mind about that.)

I will admit that the first carp I caught on a fly rod was an accident and that, after I saw it and realized it wasn't an enormous largemouth bass, I was pretty disappointed and even a little hesitant to touch the thing. And when I first stumbled upon a couple of local fly fishers who were actually catching carp on purpose, I thought it was either a joke or maybe another little campaign in the sport's ongoing class wars.

But either way, I figured I'd better try it, and when I did, the most natural thing in the world happened: My aesthetics adjusted themselves to fit the situation. I mean, the fish were big (a 5-pound carp is nothing special), they were spooky and sometimes discriminating, the fishing itself was visual and stealthy and I couldn't catch them at first, even though a carp-fishing dentist I know had given me the dressing for his secret, killer carp fly.

Beyond that fly pattern, advice was hard to come by. There was no hot young carp guide down at the local fly shop, no standard carp-fly selection in any tackle catalog and no book entitled *Selective Carp*.

I guess that was the most exciting part: So few people fly fish for carp that very little is known about the sport. If you want to learn how to do it, you have to pick the brain of one of the rare people who's into it, or just go out cold and try it for yourself. In *Carp in North America*, published by the American Fisheries Society, Ronald J. Spitler says, "When it comes to fly-fishing [for carp] we are drifting a bit into the unknown . . ." I don't know about you, but I kind of like the sound of that.

Where I've fished for them the most—in the warm-water ponds and reservoirs of northeastern Colorado—you can usually find carp tailing like bonefish in the shallow flats on hot summer days. They're beautifully camouflaged against the silty bottom, but you can pick them out by the faint, lazy puffs of mud they blow through their gills as they suck in food, or by their tails waving slowly under the surface like big brown flowers. In deeper water you can sometimes locate them by the trails of tiny bubbles they leave while feeding. (I once asked a carp fisher what exactly caused those bubbles, but he didn't know. Apparently, further study of carp physiology and pond bottom ecology is needed.)

Anyway, then it's a matter of casting a weighted fly ahead of a fish, letting it sink to the bottom and retrieving it in front of him, slowly or briskly, depending on his mood. I'm told it's just like fishing crab flies for bonefish, right down to sounding a lot easier than it really is.

Sometimes you'll spot pods of four or five carp slowly cruising off the bottom in clear water. They're as easy to spook as brown trout would be in the same situation, but if you cast quietly and far enough ahead of them, one may peel off and take a slowly sinking or gently retrieved nymph.

And, naturally, rising carp will take dry flies. By the way, a carp rising to insects or whatever floating on the surface is said to be "clooping."

When it comes to choosing fly patterns, the boilerplate logic of fly-fishing works as well as anything. That is, the more convoluted logic and poetry you can cram into it the better, but unless you have a better idea, just copy the food organism.

Carp feed mostly on aquatic and terrestrial insects, crustaceans, crawdads and such—pretty much what trout would eat in the same water. For tailing carp, I've had my best luck with size 8 or 10, drab-colored, weighted flies tied upside down so that their hooks ride up. This keeps you from fouling on the bottom and, since the fish comes at the fly from above, you want the hook on top anyway— a nice coincidence.

One of my favorites is the Tarcher Nymph, invented as a trout fly by Ken Iwamasa of Boulder, Colorado. Tom Austin, lately of Austin, Texas, does well with bonefish flies like Crazy Charlies and Epoxy flies ("Carp don't know there ain't no crabs and shrimp in here," he once told me), and

Steve has come up with a neat little Clouser Minnow variation he calls a Bloodshot Charlie—one of only three or four
patterns I know of that are tied especially for carp.

The carp I've caught, and seen caught, on dry flies ate
trout patterns that more or less copied what was on the
water: grasshoppers, mayfly spinners and so on. Then
again, the first carp I ever hooked on a dry fly took a #14
Royal Wulff, even though he seemed to be eating cottonwood seeds.

I didn't know about it then, but one of the carp patterns I've run across *is* a cottonwood seed. Another is a
deer-hair mulberry. Like the man said, "we are drifting a bit
into the unknown."

I guess I didn't do this entirely for its own sake right at first.
In the beginning, it was just a hoot to do something that
some of my colleagues considered beneath their dignity,
although, to be fair, few of my real friends worry much
about dignity, and most of them who aren't into carp respond the way A.K. does. "I think a guy should do whatever the hell he wants," he once told me.

"Do you want to go carp fishing tomorrow?" I asked.

"No."

Okay, but then, when I couldn't catch one right away,
hooking a carp fairly on a fly became a mildly interesting
problem. Then I caught a little one, weighing maybe 3 or 4
pounds, and it nearly took me into the backing on a 6-
weight bamboo rod and put a set in one of the tips. When
I took the tip over to Mike Clark's rod shop to have it
straightened, he asked, "How'd you do this?"

"On a big brown trout," I said.

"Bullshit," he said. "You did this on a carp,
didn't you?"

●

It turns out that as a fly rod game fish, the average carp is far bigger than the average bass or trout and more widely distributed than both put together. He can be difficult to hook, and he'll usually fight with great strength. In the best carp water you stand a better than even chance of hooking and landing a 10-pound or bigger fish and, since most American fishermen (and especially fly fishermen) don't much like carp, you'll probably have the best water all to yourself.

You know how other fishermen sometimes casually drift over in your direction when they see you catching fish? They do that when you're catching carp, too, but when they see what you're into, they just drift away again. I wish I could make them do that with trout.

Oddly enough, America is one of the few places where carp are generally disliked. In Europe they're highly regarded as a food and game fish and were once reserved only for royalty. In China and Japan they are traditional symbols of strength and nobility. Poets write about them, painters paint them and samurai warriors once rode into battle carrying carp banners.

Carp were introduced to America in the late 1800s to replace some of the native fish populations that we had all but destroyed through pollution, commercial fishing and general habitat destruction. They did well because they were hardy enough to live in the now warm, muddy water that other game fish couldn't handle, and they were well received at first.

But by the early 1900s carp began to fall out of favor as a food fish, probably because Americans didn't understand how to raise them commercially. In Europe, carp for eating were kept in clean, cool water, but here they were farmed in, or caught from, any old hot, murky pond, and they tasted like it.

We eventually came to miss the fish the carp had replaced, but, although it was our fault the water wasn't clear and clean enough for them anymore, we somehow managed to ignore that. According to Rob Buffler and Tom Dickson, in *Fishing for Buffalo*, the American prejudice against carp developed as follows: First we trashed our waters to the point where nothing but carp would survive in them, and then we blamed the carp for trashing the water.

That's unfair, but I guess it's not all bad. The thing I like most about fly fishing for carp is, it's not popular and, with any luck, it never will be. In a way it reminds me of the way fly-fishing itself was way back before it became fashionable. If you were heavily into it, you were considered sort of a nut, and those of us with antisocial tendencies felt pretty comfortable with that. If nothing else, people would leave you alone, and being left alone is one of the great underrated pleasures of life.

Once Steve and I were out in a boat, casting to some big carp that were feeding up against a dam face. A couple of guys wandered out on the walkway above us and watched for a while. Finally one of them called down, trying to be helpful, "Them are carp, you know."

"Yeah, we know," we said in unison.

"Okay," the guy said, and he and his friend walked away.

So, although I've come to think of these critters as big, handsome, graceful, intelligent, wary fish with a kind of quiet, understated classiness about them, they're still "just carp" and most people can't understand why you'd want to catch them. It makes it hard to take all this seriously— and that's how fishing should be. If people don't occasionally walk away from you shaking their heads, you're probably doing something wrong.

In fact, the only fishing contest I've seen that makes any sense to me is the Big Lip Invitational, fly-fishing's only carp tournament, held every summer in Fort Smith, Montana. Steve and I have fished in it as a team for two years now. At first we just saw it as a joke, but after the first one we began to see it as a more refined, intelligent joke: a genuine tournament that is, nonetheless, a spoof on tournaments.

The saving grace is that there's no prize money. The winning team (the one that boats the most carp) has their names engraved on the traveling carp trophy and gets to bask in ten or fifteen minutes of local glory before the picnic breaks up and everyone goes home. That's it.

There are also awards for the biggest carp, the carp with the biggest lips, and a few booby prizes for things like the carp with the *smallest* lips. The rules themselves are simple: two-person teams, fly-fishing only, catch and release, no motors, no chumming, carp must have both lips to qualify.

The field is small—there were sixteen boats in 1993, a few less in '94—and the entry fee is just enough to cover a picnic supper and official T-shirts.

Of course Steve and I—not to mention the other Colorado team, Larry and his wife, Donna—have our own T-shirts. The motto reads, "Carpe Carpio," which we thought was Latin for "Seize the Carp." We learned later it should have been "Carpe *Carpium*," thought about changing it, then decided that a grammatical error in a dead language was somehow appropriate for an event like this.

The contest began six years ago as the logical extension of a typical guide's day off. Some of the people who guided trout fishers on the Bighorn River below Yellowtail Dam took to going up above the dam to Bighorn Lake to fly fish for carp on their days off—to relax, to get away from the crowds and to have some yuks. It was fun, it wasn't easy and, guides being guides, some discussions arose as to who was the best carp fisher. Hence the tournament, organized by the Bighorn Trout Shop in Fort Smith.

A few teams from out of state have entered in recent years, but this is still essentially a small, local event held in a sleepy little fishing town in southern Montana—sort of an elaborate guides' day off. It draws no spectators, teams aren't sponsored by tackle manufacturers and this is probably the only thing resembling press coverage you'll see on it. And, although more than one fisherman in Fort Smith or at the nearby Cottonwood Campground will tell you, "We take our carp fishing seriously around here," something in his manner will suggest that isn't completely true.

Considering that the winners of this thing probably qualify as the fly-fishing-for-carp champions of North America, it's all surprisingly casual, although this year we did receive a warning. A guy took us aside and said, "Keep an eye on your boat." It seems that the first year we were newcomers and so had been treated as guests, but by coming back a second time we've become regulars. "Someone could, you know, steal your drain plug or hide your oars," the guy said.

Apparently tricks are played now and then, although it's not always clear what's a practical joke and what's not. On the morning of the last tournament, John Keiser showed up with a primitive-looking carp painted down each side of his drift boat. "Is that a case of vandalism?" I asked. "Oh no," he said proudly, "I did that myself." Someone standing nearby said, "You'll be able to wash that off, won't you?"

Incidentally, hanging on the wall of John's trailer is the only mounted carp I've ever seen in the flesh. It's huge. He says it weighed 20 pounds. Actually, he said, "All I know for sure is, it bottomed out a 15-pound Chitillion scale. Twenty anyway, maybe more."

I don't know if a mount indicates seriousness or not. If I remember right, that *was* the only stuffed fish in the place, but I guess that's understandable. After all, once you've got a 20-pound carp on the wall, even a 10-pound trout would look puny by comparison.

Steve and I have never won the tournament, but then we've only been in competitive carp fishing for two seasons, so we're still rookies. The first year we were in a three-way tie for second place, which was not a bad showing for a couple of newcomers. Last time we finished farther back, but I caught the biggest carp: a $6\frac{1}{2}$ pounder on a dry fly, for which I was awarded a set of carp notecards.

Still, we plan to keep at it until we can bring the traveling trophy—and the glory—back to Colorado for the winter, although it's always in the back of our minds that no one really cares much one way or the other.

But the best thing about the tournament is the fishing itself. The water in Bighorn Lake is gin clear and cool; the banks are either rubble rock or sheer cliff and there's no bottom feeding, because, at the lower end of the reservoir where the tournament takes place, the bottom is 400 feet down. This is by far the best dry-fly carp water I've ever seen.

The best way to find carp that will take dry flies is to cruise around the shoreline, looking for their snouts quietly poking up through windblown rafts of organic and semi-organic matter where insects, among other things, collect.

This stuff is not exactly classic trout-stream foam and I didn't know what to call it until Steve suggested "schmoots." I like the sound of that and, after all, we do need the terminology. This is a fairly new sport, but it's still fly-fishing, so we have to be able to say things like, "It was a hot, windless afternoon and carp were clooping in the schmoots."

Any bug is fair game for a carp, and matching the hatch does work, but on warm summer days a fair number of grasshoppers get on the water, and Steve and I have found that a small hopper pattern or a light Elk Hair Caddis (either in about a size 12 or 14) is a good bet. The contestants in the Big Lip Invitational are pretty secretive about their fly patterns, so I can't tell you what the real pros use. Last year one guy went so far as to spray paint the lid of his clear plastic fly box so no one could even catch a fleeting glimpse of his carp selection.

Carp feeding on the surface are fairly easy to spot—at least once you know what to look for. The rise is so subtle it usually leaves no ring, even on dead smooth water, and that round, dark nose looks like a waterlogged pinecone bobbing on a gentle swell.

The trick is to put the fly in front of the fish, close enough that he'll see it, but not so close that it will spook him. It takes steady nerves. Carp don't charge the fly, and the actual take is slow and deliberate. The fly disappears, you tighten the line slowly until you feel pressure and *then* set the hook.

The fishing is delicate, demanding and visual, and the carp fight unusually hard in that cool water. Several times now I've been taken well into the backing by carp that weren't all that heavy. Fish over 10 pounds are sometimes landed in the reservoir, but most run around 5 or 6 pounds.

That's not terribly large for carp, but it's bigger than the average trout caught in the Bighorn River.

The local guides have mostly kept this to themselves, but I did hear of at least one party of paying clients who were taken to the reservoir for carp after several good days in a row on the Bighorn. One of these guys hollered, "Whoo, hoo, hoo, hoo!" every time he hooked a carp. He'd done that with trout on the river, too, but up at the reservoir there was no one to hear him so, the guide said, "It wasn't quite as embarrassing."

This last time, Steve and I arrived a couple of days before the tournament and checked into the campground. We planned to spend a day scouting the lake before the contest and maybe a day floating the river for trout. But then after a great day of carping with caddis and hopper patterns, and considering reports that the river was only fishing well with nymphs, we asked ourselves, "Why nymph fish in a crowd when you can catch bigger fish on dry flies in solitude?" and headed back to the lake.

Come to think of it, I never have gotten around to fishing for trout in the Bighorn River. I should do that one of these days. I hear it's actually pretty good.

14

Travel

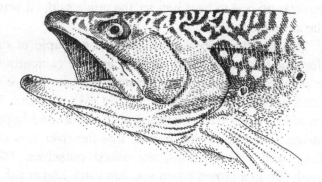

*I*f you're a fly fisher, you *will* develop a serious itch to travel if you haven't already. It comes with the sport: the nagging certainty that, even if you live five minutes from one of the best trout streams in the country, the fishing must be better somewhere else—or if not better, then at least different in some tantalizing way.

Be prepared to be misunderstood by nonanglers on this point. Not long ago I went to Labrador with A.K., who caught, among other things, a 6½-pound brook trout on a dry fly—a genuine trophy in anyone's book. Not long after we got back I watched him land a 7½-pound rainbow in a river just a few hours' drive from home. Sometime later his wife asked him, "Why did you have to go halfway to the Arctic Circle when you can catch a bigger fish at home?"

The answer is, "Precisely *because* it's halfway to the Arctic Circle."

Any fly fisher worthy of the name can rattle off a dozen lakes, rivers, streams, keys, coasts and beaver ponds he's heard about and would like to try, places where the fish *may* be bigger than they are back home, and where they're certainly different. The real problem is paring the list down to a manageable size.

The species of fish you have a soft spot for will give you a good general direction here, and in fact many anglers have their own personal "cross the street" analogy to fall back on, as in, "I wouldn't cross the street for lake trout, but I'd go to hell and back for Atlantic salmon."

(For you lake trout fans, that's just an example, okay?)

And I think it's best to forget about what's fashionable this season. If the fish and the location you're interested in aren't splashed all over the current fly-fishing magazines, so much the better. That just means the guides won't be as busy and the waters won't be as crowded.

In my business of writing stories about fishing, it's always tempting to try to sniff out the new hot spots, if only for the scoop, and then frantically bang out the stories before someone beats you to it. But then as an actual fisherman my tactic has usually been to hang back while the jet-set, fun-hog, been-there-done-that contingent invades and pillages a new location. I write and fish because I enjoy both. If I wanted to live a life full of pressure and urgency, I'd get a real job.

I also thoroughly enjoy the kind of country I'm familiar with (after all, it took me long enough to *get* familiar with it) and don't have a taste for the exotic for its own sake. People who do say that travel to strange new places is broadening, and they're absolutely right. I have done some of that and it's been damned educational. You get to see how people do things differently from how you do them and still seem to get along; in fact, they often get along a whole lot better. And you see how Americans are viewed, which, as often as not, is with a combination of amusement and charity.

But there's nothing wrong with intimacy either, and I've noticed that almost all of my travels take me north, through the overlapping ranges of the North American ice-age flora and fauna I know and love: to where there are brown instead of black bears, spruce grouse instead of blues, black spruce trees instead of Engelmann; to where the brook trout, rainbows, cutthroats and such may be bigger, but where they'll often eat the same flies they take back home, cast on the same fly rods.

So far I've resisted saltwater fly-fishing, even though it's become so stylish it's hard to hold up your end of a conversation if you haven't done it. But it can be terribly expensive, I don't have the tackle and my least favorite kind of weather is the hot, humid, oppressive variety.

And then every time I begin to weaken a little, I meet an adrenaline junkie who says, "Once you get one of those silver torpedoes on a fly rod, you'll never want to mess around with trout again," or words to that effect. And I always think, Right, that's just what I need, something to bugger up one of the few remaining loves of my life.

So I usually go north because that's where I usually feel like going. Others hanker to go south, toward the equator, and still others will go anywhere just *because* it's anywhere. That's up to you and it's the easy part. The hard part is choosing a specific destination and deciding on the style and pace of the trip. Sometimes one will pretty much determine the other, but you'll often have the choices of going

in cold and figuring it out as you go along; hiring a guide
for at least part of the trip; or doing the full-blown week at
a fishing lodge.

I've done it all three ways, plus a few ways in between,
and they've all had their charms, but be careful of roughing
it just to save money. You might find, as I have on occasion,
that after driving 600 miles (or flying and then renting a
car), plus eating in cafés and sleeping in motels, it wouldn't
have cost much more to stay at a lodge. The best reason
for roughing it is that you like it that way.

I do like roughing it, and so do most of the friends I
travel with. We like the cafés and roadside camps, navigat-
ing with maps, changing plans on last-minute whims, stopping at little bait stores to buy nonresident licenses and
trying to figure out if the toothless old bird behind the
counter is really giving us a good tip or sending us on a
snipe hunt. The long, lonely drives are the kind of shared
hardships that make you feel like you've really gone someplace and that you are, in fact, a long way from home,
being self-sufficient. Even a breakdown in your own
pickup truck is more interesting than being stranded in an
airport, if only because you can do something about it.

If nothing else, a road trip amounts to several days of
running conversation with friends, and since good talk is
so hard to come by these days, that in itself is worth the
effort.

On the other hand, an arranged trip can have its advantages, too. There's something neat about knowing exactly
where you're going, how you're going to get there and
how long you'll be staying, having a printed itinerary from
a travel agent, being met at the airport by the head guide,
having someone else do the cooking. If the camp van

breaks down halfway to the lodge, you're still stuck, but figuring out what to do next is someone else's problem.

Barring a catastrophe, all you have to do on a trip like that is fish and ponder whatever comes to mind. Your most momentous decision will be whether you want to go for rainbows again today, or grayling, or maybe try for some char. You can leave your watch in camp and discard your sense of logistics. At lunch the guide will hand you your sandwich, and someone will tell you when it's time to pack up your stuff and go home.

I don't travel or fish to "get away" because my life at home isn't something I need to escape from, but I do find that I think more clearly on a trip. Or maybe "think" isn't the right word. What sometimes happens is, things I've actually given up thinking about just slip into place of their own accord, providing either the answer or, more likely, the realization that an answer is not required.

A couple of seasons ago I was in a Mackenzie boat on the Bow River in Alberta. We'd just drifted around a big, lazy bend, and there was a beautiful gallery grove of mature cottonwoods, lit up by the late afternoon sun, with a flock of twenty or so white pelicans bobbing in the water in the foreground. The guide was pissed at the birds because they scare the trout and he wanted me to fish that backwater, but I thought they were real pretty, and suddenly, out of nowhere, I realized I didn't have as much against computers, virtual reality and all that crap as I thought I did, although that had been the farthest thing from my mind. It began to occur to me that as people spend more and more of their time gazing into boxes with glazed expressions and becoming more and more docile to make things easier for the machines, maybe those of us who are still a little bit self-sufficient will be able to take the world back.

"Goddamn pelicans," the guide said.

I said, "Don't worry about it."

Over the years I've gone on some great trips based on little more than a hunch and maybe a story from someone I thought I could trust, but I've also researched new places in considerable depth, which is easy enough if you're able to talk to strangers on the telephone.

I've called the Division of Wildlife (or whatever they call it) for the state or province I was interested in, then checked with the tourism board, a guides and outfitters association, a couple of chambers of commerce and maybe a few local fly shops for good measure. Then I've topped it off by calling one of the travel agents that deal exclusively in fishing trips to ask, for instance, "Where's the best fly-fishing for grayling in the Northwest Territories?"

Usually, after discarding the claims that sounded too good to be true—and therefore probably were—I've ended up with a short list of guides, outfitters, lodges or whatever.

Speaking of which, you *will* have to sort out some claims. After all, you're now involved in fishing and advertising, two of the three fields of human endeavor where the truth is most likely to be wounded or even killed. (The third, of course, is politics.)

In my experience, hard sells are a bad omen. Remember that good fishing lodges and guide services are among the last businesses that still make it on plain talk, results and a good reputation.

Beware of statements that sound good but also seem to leave something important unsaid, like, "We have a 56-pound salmon mounted on the wall at the lodge" (that was found washed up on the beach, dead of old age, in 1937).

The same goes for photos in the brochure. Okay, the fish is huge, but is the guy holding it wearing spats and standing in front of a Stutz Bearcat?

What you really want to hear about is last season, and if they say, "Well, a guy caught a 12-pound brown trout," your reply should be, "Good for him. How did everyone else do?"

If you encounter too much obfuscation, find another outfit. There are lots of them.

Unless they've been highly recommended by someone you know well, don't patronize a lodge or guide service that can't or won't supply you with references. And *call* the references. It's true that a lodge won't give you the name and phone number of someone who fell in the lake and nearly drowned or who didn't catch any fish because he was in a coma from mosquito bites, but you can still get valuable information, like, "Sure, the fishing is great, but the cabins leak, the food stinks and the guides are surly."

On the other hand, it's possible for the accommodations to be *too* good. You'll run across resorts that can't say enough about their lovely rustic lodge: sumptuous rooms filled with antiques and lavish, gourmet meals. As you'd expect, a place like this will be more expensive, but the fishing may or may not be any better than at the funky, comfortable little joint a mile farther up the same river.

This kind of outfit may even have a different view of fishing than you do. I stayed at a fancy lodge in the Rocky Mountains once, and I knew I was in trouble the first day. The fishing had been slow, but late in the afternoon a hatch of caddis flies came on and some large brown trout began rising. I'd landed a few fish and was tying on a fresh dry fly when my guide said, in an apologetic tone of voice, "Uh, if we leave now we'll just get back in time for cocktails."

We dragged in about ten-thirty that night, having

missed both cocktails and dinner. While the lodge manager scolded my guide, the chef was roused to make me a cold sandwich from the leftover venison crown roast.

In the end it worked out surprisingly well. I asserted myself as politely as possible and the staff made allowances —without grumbling—for a client who actually wanted to fish.

When it comes right down to it, how posh the lodge should be is a matter of personal taste and budget, but one question you must always ask yourself is, Am I going all that way to fish, or to eat, sleep, have cocktails and look at antique furniture?

Timing is also important. A lodge or guide service may operate for six months out of every year, but the fishing will change drastically during that time. Maybe there's a hot six weeks in the middle of the season when conditions are perfect, and then perhaps another couple of weeks right at the end when the fishing can be absolutely glorious, but when you also stand a better than even chance of getting shut down by foul weather. Or something like that. Every place is different.

If the lodge manager tells you that every single week of the season is just great, you've either stumbled upon the cosmic fishing hole or the guy's trying to fill up some marginal slots.

One sure way to tell when the best weeks are is to see which ones are already booked by return customers. You may have to wait an extra season to take advantage of that, but then fishermen are supposed to be patient, right?

Now I don't mean to give you the wrong idea here. Most of the professional fly-fishing types I've met are honest, hardworking people who are simply trying to properly extol the virtues of their lakes and rivers. But, like all fishermen, they remember the good days more vividly than the poor ones.

Of course there's another side to all this: You have to tell whoever you're dealing with exactly what you want, and to do that you must first get that straight in your own mind. Do you want to fish big rivers from a boat, or small streams on foot, or lakes, or a little of all three, or don't you care one way or the other? Do you want to catch lots of fish or a few trophies? Are you after one particular species or a grand slam? Do you envision a relaxing trip, or would you prefer a guide who will either get you into fish or kill you in the attempt? Do you use dry flies exclusively, or would you just as soon fish with whatever's working?

I tend to be a dry-fly fisherman myself, and I remember arriving at a remote lodge in western Canada that had advertised blanket hatches of mayflies and caddis, only to be told we'd be fishing streamers on sink-tip lines because the early hatches were over and the late ones wouldn't start for another six weeks. In the stunned silence that followed I realized I'd have known that *if I'd only asked*.

That one worked out okay, too. I got an education in streamer fishing, caught wild Kamloops rainbow trout and Dolly Vardens, and fell asleep each night to the sighing of the wind and the giggling of loons. After all, what other choice did I have?

Still, you want what you want—or at least you think you do—so don't be shy about calling someone with a list of reasonable requirements. They're used to it and they usually appreciate it. They don't want the wrong client any more than you want the wrong guide.

It's also a good idea to be honest about things like your physical condition and your skills as a fly fisher. If you'll be expected to hike 20 miles a day or cast at tournament ranges into a strong wind, it's best to know that beforehand.

Most lodges and guide services will provide you with a list of things you should bring, usually including recommended fly rod weights, types of line, leaders, fly patterns, waders, clothing and so on. My advice is, bring what they suggest, because you'll probably need it.

Be sure to ask about special baggage restrictions. If you'll be going into a remote area by floatplane or helicopter, expect a weight limit of something like 40 or 50 pounds, which, in fact, should be plenty for most fishing expeditions.

It's almost always best to go as light as possible, and the real trick to packing for a fishing trip isn't so much to bring what you need as to *not* bring what you *don't* need. Most people pack too many clothes. Rather than a complete wardrobe for all the weather conditions you might encounter, try the layered effect with a light canvas shirt and a heavy wool one, plus long johns, sweater, down vest and a good rain slicker: stuff you can wear a few pieces at a time or all at once as needed.

As a chronic overpacker myself, I know it's possible to pare things down nicely by just asking the obvious question about each item you're thinking of taking. For example, "Do I really need this whetstone, or should I just sharpen my knife before I go?"

Different destinations will require at least slightly different gear, but there are four things I always take regardless of what the lodge specifies, all of which, at one time or another, have been worth their weight in gold: a spare rod, spare line, rain gear and bug repellent.

And always bring a nice fat book. In a stormbound lodge many miles from the nearest town, you can either read it or sell it for a hundred dollars.

•

Naturally, some brochures are more helpful than others. For instance, I have some literature from a lodge in British Columbia. It says to bring "a fly box with an assortment of wet and dry flies for rainbow and cutthroat." What? As a veteran fly fisherman, I can tell you there's hardly a fly pattern in existence that hasn't, at one time or another, been used to catch those two species of trout.

This place also lists (in the same almost useless way) suggested tackle for spin fishers. That's another bad sign. There's nothing wrong with spin fishing, it's just that few things are sadder than a sport with a box of dry flies paired with a guide who only knows how to troll hardware. Fly-fishing has never been more popular, and there are plenty of places that specialize in it.

Then there's this other brochure that includes a separate sheet listing specific fly patterns, colors and sizes, broken down into four roughly six-week-long time slots through the season. It's on a separate, photocopied sheet so it can be updated easily.

It doesn't take a genius to spot the more competent outfit.

If the recommendations for gear and tackle in the brochure seem too vague, don't be afraid to call and ask for a clarification. If the clarification seems vague also, consider the possibility that these people don't know what they're talking about.

Finally there's the matter of your own attitude, which can make or break a trip. There are sports out there who seem to think a fishing lodge is a kind of theme park where the rides always leave on time and where Mickey and Goofy will appear on schedule, rain or shine. It's not like that. If it was, it wouldn't be any fun.

The best lodge in the world can only put you on good water with a competent guide in a boat that doesn't leak. The rest is up to you and whatever gods there may be. So you pick the best place you can find in the best area at the best time of year, while bearing in mind that this is real life, and in real life there are days—or even weeks—when the fish just don't bite.

Sometimes things won't be quite as you expected them to be, and if something is either puzzling or clearly unacceptable, you should go ahead and speak up. On the other hand, try to keep an open mind. A friend of mine says, "If a trip was entirely predictable, you wouldn't have to go," and it's not unusual for the most surprising things to be the sweetest. After all, great fishing is like great poetry: It makes the hair stand up on the back of your neck, and if you didn't see it coming, so much the better.

At a remote fishing camp late last season an old friend and I got a guide who scared us a little at first. He looked like an ax murderer who'd slept in his clothes, had hollow-looking, unblinking eyes and he'd mumble a few words only when he thought conversation was absolutely necessary, which in his opinion was almost never.

But after two hours on the water it became obvious that this guy was a Zen master among fishing guides. His battered canoe did precisely what he wanted it to without so much as a lurch or a gurgle from the paddle; he knew where the big trout would be and he knew what they wanted before they did; he could net a fish so deftly it never knew it had been caught; and he could start a one-match fire from wet twigs and brew perfect oolong tea in a used bean can—all pretty much without comment.

We realized we were in the presence of greatness: an authentic, supremely competent backwoodsman of the old school who just happened to be a little on the shy side.

When my friend and I booked another week at the same lodge for this year, we asked for our old guide back.

So my advice is, do the research, ask the questions and in general cover all the bases you can. Then go to a place you've always wanted to see in hopes of maybe having a little adventure there, but try not to be much more specific than that.

And do not, under any circumstances, sit down on the flight home and figure out what the fish cost you per pound.

CHAPTER

15

Winter

Winters can be great here in the Rocky Mountains. It's never unrelentingly one way or another, but in a normal year we'll see dank, Midwestern-style cold with sticky wet snow that freezes at night to a crust you can almost, but never quite, walk on; dry, arctic cold with powder that eats snowshoes up to your knees; dark, airport-closing, pipe-splitting blizzards followed by blue stillnesses, which are followed by warm, hurricane-force winds and unexpected thaws that, in turn, are followed by avalanches.

As I write this, it is, in fact, Avalanche Awareness Month here in Colorado.

Naturally there are some thin-skinned types who whine about all this, but most of us just figure they're victimized by deep character flaws that are probably beyond their control. Unless we're cooped up with them for long periods of time, we at least try to be polite.

A good, hard winter bodes well for water in the trout streams the following summer (although a heavier than usual runoff may postpone the trout fishing a little, and there are always those who worry about die-off in the deer and elk herds), but it's also beneficial in its own right. Fresh snow is helpful for tracking rabbits and hares, and it can make pheasants bunch up; the cold freezes the lakes so you can ice fish if you get that desperate for some sport; low, wet clouds can make the late-season geese fly in range and so on.

Things are seldom what we think of as perfect, but they're often just as they should be, and there's almost always some good in that.

I like winter, and this is one point where my girlfriend Susan and I disagree. She's a Spanish/Norwegian hybrid, but the Spanish is dominant, so she doesn't do well in the cold. I'm a German/English mutt—strong on the German —so I do.

Last night at ten o'clock, it was exactly 10 degrees by the thermometer outside the kitchen window, and for some reason I enjoyed the apparent symmetry of that. Susan didn't. I was sitting around in shirtsleeves, drinking something nice and cool, while she was right next to me on the couch, wrapped in a sleeping bag and cuddling a cup of hot tea and a warm cat. She wasn't whining, but she was looking miserable. As I said, it's genetic.

I live in a drafty old house with a woodstove and a weak gas furnace as backup, so you do feel the weather inside. Even *I* won't go barefoot, what with the cold winds that sometimes blow near the floor, but I guess I don't really mind that, even though it's not energy efficient and therefore politically incorrect.

I suppose there are some things I could do to winterize the place a little, but that would seriously cut into the hunting and fishing time—not to mention the fly rod and shotgun budget—and if there's a single thing I've learned in life it's that one must keep one's priorities straight.

I like winter, and I like being out in it hunting, snowshoeing, fly-fishing in the handful of rivers that stay open and even ice fishing now and then. Susan says this is where I begin to flirt with that fine distinction between just being eccentric and being downright nuts.

Granted, it doesn't always *look* like fun to the objective observer. I'll stumble home, beard encrusted with ice, face blue, feet and fingers numb, maybe with a dead rabbit or game bird or some stiff fish, and she'll just shake her head. Don't get me wrong, she loves to eat wild game and is always glad to see it, but when it comes to going out in the cold and wet to get it—and enjoying that—there is no comprehension, no sympathy.

I guess it *is* hard to explain: doubly hard without getting all mystical and macho about it. There's just something about honestly encountering conditions as they are, not beating them, but slipping in neatly and feeling more or less at home. The idea that humans can profit from nature has been a dangerous one for nature, but when the profit is nothing more than a couple of trout, birds or bunnies for dinner and it's garnered on foot, using simple hand tools and weapons, it at least seems honorable.

A few Christmases ago there was a commercial on TV that had me fuming for days after I saw it. A fat woman was complaining about the holidays because there was all this food around and she always gained weight. (The ad itself was for a treadmill, or maybe diet pills.) I guess we're that spoiled now. Half the world is starving, including some of our own citizens, and fat women on the tube are complaining about too much food.

It's possible that the blood sports are largely symbolic now—which is why it's preferable to catch your trout one by one on dry flies rather than to just dump Clorox in the river—but I think it's enlightening to go out and work for some of your food. The pain you feel when the fish won't bite, the pheasants flush a hundred yards in front of the dog or the geese fly out of range of your fowling piece is a reminder of real hunger; not the kind you feel on a post-holiday crash diet, but the kind that comes when there's no damned food.

I got out of my funk by convincing myself, on a pheasant-hunting trip to Nebraska, that the TV lady was, after all, just an actress reading lines for money, which she would use to buy groceries.

It was cold and beautiful in Nebraska, hiking the swales and gullies around the cut corn with Steve and his dog Poudre. It was late in the season, when most hunters had gone home, but the birds were still spooky. We were happy to get a few pheasants and a handful of quail, although if we'd sold them, we wouldn't have made enough to pay for the motel room, let alone meals and shells. Hunting and fishing may be symbolic in some ways, but next to the symbolism of money they look like stark reality.

•

It's almost always beautiful outside in the winter. If you stay away from things like heavily used cross-country ski areas, where herds of sheep in neon clothing congregate, there's a wonderful stillness to things: the Japanese sparseness of a raven perched on a black snag on a snow-covered hillside. It's serene, comforting and always at least a little bit dangerous.

You want to get your share of fish or game and you can't mind a little normal discomfort. On the other hand, you know that, for instance, falling in the lake in shirtsleeves in July is one thing, while going through the ice in four thick layers of clothing in January is another. So beyond the satisfaction of getting where you want to go and collecting some game if you're lucky, there's the added satisfaction of being able to take care of yourself in a situation where some care must be taken.

If you pay attention, you can learn some useful life skills, such as caution, judgment and how to feel confident within your own limitations. At some point—usually after you've already made a few notable mistakes—you no longer have to ponder questions like: Am I a wuss if I go in now, or am I a fool if I stay out? It's like wondering if you should quit drinking: If the question has come up, it means you should.

A few weeks ago, when two friends and I spent nearly all day hunting and I shot the only snowshoe hare, I tried to explain the profound symbolism of it all to Susan.

"The thing is," I said, " 'there will be hunger in the other lodges tonight.' "

"No there won't," she said. "They'll just call out for a pizza."

"Well, I mean, *figuratively.*"

I've noticed that about warm-weather people: Their sense of poetry seizes up at about 40 degrees.

Once she said, "You guys complain about the cold, too, you know. You come home and talk about how awful it was."

"Yeah," I said. "That's part of it: recognizing your human frailty in the face of higher natural powers. I guess it's a man thing."

"Why isn't it a man thing to go to the Bahamas?"

Well, because you don't suffer in the Bahamas, and suffering in the pursuit of sport is meaningful. If nothing else, some modest hardship seems to indicate that there's a little more to this than just dim-witted fun, although how *much* more is a matter of personal choice.

I have friends who feel that hunting, fishing or just trekking in harsh, difficult conditions can lead you directly to the true meaning of existence. And I have other friends who just say, "If you wanna shoot some geese, your feet are probably gonna get a little cold."

I'm afraid I tend toward the more serious side myself, especially in the winter, when even active people spend too much of their indoor time thinking and not enough tying trout flies. The little deaths in sport seem even more real when you hurt a little yourself and when your own core temperature is a bit low. And if it takes all day to get one snowshoe hare—not to mention more burned calories than a 2-pound bunny can replace, even with white wine and sour cream sauce—then that just shows you how things really are: Modern comforts are an illusion; in the real world, subsistence is a full-time job; all food was once alive and so on. Things like hunting and fishing are important because the big, dark hole of mortality is at the center of it all.

See what I mean? Serious.

I enjoy my thoughtful friends—we have some great long talks about this stuff—but in the winter, as I begin to drop into that pensive mood, I think I value those other guys a little more. You know, the ones who hunt and fish for no other reason than that they hunt and fish. The idea of Meaning with a capital *M* is not unknown to these people, they just figure that if it's really there it'll eventually become evident. Meanwhile, one must be concerned with more practical things like warm boots, good gloves, sharp augers, bait and ammunition.

And it's also probably good for me to be with a woman who sees game in terms of wine, warmth and great meals with friends instead of some kind of grim enlightenment. I mean, the big, dark hole is always there, but you don't have to keep staring into it.

16

Little Flies

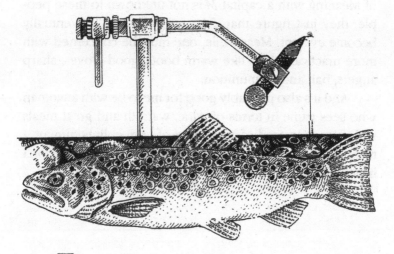

*T*his afternoon I've been casually tying first #22 and then #24 Blue-winged Olive parachutes, working my way down to the #26s. On a good day I actually *can* tie a passable size 26 dry fly, but I have to sort of sneak up on it.

By "casually" I mean I'm stopping now and then to get more coffee, poke the fire in the woodstove (whether it needs poking or not) and stir the pot of slow-simmering game stock: the kind of little rituals that, along with an enforced nonchalance, make me ready to wipe off the drugstore magnifier glasses and calmly tackle an even tinier hook.

Outside, it's snowing steadily; a heavy, wet snow that's more glassy than pure white and that falls straight down like rain, only a little slower. It's classic Blue-winged Olive weather—good for fishing them, maybe even better for staying inside and tying them.

It's a familiar scene, but if I were just dropped here suddenly, I couldn't tell, from either the weather or the flies, if it was late fall or early spring, although what's simmering in the pot might give me a clue. (By spring the wild-game menu has usually come down to the winter's last snowshoe hares.)

On some of my favorite rivers here in Colorado, those two seasons—let's say, roughly, October into November and March into April—are almost mirror images of each other. The weather at either time can be anywhere from comfortably cool and bright to penetratingly chilly with wet nimbostratus clouds lying halfway down the nearby peaks to just plain cold with snow. It's always beautiful, but most days are some kind of struggle.

As far as the hatches go, once the #18 Blue-winged Olives begin to thin out in the fall, the mayflies gradually slip down in size, first to about a size 22, then 24 and finally to some honest 26s, bugs smaller than some of the true midges that start about then and peter off sporadically through the winter.

In early spring it's the other way around. The mayfly hatches sputter along in the tiny sizes for a while—each with its own matching spinner fall—and then gradually swell into the size 18 Baetis again, which by then seems huge.

Well, let's say something like that *usually* happens,

although they'll tell you at any local fly shop that there are
no guarantees on fly size or hatch schedule. All trout
streams have their moods, and Western tailwaters in the
cold months can get pretty spooky.

That's probably why these little mayflies sometimes
fall through the cracks of the standard hatch charts into
the area of, "Well, you might actually want to have your
Blue-winged Olives in 20s and even 22s as well as 18s, just
in case," but these days a whole mess of fly fishers are onto
them anyway, enough to sometimes mob the water a little
at what were once sort of chilly and lonely times of year.

It seems like a lot of people are turning in that direction now: purposefully sniffing out difficult, unpredictable,
off-season hatches, not so much to stretch the season as to
avoid the crowds. I can remember when you could plan to
have the rivers pretty much to yourself between the beginning of duck season and about April or so, but between
then and now one of the many changes I've seen in the
fly-fishing business is the proliferation of warm, waterproof
coats and supposedly miraculous long underwear for foul-
weather anglers.

It's still hard to find commercially tied Blue-winged
Olives smaller than a size 20 or 22, but maybe that'll come.

Among those who worry about these things, there's some
debate over what species these smaller bugs are. I've heard
Pseudocloeons and *Paraleptophlebias* nominated—and
Latin words with lots of syllables do have a nice ring—but
unless you're a mad colorist fly tier like A.K., they're just
generic Blue-winged Olive Duns in assorted miniature
sizes with either pale olive or rusty spinners, which are
sometimes on the water at the same time.

There have been times when I've seined the water out

of frustration and found what looks, to the nonscientific eye, like anything from a two- to a six-part overlapping multiple hatch/spinner fall. You think these minute differences in size (and yes, A.K., maybe even color) couldn't possibly make a difference to the trout, but then if that were true you'd be catching fish now instead of standing up to your armpits in 38-degree water, looking at a net full of bugs.

And on some days, like the one last week when I was fishing the South Platte River with A.K., Mike Clark and Pat Leonard, the entire sparse, mixed hatch is channeled down the harrow, complicated currents along a far, rocky bank; the water is low and clear; the light is dull, so visibility is poor; the wind is whipping, so accurate casting is tough; it's cold, so you're trying to tie #24 flies to 7x tippets with stinging fingers; and you can stand in one place in the cold water for so long your feet go numb. You hope they're frozen, because the only other possibility is that you're having a stroke.

I don't know why I enjoy this so much. Maybe it's because I see it as a moral victory for a pampered American to come to love anything that's excruciatingly difficult and that doesn't involve money. Or maybe it's just that I spent a long time thinking this kind of fishing took so much skill and finesse I'd probably never be able to do it; thinking that because it's what some people told me, so that, for a while at least, I was afraid to even try it.

Luckily, I fell in with A.K. while I was still just young and impressionable enough to learn some new things. I noticed right off that he'd happily try for fish that seemed impossible, the same ones I'd pass up, looking for something I thought I could handle. I don't think he felt especially skillful or confident, it's more like he was just curious, but satisfying that curiosity over and over again had actually *made* him skillful and confident, whether he realized it or not.

And of course sometimes those fish *were* impossible, but he always figured the worst thing that could happen was, you'd lose your fly, and since he tied flies for a living at the rate of several dozen an hour, that wasn't a catastrophe.

Fishing small flies effectively does take a little doing—or at least some getting used to—but it's not as hard as it's often made out to be. I actually fly fished for quite a while before I realized it was possible to get snookered by certain writers, fly shop clerks and self-styled experts: people who, in order to make money or jump-start their egos, wanted to make this look like only a genius could do it.

But then I began to run into some real experts—you know, people who just knew how to catch fish. They'd show you a little trick here, maybe a new angle there, and say things like, "Just keep foolin' around and you'll get the hang of it."

Twenty-some years later I'm still foolin' around, and I *do* think I'm starting to get the hang of it.

There have been some so-called advances in fly tackle, but it's surprising how little difference most of them make. For instance, tippet material has gotten much stronger in recent years, so where you were once likely to break your light leader on a big fish, you now stand an even chance of bending your hook. There's a book out now with page after page of hook test graphs to illustrate the phenomenon.

Okay, but I guess it doesn't matter to me what breaks first, because either way the fish is lost. What it comes down to is, advances or not, a #24 fly on a 7x tippet is a more delicate rig than, say, a #2 lemming on a 0x. Beyond that, it's just fishing.

•

A.K., Mike, Pat and I all did pretty well the other day on the Platte. That is, we each missed some strikes, broke some fish off and actually landed a few during a sparse, mixed hatch of tiny bugs that lasted, off and on, for a couple of hours.

There have been a few times when I've caught lots of trout on light tackle and tiny flies, but I've learned to count a few fish as a clear success. More than one is always nice, because a single fish could have been an accident, but, if nothing else, a good fishing yarn has some drama in it, and too many fish can make it seem too easy.

Naturally, my best fish was one I *didn't* land. I think it was a brown trout, although I can't be sure. A.K. pointed him out to me, said he'd been casting to him for an hour but couldn't get him to take. Now, a trout A.K. can't catch is a hard one indeed, but as long as you manage not to spook the fish, you have virtually as many tries as you have the patience for, while the trout only has to make one mistake. So, however desperate things look, the odds can still be in your favor.

What you're aiming for is a kind of serene determination. It helps a lot if you just see it as an interesting problem instead of a matter of life and death, and you accomplish that by not counting fish in order to keep score. I guess that's something else I picked up from watching A.K.: I've met a few since, but he was the first fisherman I knew who would really rather catch one difficult fish than ten easy ones.

This trout was rising sporadically in the kind of spot that presents an almost impossible dry-fly drift. There was a cleft in the jumbled, rocky bank that cupped a little eddy where the current piled up, swept backwards upstream and then spilled out into the mainstream again in a lazy, egg-shaped whirlpool.

Even from the best casting position I could get myself into, a good drift to most of it was beyond me, but the trout was moving around in there, and every now and then he'd poke his nose up in a little slip of smooth current on the near side that I *could* get a drift to if I did everything just right.

So I tried something that was either an easy way out or a brilliant tactical maneuver: I just kept putting my size 24 Olive Quill parachute in the one spot where I could get a decent drift, and the fish finally came out and ate it.

I'd thought this was a big trout—which is why I spent so much time on him—but when I set the hook he flashed sideways in the current and I caught a pretty clear glimpse of him. It only lasted a split second, but he looked about the size of the blade on a canoe paddle.

As I said, I think it was a brown, but something about his size canceled out whatever I might have made out of his color.

I'd hooked him along the far bank, and on the first run he blasted downstream and out into the open water of a long glide. If he'd stayed there I'd have had an even chance, but he didn't like it when the bottom started to shallow up on the near side, so he ran back upstream and began boring under the rocks along the far bank.

I felt my leader ticking against the boulders over there, but the light tackle wouldn't let me put on enough pressure to haul him out. I pulled as hard as I thought I could, but it was only a matter of seconds before the fish sawed my tippet in half against the rocks. When I reeled in what was left of my leader, a good foot of it felt like it had been sandpapered.

This was a fish that could have been landed on a #24

hook and 7x if he'd been a little dumber or I'd been a little smarter or the rocks had been a little rounder or whatever, but as it was—in a world where there's still some natural justice—he was one that deserved to get away.

I caught myself laughing out loud about it. A.K. does that a lot, and people have asked me about it:

"How come the guy laughs every time he loses a fish?"

"I guess he's having a good time," I say.

That's a fair question, though, and it took me a while to figure it out myself. At first, quite a few years ago now, I just thought he was nuts. I still think he's nuts, but I've also come to see the logic of it. Fact is, the heartbreaking loss of a great big trout really is kind of funny.

The hooking, playing and losing of that fish probably took less than half a minute and A.K., who was fishing just upstream with his back to me, missed all but the very end of it, when I started giggling. The sound of laughter carries a long way on a trout stream—it's easier to hear than a screaming reel.

He called down to me, glancing over his shoulder, "Did you hook that fish?"

"Yeah, briefly."

"Well, good for you," he said.

CHAPTER

17

The Voice

Nick Lyons, the famous fishing writer, editor and publisher, once said, "It's good for the soul to have a closed season," or something very close to that. He was talking about being away from fishing for a few months out of the year so you can calm down, let the past season sink in and get to all the backup chores, which range from oiling your reels to pondering the meaning of it all.

He's right, a little distance now and then *is* good for the soul, but it makes me nervous when that's mandatory. I prefer things the way they are here in Colorado: The fishing season never officially closes, so time off is more a matter of weather and limited possibilities, and if neither of those things bother you—and your soul seems to be in decent shape—you can go fishing anyway.

I get more deeply into winter fly-fishing some years than others. Sometimes I see it as a sport in its own right, which it is, and other times I just consider it to be symptomatic relief from the shack nasties, which is just as true. I don't know why I go—when I go—but I'm afraid I know what keeps me from going at times: laziness, complacency, squeamishness about a little discomfort, all of which I sometimes try to disguise as "too busy with some very important projects." Of course that doesn't fool anyone. It's the rare fisherman who doesn't see through "busy" as an excuse.

Luckily, this is a cyclical business that seems to affect my friends and me in the same way, so either a bunch of us are up for it or none of us are. No explanation there. It's just that in some mysterious way we share a loose, leaderless group consciousness, sort of like a pack of lemmings.

This last winter we got out quite a bit. In January, Mike Clark and I just decided we had to go fishing and spent a day up on the Blue River. It was okay. We caught a few trout, and I lost a hog rainbow—probably a 5 pounder—because I didn't notice that the line had frozen in my guides until I got the fish on. There was an instant of elation, followed by confusion, followed in turn by an overwhelming helplessness: the kind of thing a fisherman gets used to.

I'm usually only good for one winter trip to the Blue. It's a nice stream with some big trout in it and many miles of water to fish in the summer and fall, but the only stretch of it that fishes well in the winter flows right through the town of Silverthorne, and it's just too strange. The Interstate 70 bridge thunders over the best pool on that upper stretch, and there are places where you'll slog up out of the river to pee and find yourself in a shopping center parking lot.

That makes me sad, because I remember Silverthorne from twenty years ago, before the Interstate came through. Back then it was sleepy, comfortable and not on the way to anywhere. My fondest and most vivid memories are of the bar, but if I remember right, there was also a café, a gas station and a few scattered houses and cabins. This was *only* twenty years ago (or was it twenty-five?) so of course the main form of transportation was the pickup truck, but the bar still had a hitching post out front and you had to be careful not to step in a pile of road apples in the parking lot.

At the time, I was living in the mountains near the town of Montezuma, about a forty-minute drive up a dirt road from Silverthorne. Some friends and I were staying in a cabin up there and working in a struggling silver mine.

It was a classic shoestring operation. The vein of wire silver had run out, leaving behind it a little lead and a little nickel, but the guy who owned the claim was convinced the silver would turn up again if he just kept digging. His investors weren't so sure, so he was reduced to getting a few of us hippies to work for shares and a free cabin to live in. The free cabin was all we ever saw on a regular basis, but it wasn't a bad life. We had good hard work to do, plenty of fresh air (both inside and outside the cabin), peace and quiet, game and fish to eat and a drunken game of pool in Silverthorne now and then.

At that time, Montezuma had five year-round residents. One was the postmaster for life and the other four amounted to the town council. That fall, as I was preparing to head down to civilization for the winter, they told me that if I stayed on till spring it would be my turn to be mayor.

Looking back on it now, I realize this wasn't an honor —all they were trying to do was stick me with some paperwork. Still, it was tempting at the time, but the mine had closed, there was no money, the cabin had been cold and drafty even in summer and, although I didn't know it then, my boss and landlord was only about six months away from getting busted on some kind of investor fraud rap.

I'd been happy living there, but my friends had already left and I knew if I stayed the winter I'd starve, freeze or go insane. So I shot one last game of eight ball in Silverthorne, stepped in something in the parking lot on the way to my truck and drove over to the East Slope, where I arrived with ten bucks in my pocket and horseshit on my boots, looking for work.

I never went back to Montezuma, but I *have* been to Silverthorne and it's become a real dump: rows of factory outlet stores, penal colonies of cheap condos crawling up the slopes, strips of fast food joints manned by surly teenagers—the full catastrophe. The fishing through town is better than ever because of the catch-and-release regulations —and that's good to see, because the fishing usually goes first—but I keep seeing the place through a haze of time and nostalgia, and the whole scene is just too surreal.

Still, Mike and I had gone fishing and caught some fish—even if the ambiance was all wrong—so we were

suddenly into the winter program, and over the next couple of months we made regular trips to our old haunts on
the South Platte River, sometimes with A.K., Pat and/or
Mike Price. The Platte can be crowded—even in winter—
and below Cheesman Canyon there's a paved, two-lane
county road running next to it, but compared to the Blue
at Silverthorne it's like wilderness. Anyway, the ice had
been broken and suddenly the whole gang was fishing
again.

Now, on any tailwater trout stream in midwinter it's possible to catch no fish or damned few. Typically, you nymph
fish steadily all day and, usually sometime in mid- to late
afternoon, there's about a forty-minute window during
which you catch all your fish for the day. Maybe someone
lands as many as three trout and, judging from the other
fishermen you've seen and the few you've talked to that
day, that probably qualifies him as top rod on the river. On
the drive home you gang up on him and tell him being top
rod means he has to buy dinner. Now and then it even
works.

Except for that forty minutes or so, the river is dead.
You don't see many fish, and those few you do see are
sitting on the bottom like waterlogged branches, not feeding, not moving, possibly not even entirely conscious.

That happens a lot in the winter, so you learn to fish
casually and at a reasonable pace so you're not all burned
out and frustrated when something happens—who knows
what?—and, for a few minutes at least, the fish bite.

Most days it really does happen. Everyone who has
anything resembling the right fly in the water catches a fish
or two before it shuts down again. You'll hear theories
about why that happens from people who have a patholog-

ical need for theories—the most popular one now has to do with drift migration patterns of aquatic insect larvae—but no theory makes it predictable or explains the days when it doesn't happen. In the end, it's a matter of blind faith and a light rod you can cast all day.

Now and then there's a hatch of midges or, rarely, some tiny mayflies, but mostly it's nymph fishing. I almost always fish a brace of nymphs now, and I try to imagine that kind of rig doubling my chances of having the right pattern, but that's not statistics, that's faith again.

On some trips I'll change flies furiously, and on others I'll tie on something that feels right and fish with it all day. It's a matter of mood. Changing flies is something to do, but then searching for the right patterns when the fish aren't biting can seem like nothing but an exercise in knot tying.

And there are lots of flies to pick from: Pheasant Tails, Hare's Ears, RS2s, Miracle Nymphs, Buckskins, Brassies, String Things and a whole mess of patterns that, like the suspects in drive-by shootings, have descriptions but no names, say, a generic black midge pupa with a body of dyed goose biot and stubby gills at the butt made of Hungarian partridge flue. The body of a red midge larva can be made of dyed goose biot, floss, dubbing or wire, and as unlikely as it seems, there are days when the fish will bite one, but not the other three.

In the hope of hooking two or three fish a day on average, there are tiers around here who spend years exploring the permutations of no more than three materials wound on or lashed to a size 20 or smaller hook, either coming up with new patterns or adjusting old ones.

Like the good old Miracle Nymph. It's nothing but a white floss body ribbed with copper wire, but then someone noticed that when the fly gets wet the color of the thread underbody bleeds through a little, giving the thing a barely noticeable gray, olive, yellow or rusty cast. Ed swears this makes a difference. I can't imagine that it does, but when I tie Miracles I faithfully change thread color after every six flies as a kind of observance.

Almost all winter regulars on the Platte eventually fall into this sort of nitpicking program, and we locals like to say that over the years of catch-and-release regulations and matching the hatch, the fishing there has gotten progressively more technical and stylized, although it's never clear whether we're talking about changes in the trout themselves or in the fishermen.

A.K., Mike Clark and I went down to the Platte in early February and had a typical February kind of day. The weather was warm and bright for the time of year (it was the middle of one of our regulation midwinter thaws), the water in the river was low and cold and the wind was howling.

Not the best of conditions—calmer, cooler air, less sunlight and somewhat warmer water would have been much better—but then when you go fly-fishing in winter you keep your expectations reasonable: You'll spend a nice day on the river and maybe you'll even catch a trout or two.

We fished near the little town of Trumbull, and in six or seven hours we managed to land a few trout and hook and lose a few others. All in all, a fairly respectable performance.

When it was all over we had burgers at the Deckers Bar (the only hot food for 30 miles in any direction, but still good) and talked over the day's fishing. We've all fished this river for a long time now, and I said I remembered the winter fishing being a lot better.

A.K. said he remembered that too, but he also remembers that in years past we spent a lot more time down there in January, February and March than we have in recent seasons, and that's important. Much is made about the skill it takes to catch trout on a fly rod, but putting in a lot of time also helps. Winter fishing is unpredictable, but there *are* great days, and the more time you spend on the river, the more likely you are to stumble into one.

And you also have to admit to yourself that memories —especially the good ones—are selective. When I'm casting back ten or fifteen years, I have to remind myself that the days when the trout rose eagerly to dry flies or ate nymphs steadily for three hours straight stand out more clearly than the days when they didn't.

Not long ago I said to Ed that I thought the Platte was getting awfully crowded these days, even in the off-season. Ed's an old South Platte hand and he said he felt that too, but added that, honestly, he thought he *should* be able to remember days when it wasn't crowded, but he's not sure he actually does.

I *can* recall days when I had long stretches of that river all to myself, but Ed is probably right: That was as rare fifteen years ago as it is now.

I guess after a certain age you have to become aware of the dreaded good-old-days syndrome. That comes from having so many recollections stored away that when someone mentions the name of a favorite river you don't do a complete inventory of your memories; you just do a quick edit and come up with something like the South Platte's greatest hits.

After we exhausted the subject of memory, Mike and I

got off on a tangent, giving A.K. some grief because he hadn't been able to go fishing much that winter. He really *had* been too busy, flying around the country to sportsmen's shows to promote his new line of fly-tying tools, but the three of us agreed quite a few years ago now that if any one of us started to take himself seriously, the other two were supposed to straighten him out. I told A.K. that having a corporate address in an eastern city put him on pretty thin ice, but I smiled when I said it so he'd know I didn't really mean it. He told me—also smiling, but not in quite the same way—that he'd be done with the shows by April, at which time he would proceed to fish circles around me.

Fair enough. After all, this happens to all of us from time to time: We actually do get busy with something and miss some fishing. But the trips continue even if you can't go, and you know your friends are out on the water while you're—I shudder to use the word—working, and on the days that doesn't drive you crazy, it's kind of comforting.

By the time the burgers arrived, we'd worn out the subject of being busy and were planning a trip to the Henry's Fork in Idaho for the coming summer.

A.K. and I had pretty much given up on the Henry's Fork after the 1988 season, when drought, low flows, poor management and a few other elements combined to all but wreck the fine old fishery there. In August of 1987 we'd had our best fishing ever on the Fork—enormous rainbows eating dry flies day after day—but in '88 it was so bad we left after two days and ended up on a spring creek a day's drive to the north.

But now the word is the Henry's Fork is coming back nicely. Maybe not quite like the old days, but as I just pointed out, once you get some distance on them, maybe the old days can't really be trusted.

Anyway, it's been seven years now, and we think we should give it another try. Maybe in June for the famous Green Drake mayfly hatch.

True, our friend Mike Lawson (who runs a fly shop on the Henry's Fork) said last year's Green Drake hatch was poor, but then that was last year. When it comes right down to it, there are no guarantees except that every season is a new beginning.

A few weeks later, A.K. was off doing a show somewhere and Mike Clark, Pat and I were back on the river. Once again, it was warm and breezy and the sun was shining: a fine day to be hanging around on a trout stream, but not so good for fishing. Warm days are the most comfortable—and it's a good thing, too, because you'll probably spend a lot of time sitting on convenient logs and having long talks —but the cold, cloudy days fish the best. You know this, but if you get out enough you have the leisure to rediscover it every season.

Thinking back on it, as I'd been doing lately, I could remember my best winter fishing days as agonizing. Numb feet, stinging ears and fingers, the line frozen in the guides and sometimes even on the reel. You can chip ice from the guides—carefully—but if you don't have a fire going, you have to stick the reel in your armpit to thaw it out, which can be really startling. If there *is* a fire, you have to remember that cork grips and reel seats can be singed and plastic fly lines and leaders can melt. That kind of thing.

When you pick a day that's too nice, you gut it out and fish anyway because, assuming you're in the right place and have something like the right flies tied on, there will always be that forty minutes to look forward to. But then off-season fishing is off-season fishing. If the best thing about it is the weather, you might as well enjoy it.

At the right times of year—not to mention certain outstanding but unpredictable days at the *wrong* times of year—the South Platte offers up glorious hatches and many fish. On the slow days you experience something like what invariably happens in a marriage or a long cohabitation: You see your favorite sex object looking decidedly unsexy and, although you do notice, it doesn't seem to make any difference. In the one case, you don't wish for a different woman, and in the other it doesn't occur to you that you shouldn't have gone fishing.

By about three in the afternoon that day, I had wandered away from Mike and Pat and was fishing alone on a piece of water we call The Duck Pond. This is a long, braided run that usually has a lot of trout in it. If there's any feeding going on, the fish will nose up into the head of it. If not, they'll usually fall back to hold in the slower water.

I'd worked the upper end and was slowly fishing my way down the run, being as methodical as possible for that late in the day. I was casting listlessly—doing what I came to do and trying to get used to the idea of getting skunked—when I hooked a fish. It had been so long since I'd had a strike I couldn't recall what to do at first, but I finally got around to setting the hook.

The fish felt okay at first—strong and quick—but after the first run it started to feel both weak and too heavy. Then I saw that it was swimming sideways and I knew it was foul hooked.

I thought, Bummer, the only fish of the day and I didn't get him fairly, so I can't count him. That's crucial, by the way. A fish that's not hooked in the mouth isn't caught fairly and can't be counted, period, no room for discussion. Even a single lapse out of desperation here will start you down the road to becoming a despicable, unprincipled fish hog.

But I'd forgotten that I was fishing a brace of nymphs. When I got the trout to the net and went to unhook him, I found that he had one fly under his pectoral fin and the other in his mouth. Okay, this was a somewhat delicate point, but I figured it was unlikely that he'd gotten foul hooked, then realized he was hungry and eaten the other fly, so he was a fair catch. What a relief.

It was a pretty fish, too—a chunky, beautifully colored brown trout about 15 inches long. I remember thinking, This would be a paltry reward for a whole day's fishing if I was thinking in terms of rewards, and then thinking, What the hell do you mean by *that?* Maybe that it's a lot easier to claim you're not in this just to catch fish after you have, in fact, caught one.

A young guy, maybe eighteen or twenty years old, had watched me land that fish, and after I released it he came over to talk. He asked how the fishing had been, and I said it had been pretty slow. Then he said, a little shyly, I thought, "Well, I'm real new at this, but I haven't caught a fish all day."

I remembered the feeling from when I was just starting out: If you're not catching fish, you automatically assume it's because you're not good enough.

I said, "Well, I'm not new at this at all, and that fish you just saw was my only one today."

"Really?" he asked.

"Yeah, really."

I think that made him feel better, and I felt pretty good too, because I hadn't listened to the voice. You know, the one that whispers in the ear of every fisherman at a time like that, especially on catch-and-release water, where, however many fish you've caught, you won't have any with you: the voice that says, "Go ahead, tell him that last trout makes twenty so far."

18

Guides

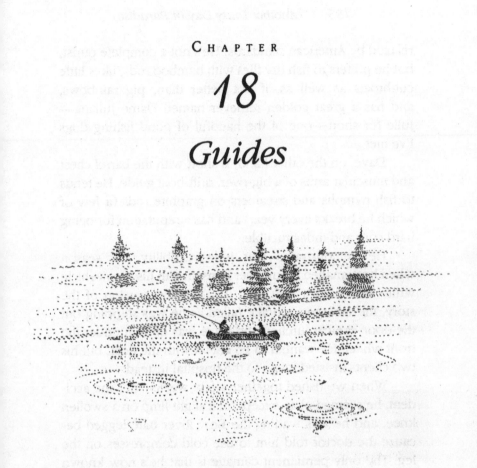

On a recent trip to Alberta, Canada, I did some fishing with Dave Brown and Peter Smallman. These guys are partners—Dave is a guide, while Peter runs the two Smallman's Fly Shops, one in a shopping center in Calgary, the other above an ice-cream parlor in Cochrane. They're the kind of odd couple you sometimes see in the fly-fishing business.

Peter is tall, precise, a little reserved and profoundly

relaxed by American standards. He's not a complete purist, but he prefers to fish dry flies with bamboo rods, likes little cutthroats as well as, if not better than, pig rainbows, and has a great golden retriever named Dame Juliana—Julie for short—one of the handful of good fishing dogs I've met.

Dave, on the other hand, is short with the barrel chest and muscular arms of a big-river, drift-boat guide. He tends to fish nymphs and streamers on graphite rods (a few of which he breaks every year) and has a reputation for being hard core and indestructible.

He demonstrated that indestructibility last season when he managed to run over himself with his own vehicle while launching a drift boat. In the short version of the story, the emergency brake failed as he was stepping out the door, the car lurched and Dave was thrown under the front wheel. He wanted to go ahead with the float, but his two clients insisted he go to the hospital instead.

When we fished together a few weeks after the accident, he seemed okay except for a slight limp on a swollen knee, and he was wading the Bow River bare-legged because the doctor told him to use cold compresses on the leg. The only permanent damage is that he's now known as Dave "Speed Bump" Brown.

Dave and Peter seem to have one of those nearly ideal partnerships. Labor is divided according to temperament, the two of them apparently get along well and, as Dave told me, "If a customer can't relate to one of us, he can probably relate to the other."

Naturally, everyone loves Julie.

Sometimes the best thing about a fishing trip, looking back on it, wasn't so much the good fishing as it was hanging around with the guides. Guides still seem exotic to me, probably because I spent so many years fishing before I ever went out with one. I mean, I was young and poor, with more endurance than sense and more time than money. Guides were a luxury I just couldn't afford.

The good part of that was, I learned how to fly fish in the hit-and-miss, trial-and-error way that makes things stick, and I learned patience, persistence, acceptance and probably a few other good things, too.

The bad part was that, lacking instruction, I developed a few bad habits, some of which I'm struggling with to this day, and I missed out for years on all those neat, practical, all-but-obvious little things a guide can teach you if you just pay attention. In fact, although people have been trying to tell me what to do all my life, the only ones who've been right on anything like a regular basis were fishing guides.

By now I've fished with a fair number of guides and am able to count some among my friends, going back to fish with them again as much for the company as for the fish. Taken together, fishing guides do constitute a distinct breed, but they're not all the same, as some claim. Far from it, in fact.

Many American guides—especially the younger ones —consider themselves to be a combination of teacher, coach, chauffeur, valet, tour director and therapist. They say that's a fairly recent development, caused by the huge number of beginners who are now flocking to the sport.

Once, not all that long ago, a guide could assume that the average client more or less knew how to fly fish, or at least that he could cast a little bit. But now, I'm told, you have to be ready for the sport who has only the vaguest idea of what he's doing, and you have to be prepared to do as much of it for him as possible, while trying to convey the idea that, as long as he's holding the rod, you can't do it all—regardless of how much he's paying you.

And you may also have to patiently explain to him that, although you know the river well enough, you are not actually in control of the fish or the hatches or the flow or the weather or the mosquitos. It's fishing: sometimes it goes well, sometimes it doesn't, and whining isn't gonna help any.

Almost every guide I've ever talked to refers to this as "baby-sitting."

Too much baby-sitting can lead to a kind of smothering, even intrusive style of guiding that makes you feel more like a spectator than a participant, but, to their credit, most of these guys will gladly back off to a polite distance if they can.

On the other hand, I've been with some guides from the old school who figure how good a fisherman you are is your own affair. They'll take you to where the fish are, maybe even point them out to you, but otherwise you're pretty much on your own. If they think you look like you know what you're doing, they'll stand around holding the landing net. If not, they might decide to take a little nap.

I've seen some clients get upset at this, seeing it as either laziness or stupidity, but from the guide's point of view it's the logical course of action. He assumes you're competent—a gesture of respect many Americans no longer recognize—but if it turns out that you came all that way and spent all that money to fish, but you don't know *how* to fish, well, that was your mistake, not his.

And then of course there's the luck of the draw. On another trip to northern Canada, a guide told me, "It never fails. When we have a crappy week, the camp is full of good fishermen. And when the weather's great and there are hatches all over the place, we get guys who can't get their fly out of the damn canoe."

You have to remember that, as a client, you are the raw material, and not even the best guide can make a silk purse out of a sow's ear.

Of course the very best guides I've seen don't *have* a style. They take stock of you within the first half hour on the water and adapt themselves accordingly: either leading you by the hand, leaving you alone or something in between. Somehow they manage to balance the amount of help you want with the amount you need (not always the same thing), and in ways often too subtle to describe, they maneuver you into catching fish you wouldn't have caught without them, but that you nonetheless caught all by yourself.

As you drift along in the Mackenzie boat, your guide suggests that you throw an upstream mend in your cast up along the bank. You can't quite manage it at first, but then your drifts improve as you get the hang of it and you start getting strikes.

But, thinking back on it, did you really get the hang of it, or did the angle of the boat change in such a way that the half-assed mend you were capable of was enough to get the job done?

The guide would probably like you to notice and appreciate something like that, and maybe even reflect that appreciation in your tip at the end of the day, but chances are he'll be too diplomatic to point it out. In fact, if it wasn't for fishing guides, diplomacy could now be a lost art in everyday life.

•

Ed started guiding a few years ago, for a shop down in Colorado Springs, and since then I've noticed a slight change in him. He was always a good fisherman and a courteous and generous partner, but lately he's developed a kind of extra polish.

For one thing, he can now spot fish like an osprey because that's what good guides spend so much of their time doing. Some people think guides are professional fishermen, but they're not. They don't fish; they try to help *other people* fish, which is an entirely different story.

So we'll be walking a bank now, looking for trout on a river we've fished together off and on for twenty years, and I'll say, "There's one."

Ed will look, cock his head a little and say, "Actually, there's six . . . No, seven."

"Huh? Where?"

Maybe it's just my imagination, but he also seems a little more easygoing now, less likely to care if he catches fish, more genuinely pleased if I do, and more likely to do something like fish a dry fly all day because that's what he feels like doing, even if his best shot at actually catching something is with a nymph. Some guides go on automatic pilot whenever they're near water, even on their days off, but most just enjoy the lack of pressure and fish with what looks like a sense of relief.

And now, if I ask Ed what's new, he might say something like, "I had a client last week who'd never fly fished before and I got him into a 23 incher."

It's permissible for the guide to take credit for that, but it's also expected that in another kind of situation he'll say, "Well, there was a nice hatch and I had some good fishermen, so we did pretty good."

I don't mean to say Ed has actually changed. We're still just old friends who travel, camp and fish together in the same old way. It's just that if I went fishing with him now for the first time, I might notice that distinctive humorous, calm detachment and think to ask, "By the way, do you guide?"

On my last day in Alberta, I floated the Bow River with two guides, Mike and Tony, on an unofficial basis—that is, we all fished, and none too hard, either. It was 32 degrees Celsius (about 90 Fahrenheit) and we were fishing dry flies, even though the Bow in summer is known primarily as a nymph river with the chance of an evening hatch.

I've noticed that off-duty guides are often willing to do something like that: I mean, deal with the kind of self-imposed limitation that will probably get you into five or six fish instead of twenty or twenty-five, just out of curiosity.

There was plenty of time to talk, and I heard some good guide stories. Without going into detail, there was the guy who had never fished before but fully expected to catch a hundred trout; the guy who wouldn't listen and never hooked a fish; the guy who whined from dawn till dusk and also never caught a fish; the guy who showed up drunk in the morning and proceeded to get drunker; the guy with the heart condition who kept passing out and so on. Clients from hell: Any professional guide can tell you about dozens of them.

Somewhere during a session like that I always wonder if I've turned up in some guide's stories as the outdoor writer who spent all day getting tangled in his line and breaking flies off in fish. Probably.

Then again, I have to repeat one of the best compliments I ever got. I was sitting around with a guide after a day on the water, and he was talking about different types of clients: intense, laid back, desperate, philosophical, good, bad and indifferent.

"So," I asked, "given the choice, what kind of client would you rather guide?"

"I'd rather guide a guy like you," he said, "but guys like you don't usually *need* to be guided."

What can I say? Fish long enough and you're bound to have that nearly perfect day, complete with a competent witness. Then again, if that guy compared notes with the last guide I was out with, they might conclude that there are two middle-aged, bearded fishermen with the same name.

That day on the Bow River was one of those good days of fishing when damn few fish were caught. We were casting dry flies on a hot, bright day when any fisherman with his wits about him would have been dredging with nymphs, and for me it was the last day of a long, rambling trip that had gone through Wyoming, Montana, Alberta, British Columbia and back to Alberta again. If the truth were told, I was getting a little road burned. About all I was still good for was watching the scenery and missing the odd strike.

Actually, I think Mike said something about that. What was it? Something about how with most clients you have to beat them over the head to get them to look at the scenery. It wasn't a complaint, just an observation from a guy who spends who knows how many days a year guiding. I didn't ask him how many days. Some guides are proud of the number of trips they do in a season, others don't keep track and still others don't like to think about it.

Tony once guided full time, too, but he only does it occasionally now. They say he charges a lot and is able to pick and choose his clients, most of whom are old regulars from way back. And he also gets to do something else every guide would love to do.

"I make 'em a deal," Tony said. "I say 'Look, I can take you to where the fish are and I can tell you what they're biting, but if you can't catch 'em, that's tough shit, ey?' "

19

Game Dinner

I just spent the better part of the morning cleaning up the wreckage from last night's game dinner. This one was built around, but not limited to, a brace of sockeye salmon from Alaska and a big pot of spaghetti sauce made from the last of the venison sausage and hamburger, plus the last of the dried leccinum and boletus mushrooms.

Those two kinds of wild mushrooms should be up about now, so I expect to gather some fresh ones in the next week or so. And of course deer season is coming up. I don't always get a deer, but I always *expect* to.

I suppose there are more elegant occasions for having a game dinner than cleaning out the freezer, but it's become sort of a late summer/early fall tradition around here.

It was a good group: two outdoor writers, one poet, one newspaper editor, an investment banker, a blacksmith, a librarian, a weaver, an environmental consultant, a potter, a bamboo-rod maker and Larry, who is difficult to categorize in a few words.

Naturally, everyone contributed something, from the obligatory bottle of wine to homemade ice cream with fresh wild raspberries to some recently caught rainbow trout that had been lightly smoked but still needed to be broiled.

I always enjoy the casual confusion of game dinners. I'm sort of a flamboyant cook myself (that is, I always take up more room in the kitchen and dirty more dishes than I really need) and then people always show up with things that have to be boiled or broiled or chilled or chopped or warmed up. I have a small kitchen that gets crowded easily, especially with a few bird dogs underfoot.

Last night Ed and Monica had a bunch of mushrooms they'd found that afternoon, which they dumped on the drainboard for inspection, so while I was stirring spaghetti sauce and cutting up salmon fillets, Larry was grilling his trout and Susan was baking her quiches, John Rankin held a seminar on mushroom identification at the sink. As it turned out, there were three varieties, some better than others, but all edible.

Jack was standing at the kitchen window, looking wistfully out at the bird feeders in the backyard and asking me if I'd seen fewer goldfinches than usual this year. He had, and he thought that was ominous.

Molly, the golden retriever, was cuddled up with Donna and the other Susan on the couch. By the look of it, the two women were plotting something, and Molly seemed to be in on it; leaning in, listening closely. Poudre, the Llewellin setter pup, was howling through the screen door at Steve, who was out in the backyard in the rain, grilling the salmon. Poudre hates to be left out of anything even mildly interesting.

I started talking about a recent speech in which a politician had apparently declared a religious war on people like me and just about everyone I know, and I overheard Ed say, "Oh God, don't let him get started on that. Ask him if he's been fishing lately."

Someone in the other room yelled, "So, John, you been fishin'?" I decided to take the hint and said, "Where do you think these salmon came from?"

Sawhorses and a sheet of plywood to serve as a table were being hauled inside because, as I said, it was raining. Rain doesn't *always* change things when you plan to eat outside; last time it didn't start raining until we were on our second cup of coffee. Donna congratulated me on my timing. I said that once you're in tune with the rhythms of the universe, it's easy.

Some game cooks actually plan their meals—this complements this, and both together logically and aesthetically lead to that, all transitions lubricated by the proper wines, of course—but ours are usually pretty haphazard. Someone gets the idea, makes the announcement, and then it all falls together naturally. The theme is wild food, but beyond that it's up for grabs.

Whatever is in season is usually prominent and fresh, but then things come out of half a dozen freezer chests, too, so there's this multiseasonal bounty: trout and rabbit, elk and bluegill, raspberries picked two hours ago and

dried mushrooms from last spring. When you invite someone, they'll ask how many people are coming to determine
how many fish or rabbits to thaw out, but they don't ask
about wine. They know from experience that whatever
they bring will go perfectly with something.

I will say that most of us are good game cooks in one way
or another.

Larry is a master of simplicity: largely plain deer, elk,
trout, bass or whatever, cooked just right, usually over live
coals, with great respect for the meat itself, although lately
he's been learning about sauces.

Ed is an advocate of simplicity and respect to the point
that he believes marinades to be the work of the devil and
will eat any pasta dish so long as it has "those little green
things in it."

I once explained to him, "That's parsley."

"Whatever," he said.

Steve, on the other hand, is a good tinkerer, invent-
ing dressings and sauces with a delicate combination of
thought and bravado. His roast grouse with a glaze made
from boysenberry jam, wine, butter and I don't know what
all else comes to mind. He uses expensive copper pots that
distribute the heat even better than cast iron and knows
about things like braising and poaching.

He's either the best game cook among us or just the
fanciest. When I brought a large grilse back from a recent
salmon-fishing trip, Steve volunteered to cook it. When I
mentioned that to Donna she said, "Yeah, that's my favorite
fish recipe."

"What's that?" I asked.

"You know," she said, "give it to Steve."

Donna is great at combining disparate ingredients into

of that cliff, and I knew that if the fish ran downstream from there I wouldn't be able to follow and probably couldn't winch him back up through the current. I tried to feel the shape of the bank curving out, but I didn't know exactly where the bank was. There was a riffle at the head of that bend pool that I thought I should hear when I got close. I *didn't* hear it, so maybe it was still okay. Then again, I didn't know how far out the fish was.

I felt my reel to try to see how much line was left on it, but it was hard to picture. Some, maybe lots.

The fish let himself be played back against the bank again. I couldn't hear the riffle and I hadn't felt the rush of it in the line, so I knew he was in slack water where I could get at him. I waded down—I was in the water, although I didn't remember getting in—and fumbled for the net when the angle of the line seemed to indicate the fish was more or less at my feet.

I made a mess of netting him, thinking I knew where he was, only to come up two or three times with a dripping but empty landing net. I finally managed it with the rod in my left hand, net in my right and the flashlight in my teeth.

It was a brown trout, not a bright, golden yellow one, but a washed-out, older fish; brownish ochre on the back shading to an almost bluish silver with big black spots. He'd fought like a five-pounder, but in the net he looked and felt more like four. And, yes, weight and length change at night, too. Maybe he was more like twenty inches and a fat three pounds, but he was my fish and it hurt a little to let him go.

I was stumbling back upstream, thinking I could keep fishing the dry fly, switch to the biggest black Woolly Bugger streamer I had or quit while I was ahead. A nice big fish can seem like a proper end to things, especially when it's well past midnight and you've been fishing since seven o'clock on what would now be *yesterday* morning.

Then I ran into one of my hosts, who was wading downstream looking for me. He was a big shape with a hat and I couldn't tell who it was until he spoke. He asked how I'd done.

"I got a nice one," I said, and he didn't ask how nice, knowing that this isn't always easy to explain. Instead he said, "Do you remember where the trail back to the car is?"

the food is there means that many of those present have a modicum of native intelligence and the ability to use some simple tools. That can't be said of every dinner gathering.

Of course the trick to a game dinner is to invite the right people. Most of my friends are into hunting, fishing and/or some other kinds of foraging, so we appreciate the quality of the food—which is better than almost anything you can buy—and we also appreciate that knowledge, skill, persistence, patient harmony or some other endangered human trait put it on our table. That's why I like these people so much. As my dad would have said, "They may not be perfect, but they know what's what."

So there's always some praise, maybe even a toast, because shooting a deer or catching a fish really is both more difficult and a lot more satisfying than going down to the store to buy a chicken. Game, fish and other wild edibles are all reminiscent of specific seasons; of knowledgeable, reasonably self-sufficient people roaming the countryside and of freezers filling up and emptying again as the year plays itself out.

It's not a matter of survival anymore; it's more like gourmet subsistence. Most of us couldn't afford to eat this well this often any other way, but we do because we live near open land, and have guns, fly rods, a little free time and the modest gumption it takes to get off our butts and go do something.

As Larry says, "One way to enjoy life is to live simply and elegantly within your means." (The other way is to make a lot of money in such a way that you don't spend too much time at it or end up in jail.)

Eating game also introduces you to the concept of restraint, which in turn raises some interesting questions: How much good food is enough? Is it always proper to kill your limit? How much difference is there between what you want and what you actually need? The answers aren't always immediately evident, but it's something to think about.

And then there's death itself. It's not something you want to dwell on, but it's worth understanding in a casual, everyday way. All food was once alive, and to live you've gotta eat. If there's a larger, darker question in there, it's unanswerable and therefore not worth wasting time on. It's just that all good cooking celebrates the transitory nature of reality. I mean, the morning after the best dinner you ever had, you were hungry again, right?

20

Spring Creek

As I write this, a few friends and I are planning a small, low-budget tour of some Montana spring creeks. Tentatively planning, that is. Ed is making the arrangements, and I haven't heard from him yet, so it's still up in the air and, in fact, may or may not come off.

We usually think about a spring creek trip every season and then end up actually making one about every second or third year. The problem is, some of the better known spring creeks can be booked up a year or more in advance, and since most of us can't see more than a few months into our futures, we don't always plan far enough ahead. When that happens we're either shut out or faced with going through one of the guide services that buy up blocks of days, and that can get a little steep.

That's not to say the guides aren't worth the money, because most of them are, nor is it to say that any of us couldn't *use* a guide. It's just that the expense can seem a little extravagant.

I guess one of the reasons we get along so well is that, although we all have our private indulgences (ranging from good whiskey to bamboo fly rods) we still tend to be a little tight with the money—even when we have some, which is not all the time, and almost never all at once.

As it is, six days on private spring creeks should run us about $300 apiece in rod fees, but if we sleep in that free campground on the Yellowstone River, cook our own meals and tie most of our own flies, we'll still feel like we're living righteously frugal, bohemian lives.

That's *most* of our own flies. We always drive in to one of the fly shops in Livingston to buy handfuls of the latest spring creek patterns—designed by the spring creek experts—and to get the current hatch reports, which are always a little more detailed after you've dropped some cash. I've noticed that this stings a little less as the years go by, even though the flies I buy are usually patterns I could tie cheaper and almost as well myself. But I guess shelling out $50 a day just to get on the water does sort of lubricate the wallet.

I know, fifty bucks isn't much anymore—it's a new fly line and change, maybe a good (though not great) dinner —but when you've grown used to fishing free public water, paying to get on a trout stream can be something you have to get past.

There's always been a strong populist tradition in American fly-fishing—one I've bought into from the beginning—but there's a parallel history of private waters, exclusive clubs and expensive resorts that goes back just as far, and in darker moments it's possible to imagine that we'll eventually become like Europe, where virtually all the good fishing is not only private but also hideously expensive and portioned out according to class.

Of course class consciousness isn't unheard of in America, but to our credit, we're pretty embarrassed by it.

Not so in other parts of the world, though. If you voice your misgivings about exclusiveness on a salmon beat on a private estate in Scotland, you might hear a guy say, without a hint of irony, "It's not a problem. After all, common people *prefer* rough fish."

You may be either too polite or too stunned to ask, "Then why do you need a full-time water bailiff to chase away the poachers?"

Most of the spring creeks I know of are a long way from that, even though they're private and have been for generations. Here in the West at least, there's something about the hydrogeology of them that causes them to rise in fairly level country near mountains, and they were grabbed up by the early settlers for their good river bottomland and year-round sweet water. I'm told that back then the fishing and duck hunting were secondary considerations.

But now ranching and haying don't always pay the bills—a man once told me the way to retire with a million dollars after a lifetime of ranching was to start with $2 million—and the owners of most private creeks are doing what I think just about anyone would do in the same situation. They're either keeping the fishing to themselves and their friends if they can afford that, or charging for it if they can't.

Putting envy aside, I have to say that doesn't bother me or anyone I know. I'm glad there are some spring creeks you can get on just by paying a fair price (that is, without having to beg or know someone), and frankly, if American fly-fishing does go aristocratic in years to come, it won't be because some ranch families are using rod fees to help pay their taxes.

There. That concludes today's sermon.

Naturally, the good spring creeks are few and far between. The strict definition of a spring creek is one where most of the water comes out of the ground instead of from runoff or snow melt, as in a freestone stream. If there's a good, year-round head of clear water, if the springs are deep enough to maintain a more or less uniform temperature, if the water wells up through limestone to give it the right chemistry and if the banks haven't been stripped and beaten down by cattle, you get what fly fishers think of as an archetypal spring creek: a stream with lush vegetation that supports aquatic insects in the billions and trout that grow big and fat on more food than they could possibly want. But that's a lot of "ifs."

The last time I fished a spring creek I was with Ed and it was early June. That's a good time in Montana because the hatches are on, but they're not in full swing yet and the weather can still be tricky, so a lot of fishermen wait until later in the season. The point is, there might be some open slots, so you can get on even if you haven't planned the trip a year or more in advance.

The way I remember it, when we realized we'd be going through the Paradise Valley anyway, we called pretty much at the last minute and lucked into days on two of the creeks. We called a third, but the woman on the phone laughed and said, "You mean the fifth of June *this year?*"

That was an unusually frantic trip, the kind I've been trying to avoid for the last few years, though not always successfully. I think we did eight streams in nine days—starting with the Boulder and ending on the Firehole—but I'm not completely sure of that, and when I try and call it up, it begins to swim together with other drives through that country. (As a guy said down at the café the other day, "The memory is the first thing to go, and I can't remember what the second thing is.") I know I kept a diary of the trip, but I think I left it in a motel room in Lander, Wyoming, on the way home.

But if a good part of that trip is now lost in the ozone, I still remember the spring creeks pretty clearly. The weather was cool and fitful, with periods of bright sun mixed with clouds and rain squalls. The Pale Morning Duns had begun to come off and the fish were onto them but, as I said, things weren't in full swing yet, so the creeks were almost empty.

Mobs of fly casters aren't a crapshoot on pay-to-fish spring creeks like they are on public water because most creeks only allow a limited number of fishermen per day. Still, these are small, intimate streams, and when they're booked full they can still seem a little too crowded.

I think I actually prefer spring creeks before everything really gets going. The relative lack of other fishermen is nice, and although those roaring hatches where the mayflies get behind your sunglasses and up your nose are fun, sometimes they're harder to fish than sparser, slower hatches where the fish have fewer bugs to choose from.

Then too, the trout are sometimes a little more eager earlier in the season. Now big, spoiled, catch-and-release spring creek trout are seldom what you'd call pushovers—although, like all of us, they do have their stupid moments—and they never get a real vacation because hard-core types fish the creeks year-round, sometimes at cheaper rates in the dead of the off-season. But in late May or early June the fish haven't been pounded steadily for months on end and may be a little more likely to rise to a real winged dry fly instead of some floating nymph or sub-emerger sort of contraption. That's important to me only because I think dry flies with wings are pretty.

But spring creeks are famous for snooty trout, and it's still possible to get into that old routine where the fish are feeding, but they won't bite, and you're changing from one pattern to another while fighting off a sense of impending doom.

At times like that you should avoid thinking that you paid good money to do this, and if the idea won't go away, try reminding yourself that you didn't buy fish, you just rented time on a stream that has fish *in* it.

My standard Montana spring creek Pale Morning Dun is the one you can buy at any fly shop in the area—a post-wing thorax tie with split tails and a dubbed yellow body that's sometimes called a Lawson's Thorax. I also try to have a split-wing thorax, some goose-shoulder no-hackles and some parachutes. The Montana patterns are a brighter yellow than the Pale Morning Duns we tie back home in Colorado (ours usually have a pinkish or rusty cast), and sometimes changing from one color to another makes a difference to the fish.

That's eight fly changes, which seems like a lot, but if none of those work I'll float a standard Hare's Ear or Pheasant Tail nymph, and after the obligatory stop at the fly shop I'll have a bunch of captive, crippled, ruptured and fetal patterns to try.

On a particularly difficult fish, I'll usually only go through two or three fly changes before I start to think maybe it's my drift that's bad. Then I'll try a few short casts for practice, maybe go to a lighter tippet or tie the next fly on with a Duncan loop instead of an improved clinch knot, to let it ride more naturally on the water.

Or maybe I'll change position, moving up- or downstream a little or even crossing to the other side. This takes time because you have to move slowly so as not to disturb the water with too much splashing, but it's often the best way for a mediocre caster to get a better presentation.

I always think the people I'm with are too busy with their own fishing to notice any of this, but then when I run into one of them later they'll almost always ask, smiling, "Well, did you ever catch that one?"

You tell yourself, This is why you wanted to fish a spring creek in the first place, right? People told you they were lousy with trout and bugs, but they were also very difficult to fish, or "highly technical," as some like to say; the kind of water where the really good fly casters come to do their stuff. You wanted to see that and you thought you were up to it.

If you're like most, it doesn't matter if you were up to it the first time or not. If you wired the hatch and caught fish, it was glorious; if you didn't, it was glorious in another way. Novelist Peter Hoeg once said, "When you're young, you think that sex is the culmination of intimacy. Later you discover that it's barely the beginning." Fishing is like that: Even when you catch one, it's barely the beginning.

So you sucked it up and fished a spring creek, and when it was all over you wanted to do it again, either to repeat a performance or to do better next time—and because it was just plain beautiful, as advertised.

It's possible that in true sport there is no failure, only varying degrees of success, and, after all, fishing teaches you to have the courage of your convictions. You wanted it to be tough. It's tough. Okay . . .

If you get skunked on a spring creek, you're in the same boat with some of the world's great fly fishers (whether they'll admit that or not), and if nothing else, a day will come somewhere else when the fishing is pitifully easy: You don't know what to tie on, so you start with a big Royal Wulff and it works; you cast poorly, but trout take the dragging fly anyway; you can't see to land them because of glare or darkness, but they swim into your landing net by themselves.

When that happens—and it will someday—you can think back to that blank day on Armstrong's, Nelson's or DePuy's and think, What the hell, I had this coming. Basically, everything works out well in the end if you just fish enough.

I've fooled with spring creeks off and on for years, and each time I got to fish one it was a treat. By now I guess I can catch trout as often as the next run-of-the-mill fisherman, but I'll never be a hotshot at it because I don't fish spring creeks enough and because I've gotten myself into an awkward bind on that account. That is, I'd somehow like to be as *good* as a hotshot without doing the work or having the competitive nature it takes to actually become one.

As it is, I can fish hard and experiment with patterns

and strategies for a while, but when things really get puzzling my attention sometimes begins to wander. I start trying to identify those warblers in the bankside bushes (even though I have enough trouble with that when I have a bird book and a spotting scope), or I'll find myself pondering one of the abiding mysteries of the universe like, "Why are sock sizes different from shoe sizes?"

That's when I break my own rule, because, after all, the real value of rules is sometimes found in the exceptions. I say to myself, Look, you paid hard-earned cash to be here, so pull yourself together.

CHAPTER

21

Desperation Creek

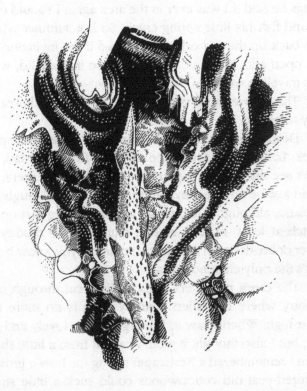

For once I don't have to make up a phony name for
the stream I'm talking about because the man who owns a
nice long stretch of it has already done that. He calls it
"Desperation Creek." Things being as they are, there may

actually *be* a Desperation Creek somewhere in the Rocky Mountain West, but of course this isn't it. Or at least not yet. I'm sure the name began as a combination joke and smoke screen, but now the owner uses it with a straight face, which is how real place names evolve.

There's no great story about getting on the stream. I met a man at a party a few years ago, and in the course of things he said if I was ever in the area again I should come by and fish his little spring creek. So last summer when I was back up there, I called and asked if the invitation was still open and, if it was, could it please include Ed, who I was traveling with.

The answer was yes, and that was that: almost too easy to be fun.

Desperation is an archetypal small Western spring creek. Looking out across the meadow from the road, you don't see the stream. If you didn't know it was there, this could just be another several hundred acres of rough pastureland, although it should go without saying that on this stretch at least, no big, stupid, clumsy cows muddy the water or break down the banks. So unless you know better, that's the only clue: no cows.

The creek meanders in its shallow cut through open country where the tallest scrubby bush is no more than waist-high. When I saw it, I thought it was lovely and perfect, but I also thought it would benefit from a little shade. Then I remembered a Xeriscaper telling me how a grove of hundred-year-old cottonwoods could suck a little stream like this dry in the summer. Okay, forget the shade. It's perfect as it is.

Our host assigned each of us half the stream—starting roughly in the middle, Ed worked upstream and I worked down—but first he took us around to show us where the fish were. Some of the spots were obvious, like a deep bend pool with a cut bank, but others were more obscure, the kinds of places where, on strange water, you'd inadvertently spook the fish if you hadn't been warned.

We'd walk from place to place far out away from the creek. Then, coming up on a spot, we'd crouch and finally kneel, and the man would outline the proven approach to each spot: "Stay low from here on down, don't get any closer than that bush and cast from your knees—sidearm." This is a guy who knows his fishing, and I could tell he really hoped we'd do well. (The stream itself is very small, but there are some big trout in it.) He couldn't tell us everything in a few minutes, but he wanted us to fully understand the delicacy of the situation.

Then he wished us luck and left, saying he was too busy to fish. Maybe he was, or maybe he just knew that three people would be one too many. Real generosity isn't always obvious.

Ed and I had been traveling and fishing for at least a few days by then, so we'd worked out most of the kinks. We were as sharp as we get and feeling confident. As we split up, Ed gave me a clenched-fist salute and advised me to "have courage."

I went to the first spot I'd been shown: a gentle riffle with a fair-sized pool below it, where four or five trout were rising. I couldn't see the fish themselves because the light was wrong, and I'm not that good at guessing fish size from rise forms. I crept over to the stream at a shallow, fishless stretch downstream to see if the bugs on the water were really Pale Morning Dun mayflies as I suspected. They were. Good.

Then I crawled up toward the pool, knelt by the bush and began working out line for my first sidearm cast. I hooked a shrub on a back cast and had to crawl back there on my knees to get my dry fly. When I was younger, I used to do this kind of fishing in roofers' knee pads. Now that I —and my knees—are older, I seem happy enough to crawl around unprotected, chewing gravel holes in my waders and sometimes hurting myself. Who knows why? Maybe I finally realized that life is going to cause some damage and there's nothing much I can do about it.

I cast for the bottom trout first. One cast was short, the next not quite so short and the third was pretty much right on. The trout moved 6 or 8 inches and took the fly daintily. When I set the hook, he wiggled once and shot out of the pool toward me. I saw him go by, heading downstream, as I was trying to gather line to take up the slack. It was a rainbow, 20 inches long or more, but by the time I got control of the line he was gone.

There were two more trout still rising in the pool, one about a yard ahead of the other. I neatly hooked and landed them both. The first was about 10 inches long, the second more like 8. I tried to make myself think: Look, they're trout, they're real pretty and you caught 'em. This is great, right? Never mind that you blew the big one.

At the next spot there were two fish rising tight to the far bank, one so close he was making a half-moon–shaped ring, the other maybe a foot out and 2 feet upstream. You naturally assume that the more difficult fish is the biggest, so I got into position and planned a cast that would put the fly almost, but not quite, on the bank, and then let it drift past the first fish and within an inch of the feeding lane of the second one.

It nearly worked. I couldn't have been off by more than a fraction of an inch, but that was enough to stick the fly securely on a wet, rubbery, pencil-sized root. Before I could think of what to do, the leader bellied heavily in the current and the two fish stopped rising.

I broke the fly off and then took a few minutes to calm down and to replace my 6x tippet and size 18 Pale Morning Dun thorax dry fly. I thought about waiting the fish out, then realized that the sparse hatch had been on for a while and wouldn't last forever. So I moved on to the next spot, where I hooked and landed a nice 14- or 15-inch rainbow out of a pod of several risers. The fish jumped twice, spooking the rest of the pool.

A little farther downstream I spotted a trout rising near the bank in a spot I hadn't been shown. It was there that I started hearing the voices: a man and a woman, clearly angry, though I couldn't make out what they were saying, and also the occasional sound of a slamming screen door. It had to be coming from the little house, half screened by Russian olive trees, about 200 yards away, just over the fence line on the next property. I hadn't noticed it before.

I cast from my knees and caught the trout on the third or fourth drift. It was a chunky, silvery rainbow about a foot long.

Then, as I was walking on downstream to the next pool, staying far back from the stream so as not to spook the fish, the woman's voice carried clearly through the still air. It said, "You *bastard!*" I could see now that they were hauling furniture from the house to a pickup parked out back. I thought, Okay, the main thing here is, this is none of your business.

I remembered the next pool. It was an L-shaped bend with a steep bank on the outside and an open gravel bar on the inside. Kneeling in the grass 30 or 40 yards away, I could see a few trout rising near the head of it; casual, sporadic dimples. I couldn't recall how my host had told me to approach this one, but it looked as though if I crept up the long leg of the L on the inside, right at the water's edge, I could get to a spot far to the side and a little below the fish. A slight right hook would keep the line out of the gravel, and the back cast looked clear.

I slithered down the bank and began crawling upstream toward the pool. The same openness that would leave plenty of room for a back cast made me feel awfully exposed, so I stayed as low as I could, on my knees and one hand, carrying the rod low, moving with an awkward, hopping limp like a dog with a bad foot.

At about 40 feet the angle of the light changed so I could see the fish. One second the stream was a dull silver sheet and the next the water was clear as air, green bottomed at a depth of roughly 3 feet, with mottled brown rocks. There were only two trout that I could see and they were both huge: easily 20 inches, possibly more. One fish was pale—probably a rainbow—and the other looked very dark, almost black. They seemed to have divided the pool exactly in half, lengthwise, and each one was dancing around in its own half, casually eating mayflies.

From next door, only about 75 yards away now, the man's voice said, "Goddamn it, that's just like you. That's why—" and then the door slammed again.

I crouched there for a few minutes, watching the two fish. Whenever I see game like this—going about their business, unaware that I'm there and that I'm about to catch them or shoot them or (just as likely) do something stupid and scare them away—I often hesitate, savoring it. In some ways, the most beautiful moments in sport are the ones just before you act. You know, open-ended, full of promise, often better than what actually happens in the next few minutes.

Then I cast to the near fish, making a few short false casts first to make sure I'd judged the range and the drift right, and then dropping the fly about 2 feet ahead of him. It was lovely. The fly went past the fish less than a foot to his right. He saw it, turned, followed it downstream and took it gently near the tail of the pool. When I set the hook, the trout shook his head and wallowed on downstream, out of the pool and into a long glide. I didn't want to spook the other fish by standing up, so I followed the run in what must have been a pretty comical knee-walk, but I had just enough time to glance back and see that the other trout was still rising.

I played the fish out in the next pool, far enough downstream that I could lurch to my feet and stand. I suppose you could say it was an unspectacular fight—no blazing runs, no jumps—but when I have a big trout on light tackle, I'm grateful for that. It means I might be able to get him.

When I waded into the water to land the trout, my boots sank in thick mud and a cloud of black muck billowed into the clear stream. My beautiful trout vanished in this crap momentarily, and I experienced panic, but it was okay in the end. The fish was covered with mud, but he was in the net.

I waded out to clear water and washed him off. He was wonderful: as deep-bellied and hump-backed as a little sockeye salmon; olive, purplish red and bluish silver with big spots; 22 inches easy, maybe 23, maybe even . . . Well, I've gotta start carrying a tape measure. Anyway, it was the biggest trout I'd seen in a hell of a long time, and I was real happy.

"You can't take that!" the woman's voice said. "That's *mine!*"

I crawled back up to the pool on knees that felt bruised and that I knew would be sore for days to come, thinking, Hardware store in Bozeman, knee pads, twenty bucks, tops. Sure enough, the other fish was still rising.

When I put the thorax dry fly over him, he executed a heartbreaking refusal rise: He saw it, turned and came for it with his mouth beginning to open and then flashed away at the last minute. It was all I could do not to strike.

The fish ignored two more good drifts with the same fly, so I knew I had to change. For no other reason than that it looked good, I tied on a Harrop's captive dun pattern I'd bought at a local fly shop a few days before. I couldn't see it on the water, but when the fish rose to take something on the surface, I thought it was about where my fly should have been and carefully set the hook.

This trout did exactly what the rainbow had done. He shook his head, ran slowly but heavily down the long run and let himself be played out in the next pool. He was almost an exact copy of the bow: let's say 22 inches, fat and heavy, except he was a lovely brown, the color of burnt butter.

When I released the fish, he cruised to the edge of the main current, belched some mud from his gill covers and then darted under a cut bank. I stood there watching that plume of ugly black muck drifting out of sight around the next bend and wondering how I'd tell Ed about this. Lead up to it? Blurt it out?

I remember my emotions about this being mixed, as they tend to be now that I'm no longer a kid. I was happy about those two big trout, but also vaguely sorry about all the mud I'd stirred up. You can't live without causing some damage, but it occurred to me that maybe over the years I'd caused more than my fair share, although I guess I'd also learned that regret is usually a waste of time. Then again, I knew that when I told Ed the story I'd leave the mud out.

The screen door slammed and the man's voice said, "Aw, fuck you!"

I almost yelled back, "Yeah, well fuck you, too!" but then decided against it. In a situation like that it's best to remain hidden; best for everyone that they never even knew I was there.

22

What Else Is There?

I used to think I was a fairly radical, not to mention up-to-date environmentalist, but when I look into the newer literature of the movement I realize that I'm not quite an antihumanist anarchist, a primitivist, a humanist eco-anarchist, a green Marxist or an eco-feminist, which are the only choices one recent article on the subject allowed. I probably *am* a bioregionalist (a pretty tame stance these days), but more to the point, I'm a fly fisherman, and that comes with its own political agenda.

My position is, we should have a clean, healthy, diverse natural environment so I can go fishing. Because fishing makes me happy.

Granted, that seems like a simple-minded goal in these grim times, but there it is nonetheless: without becoming overly romantic; without ignoring reality; given the normal limitations; from roughly now until the shit hits the fan, I would like to be, you know, reasonably happy.

And yes, maybe that *is* too much to ask. Then again, I haven't had the dreaded middle-age crisis and I don't detect one brewing. Of course I have an advantage. Half the men and a few of the women I know who've wigged out in their forties wanted to run off and do what I do now, which is fish a lot and write books about it for a living. (The other half wanted more money, faster sports cars and younger lovers, but that's a whole other story.)

These people, after a life of working and striving for money, status, influence or whatever, wanted to chuck it all and become one with nature in some kind of particularly human way, which is the only way available to us. They saw this as a more or less direct route to truth and salvation, and for some of them at least, it was just that.

After twenty-some years of listening to New Age sanctimony, I cringe a little at the mention of becoming *one with* anything, but I guess it's like saying you want happiness: corny but undeniably true.

I started to get into fly-fishing back in the late 1960s, soon after moving to Colorado from the Midwest with no real plans. You could do that back then—live without plans, I mean—and no one thought much of it except maybe your mother.

At first, fly-fishing just seemed like an elegant and practical way to catch trout, and it was also fashionable in a hip sort of way. (Ernest Hemingway fly fished. So did Richard Brautigan. And so, it turns out, does Eric Clapton, as well as a whole bunch of other really cool people who are still with us.) But there was something else, too: It was said fly-fishing was a sport to which one's life could be dedicated.

Okay, presumably that wasn't being said with a completely straight face, but it still had a nice ring to it. I'd been more or less at loose ends since junior high, when it became obvious that if my sister was going to be Queen of the Prom, I was going to be Maynard the beatnik. I guess the idea of dedication didn't interest me much until I realized it could go in some pretty unusual directions.

I'd been fly-fishing for a number of years when, in 1976, an obscure little book called *A River Runs Through It and Other Stories,* by Norman Maclean, appeared from the University of Chicago Press. By then I had it bad, and it didn't surprise me at all to hear Maclean equate fly-fishing with religion. What did surprise me was that some people thought he was kidding.

Robert Redford's movie version of Maclean's story is a good one, much better than most movies made from good literature. They say it did a lot for the sport of fly-fishing, but it also elevated me and many of my contemporaries to instant old-timer status as those who remember when *A River Runs Through It* was "just a book."

Anyway, it was right around then—in the late '70s— that I passed a kind of personal milestone: I quit my job because there was a great Blue-winged Olive mayfly hatch going on and my boss—a man with no soul—wouldn't give me the day off to go fishing. The logic of this seemed flawless at the time, and to be honest, it wasn't much of a job.

Still, it was around then that I decided I'd better become a writer, if only because I wasn't good enough to be a fishing guide or fast enough to be a professional fly tier, and all the other alternatives seemed to involve either not enough fishing or starvation. Luckily, I didn't realize at the time that becoming a freelance writer to *avoid* starvation would not be viewed as the act of a sane man.

So now, because I do write about fishing for a living, I am sometimes interviewed, and a common question is, "What *is* it about fly-fishing, anyway?" Of course the electronic media types who ask this want a cute sound bite before the next commercial instead of the real answer, and once, in an attempt to get into the spirit of the thing, I actually said, "Well, Bob, it's sort of like golf except you can eat the balls." Further proof that writers shouldn't be trusted to think on their feet.

The real truth about fly-fishing is, it is beautiful beyond description in almost every way, and when a certain kind of person is confronted with a certain kind of beauty, they are either saved or ruined for life, or a little of both.

But that's not good enough for most interviewers. "Okay," one radio guy said, "tell me why *I* should take up fly-fishing." (The thing you have to remember is, if you're not recruiting for a cause or pushing a conspiracy theory, you don't belong on the airwaves.)

Not really meaning to be a smart-ass, I said, "Actually, I never said you *should*."

•

By the time I quit that job to go fishing, I had reached the first plateau. I could cast well enough as long as the situation wasn't too complicated or the range too great, I could locate trout in a stream if they weren't doing something too off the wall, and I could at least guess at what fly to tie on. More to the point, I could sometimes manage to catch a fish.

I caught some that day, in fact—brown trout, two of which I killed and ate for supper—and it's a good thing, too. If I'd gone home that night unemployed and with no fish, I might have become discouraged and ended up in law school.

That was a long time ago, and I still can't claim to be an expert fly fisher, but then I don't have to be. I found that to write about it you simply have to *find* an expert and know what questions to ask, although you do have to fish yourself, if only so you can grasp certain intangibles.

And you don't have to be an expert to see that although what was said about dedicating your life to fly-fishing may not have been meant seriously, it turns out to be true in some extreme cases. And the reasoning is refreshingly simple: Only a few things are worth doing for their own sakes, and life is short.

Just to get good at fly-fishing—that is, to be able to catch fish as often as not in a variety of situations—you have to master the basics of fly casting. That takes a while, especially when you teach yourself, get it all wrong and then have to go back to the beginning and start all over again. In the right hands, fly casting looks graceful and effortless, but when you first try it, you think there must be something wrong with your rod.

Then you have to understand a few things about fish,

the hydrology of the water they live in and the intricacies of fly tackle, while, at the same time, avoiding the obvious pitfall of becoming a boring techno-freak.

Since trout feed mostly on aquatic insects, you have to learn a little bit about the bugs, although exactly how much information you need is a matter of debate. In fact, entomology is where some fly fishers go over the edge, endlessly arguing fine points of taxonomy when all you need is, say, a Pale Morning Dun dry fly tied on a size 22 hook instead of a size 18. At its worst, this can turn fly-fishing into what Charlie Waterman (one of the sages of the sport) has called "a small pool of trout surrounded by a great wall of semantics."

You'll probably decide to tie your own flies anyway, and this will become a much bigger deal than you thought it would.

In the course of all this, you'll learn how barometric pressure, humidity, cloud cover, moon phase, time of day, time of year, stream flow, water temperature and turbidity affect fish and bugs. Or at least you'll begin to think all that means something.

You'll learn how to wade a river and, more importantly, when and where *not* to wade. Slogging through a fast riffle one fine day, you'll suddenly come face to face with the full weight of water, which comes in at 8 pounds per gallon. Drowning is always a possibility, but you'll probably live; most do. If it's a nice warm day you'll dry out in an hour or so.

While others are concerned with more mundane matters, such as who to marry and how to make a living, you'll find yourself pondering questions like: Should my rod be made of fiberglass, graphite, boron or bamboo? Should my line be a double taper, rocket taper, triangle taper, weight forward, sink tip or shooting head? Should my wading shoes have treads, felts or cleats? Should my hooks come from Norway, England or Japan? All of which really can be important—more or less.

You'll surely start reading books and you'll learn all kinds of useful things, but you'll also find that book learning is no substitute for lots and lots of time on the water. There are fishermen who talk a good game but can't catch fish. You don't want to be one of *them*.

You may end up with a trout doormat on the front porch, a trout mailbox, a set of brandy snifters etched with illustrations of trout flies, chamois shirts with embroidered stoneflies over the pockets and a complete set of Susan F. Peterson trout china, but none of that is actually required.

You're supposed to go through a series of transitions. At first you just want a fish, and since this is a complicated sport requiring some skill, landing that first one isn't always a snap. Once you're past that, you'll want lots of fish, then big ones, and then you'll want something like the difficult or the interesting or the beautiful fish, or maybe the fish that swim on the other side of the world.

Finally, you're supposed to see that the real goal of wanting is to stop wanting altogether, so you just go to water out of curiosity and gratefully take whatever it gives you.

It's supposed to be a smooth, straight path to enlightenment—five koans solved and discarded—but I was always a poor student of Zen, the guy who couldn't meditate because he couldn't sit still, so I go back and forth in fits and starts, changing my aesthetics about as often as I change my socks on a fishing trip, that is, every couple of days whether I need to or not.

But if I don't *have* to sit still, I can sometimes manage something that approaches the sublime: that is, just fishing, without the self split in two, with one half casting and the other half watching as if from a distance. It's great. You stare into the water until you realize it's been staring back at you, and maybe you even catch a few trout. But even though I now and then fish brilliantly, I've never quite lost myself as the fisherman and become the fish, let alone become first both and then neither.

But I did come to realize that good fishing and good writing use the same skills. Whether you're after a trout or a story, you won't get far with brute force. You're better off to watch, wait and remain calm, just putting yourself in the place where the thing lives and letting it all happen, rather than trying to *make* it happen.

When a story is going badly, the best thing to do is put it away and go do something else for a while. Maybe go fishing. If the fishing is going badly, the best thing to do is sit on a rock to watch and wait. Sooner or later a crack will open just wide enough to let you slip quietly through. Eventually the story reveals its theme and the fish thinks you went away and starts rising again. The only real skill you've exercised is the ability to stay awake until it happens.

The same strategy has been known to work in politics, business and other more prosaic matters. If you don't know what to do, do nothing for a while. If you don't know what to say, let the other guy talk. Sooner or later he'll let the truth slip simply because he's not smart enough to just shut up. Basically, the world is a big, dumb trout, and you're a fisherman with all the time in the world.

Okay, maybe not. But that's how it seems when you can take things as they come.

Sometimes I wonder what kind of fisherman I'd be if I didn't write about it—or what kind of writer I'd be if I didn't fish—but when it comes right down to it, I can't begin to imagine, and by now it doesn't matter anyway.

In case you haven't noticed, fly-fishing has become fashionable lately. This kind of snuck up on me, so I can't tell you exactly when it happened, but I knew it *had* happened when well-dressed, youngish middle-aged, demographically correct people began to appear on TV casting with fly rods or looking over expensive tackle, not in those insipid Saturday-morning fishing shows, but in slick commercials hawking credit cards and painkillers.

That's how you know something has arrived in America: when they start using it to strike a subliminal chord in advertising.

Some friends and I have occasionally sat down to try to decide if this is a good thing or not, and our consensus is, maybe, maybe not. The only thing we can agree on is, it's startling to be middle-aged and back in style.

Lately, fly-fishing has been described as a "growth industry." (That's supposed to be good news, but it sounds to me like the economic equivalent of cancer.) Stories in the media tell you the newcomers are mostly well-off professional yuppies who can afford the gear and the travel, but then out on the stream you meet old folks and kids, men and women, bums and brain surgeons, polite people and assholes, conservative Republicans and radical antihumanist eco-anarchists. You get along okay with most of them (except the assholes) as long as you don't talk politics.

Some of them are better fly fishers than others, but

their station in life, their income or the amount of money they spent on their tackle seems to have nothing to do with it. In fact, how much they actually know about fly-fishing doesn't always seem to make a difference. This is what Robert Traver meant when he said, "All men are equal before the trout." If he'd written that more recently he'd have said "all persons," which is probably what he meant anyway.

I can't blame anyone for falling in love with fly-fishing, but I have mixed feelings about the growth of the sport. On the one hand, if someone decides to build a dam on a great trout stream, he'll get a lot more letters and phone calls now than he would have ten or twenty years ago. On the other hand, some of those streams are getting pretty crowded these days.

But I'm a conservationist, so, philosophically at least, it doesn't seem unreasonable to trade a little of my solitude for a larger constituency for trout streams. Then again, I've also become a cagey outdoorsman, so I know of some little creeks where I can hike a few extra miles and have my solitude and my trout anyway.

Not long ago Ed told me he thought that small, secluded freestone streams full of small trout were going to be the sport's next rage and that, in fact, some fly shops and guide services were already gearing up for that.

"Oh well," I said, "if worse comes to worst, there's always carp."

As it is now, I can still make those long, brisk walks with a day pack and rod case, unlike some of my contemporaries who have become plump and weary. They make more money than I do, but they spend it on useless shoes and expensive cars that don't even have four-wheel drive.

One of these guys—who also happens to be an old friend—once decided to have one of those helpful, friendly talks with me, just in case there were some larger perspectives on life that I'd overlooked. But it didn't go the way he thought it would and he ended up exasperated, saying, "Jeez, man, *it's only fishing!*"

To which I had to say, "Exactly! And in your case, *it's only the stock market.*" Again, not really meaning to be a smart-ass, but since that's how it came out, okay.

It was a slightly hot moment, but in the end we remained friends. He fishes now and then himself, and sees the value in a simple, healthy life, while I am not entirely opposed to money. I mean, money buys fly rods and plane tickets, right?

And, after all, we're both adults, which, come to think of it, had something to do with his point in the first place. At least he didn't tell me to grow up and get married and get a haircut and buy a Weed Whacker. He just thought that at my age I should buckle down a little, get some equity, think about the future.

Hell, I've thought about the future. I long ago realized that there won't be enough time to fish all the great rivers of even just North America, let alone the world, and that *is* sort of a bleak thought.

On the other hand, it's comforting to think that, even now, there's more good water than a guy can fish well in a lifetime, and although I'm not a kid anymore, I've noticed that I fish better now that I'm older.

It's part of the myth—or at least the accepted pose—that you're supposed to love fishing with a manic, self-destructive craziness. I guess I did once, but I found it hard to locate the stillness I was after while bolting breakfast before dawn with the guides standing around tapping their feet and pointedly looking at their watches. Of course the best guides I know don't even *wear* watches.

There was a time—back before it was a cliché—when I might have said, "No pain, no gain." Now I'd be more likely to say something like, "No patience, no peace of mind," although I *might* just be smart enough to say nothing at all.

I've also noticed that I'm getting more and more reclusive as I try to keep my own fly-fishing from turning from a sport into a business. (Not that it's an endless struggle or anything, it's just something I think I should keep an eye on.)

And I don't mean to say there's anything inherently wrong with the tackle business, either. It's just that you must be very protective of the one or two things you do for love instead of money. I mean, those are the things that give you a vantage point from which to view the rest of the world—or is it a pair of rose-colored glasses?

Anyway, I pretty much stay away from banquets, meetings and fishing contests (except for the carp tournament), and I stopped going to sportsmen's shows not long after I stumbled upon the portable, indoor trout stream at Currigan Hall in Denver a few years ago.

But I still keep meeting kindred spirits. At a party, a woman says to me, "Well, my *husband* fishes! He wishes he could just *live* on the river!" The husband is right there, bourbon and water in hand, and one glance into his eyes tells me this is true. In fact, he wishes he was living on the river at that very moment.

This is one reason why fishermen seldom laugh at fishing jokes: If they hit the mark at all (which is rare), they're too true to be funny—like the bumper sticker that says, SO MANY FISH, SO LITTLE TIME.

There does seem to be an element of desperation about it now and then, but it's a desperation that gets resolved. Fishing is the part of life that's filled with more or less regular successes, and failures that don't really matter because there'll always be a next time. You come to see that a life frittered away with sport and travel makes perfect sense, but no one trip ever tells the whole story.

So basically, I wake up one morning to find that life is strange but simple, and fly-fishing is still as important to me as it was a few decades ago, even though I still can't tell you exactly why, and even though I'm glad it's no more important than it is. It just turns out to be the one part of my life where things are right, or where it seems worth the trouble to try to *make* them right, or maybe the only place where the possibility of rightness even exists. Something like that.

I still can't tell you why I do it. I've tried that a few times and always gotten tangled up in too much sentiment or politics and ended up completely missing the point without actually saying anything I didn't mean. I've read books by fine writers who've tried to explain it. Many failed, and the best only gave tantalizing hints. Jim Harrison said, "Few of us shoot ourselves during an evening hatch." Tom McGuane said, "If the trout are lost, smash the state." Harry Middleton said he's addicted "not so much to fly-fishing but to what it sinks me in."

I think it's now more a matter of unspoken agreements among friends than pounds of fish, and that's probably why I spend more time hanging out with fishermen, as opposed to whoever all those other people are.

Among those others are some well-meaning types who don't enjoy life nearly as much as I do, but who nonetheless believe I should do things differently. They seem to think I'm a decent fly fisher and—a little bit of a temper notwithstanding—a nice enough guy, but that otherwise I'll probably never amount to anything. To that I have to ask, "What else is there to amount to?"

Dances with Trout

The world punishes us for taking it too seriously as well as for not taking it seriously enough.

—JOHN UPDIKE

1

The Lake

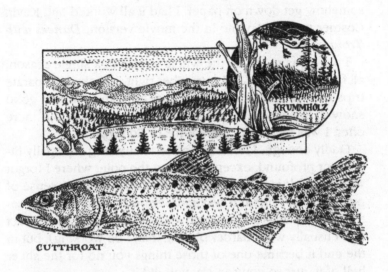

KRUMMHOLZ

CUTTHROAT

One summer, A. K. Best, Larry Pogreba and I walked up into a high mountain valley we know of to find and fish a certain alpine lake. The most recent report we had on it was ten years old but, back then at least, it was supposed to have some big cutthroat trout. This is a remote lake that's not fished much, which naturally gets you to thinking.

I'd never been to this lake, or to any of the half dozen other lakes and hanging puddles on that far southwest ridge, even though I've been fishing, hiking and hunting in the valley off and on for somewhere between fifteen and twenty years and had, only the summer before, systematically fished the entire length of the stream from the last paved county road up to the headwaters.

I'll admit right here that this was more of a writing than a

completely honest sporting proposition. I had in mind one
of those gradual revelation numbers: Fishing the stream yard
by yard, mile by mile, the details would build up novelisti-
cally until finally I would catch the last tiny cutthroat trout
sucking snowflies from the lip of the glacier and there'd be
this vague but satisfying sense of completion, which I would
somehow get down on paper. I had it all worked out. Kevin
Costner would play me in the movie version, *Dances with
Trout.*

I did manage to fish the whole stream in a single season,
all fifteen miles of it. If I remember right, it took ten separate
trips between the end of runoff in June and the first good
snow in September. Once or twice I went alone, but more
often I was with A.K., Mike Price or Ed Engle.

Oddly enough, I never got close to anything especially literary or profound, except maybe at the point where I forgot
why I was doing it. There was still an amorphous sense of
purpose that I liked. It was more serious than play, less serious than work (a distinction made more subtle by the fact
that I usually work harder playing than I do working), but in
the end it became one of those things you do for the sheer
hell of it, just so you can say you did it.

Also, I caught lots of fish. That's just good, clean fun but,
as often as it happens, it still seems like proof of something.
The trout takes the fly, the line tightens and it's like I was
blind, but now I see. I have to admit there are days when I
fish as a conscious act of revolution, but the days when I fish
for no apparent reason at all are usually better.

I thought about keeping a journal, but when it came right
down to it I didn't. For one thing, I didn't want to be bothered scribbling when I could be fishing. For another, I knew
I'd be happier relying on my recollections because the memory of a fisherman is more like fiction than journalism, that
is, it doesn't ignore the facts, but it's not entirely bound by
them, either.

When I finally did catch what had to be the last cutthroat

from the last trickle deep enough to hold one, I thought, Okay, *there*. Then I started thinking about that lake up on the ridge and the rumors about big trout. The lesson about writing had something to do with endings: like maybe they don't really exist in nature.

That was the summer that the idea of minimum flows lower down on the same drainage floated to the surface once again, as it does about every five years or so. By now all the studies have been done and the experts tend to agree: Water quality, biomass, species diversity—it's all there. Just add a proper, minimum winter flow—enough to let the larger trout live until spring—and you'll have one hell of a trout stream.

This is something a handful of us locals have been kicking around for a couple of decades now, first as part of Trout Unlimited, then as I don't know what. At one point some people started referring to us as the TLO (the Trout Liberation Organization) but that didn't stick because right about then it was becoming clear that terrorism wasn't really very funny. I suggested the National Riffle Association, but in the end we didn't need a name because we weren't an organization in the usual sense. I think we realized it was better to remain a nameless, unorganized handful of people with a more or less common vision so that the occasional good idea wouldn't have to undergo surgery by a committee.

So for quite a while now we've been trying first one tactic and then another, keeping the idea of minimum flows alive because it might eventually catch on and looking for the chink in the state and local bureaucracies that would allow everyone in power to gracefully do the right thing.

The main problem is, it's hard to get used to the level of discourse you're involved in. When you go to a bureaucrat with an idea, he looks you in the eye, smiles warmly and thinks, "Is there anything in this for me and, if not, what's the quickest way to get rid of this guy?" When you approach a politician, he thinks, "How can I be simultaneously for and against this?" not realizing that by being on both sides of a fight he'll eventually beat himself up.

When you start talking about putting water back into a stream because it belongs there, you're screwing around with one of the oldest Old World artifacts on this continent. Water law here dates back roughly to the introduction of the horse into North America. By now it's become pretty well fossilized.

The stretch of stream I was fishing that summer was at the top end of the drainage, in a wilderness area, above the dams, ditches, headgates and all the other plumbing by which too much water was being stolen from the stream and by which also reasonable people could put some back. Not all of it—just enough for the fish to breathe.

That upper fork is not exactly untouched, but it's still nicely out of the loop. If you walk far enough upstream, you can literally, that is, *physically*, leave the argument behind, and that's . . . what? Let's say, liberating. Or let's say that, without diminishing the importance of the environmental issue at hand, it can give you a larger perspective: Left to themselves, things are as they are because they couldn't be any other way, right?

One day, in the course of doing a lunch with a guy who might have been made to see minimum flows in the lower stream working to his advantage, the man asked me, "What is it you really want?" assuming, of course, that what I *told* him I wanted was a smokescreen behind which a hidden agenda was advancing unseen.

I can often wait out a trout, but I tend to lose patience quickly with humans, so I slipped and said, "What I really want is for us to disassemble enough of modern technological culture that we can become a nation of agrarian anarchist, gourmet hunter/gatherer, poet/sportsmen." That may or may not have been a mistake, but it was therapeutic.

That was also the year I began to get interested in the concept of bioregionalism: the idea that your coherent, familiar, natural habitat is much more important to you in the long run than political boundaries, not to mention much harder to define. I guess I'd known that instinctively all along, but it was only recently that I'd discovered the label and the small, backwater political movement that comes with it.

So as an exercise in visualization, I asked myself, honestly now, ignoring meaningless designations like United States of America, Colorado, Boulder County, St. Vrain Valley School District or an arbitrarily selected stretch of trout stream, where do you feel you belong? I started with the places where the water is cold enough to support trout and where I know enough to dress for the weather, overlaid the ranges of mule deer, snowshoe hares and the species of grouse I know how to hunt, added spruce, fir and pine trees and the few edible mushrooms I can identify.

It became obvious that I was fundamentally at home either in one small drainage in the Colorado Rockies or anywhere in the northern third of North America. I found that helpful. Everyone should have a rough idea where home is.

The fork of the stream and the rumored cutthroat lake are in one of those classically beautiful, high, wide but somehow still intimate valleys in the Colorado Rockies, and parts of it are nicely inaccessible. First there's an hour and a half's worth of jarring, slamming bad road. Then, at the road's end, there's a pretty good uphill hike past the stretch of stream that's fished by the four-wheel brigade. After several miles the trout change from brookies to cutthroats, some of which get unusually large for that kind of high, sparse water.

The stream itself is small, cold, steep, deep in places, shallow and braided in others and jumbled with boulders and the bleached trunks of fallen spruce and fir trees. It's mostly in forest, so the water is nicely shaded, but the dense spruce and fir needles will grab your flies and leaders on careless back casts and hold on to them like Velcro.

This does not make for graceful fly-fishing. You scramble

over rocks and rotting logs, make short, choppy casts and lose flies to snags but, because most fishermen won't put themselves through this—let alone walk that far to do it—the hardest spots give up the best trout.

This is the kind of fine little creek that grabs and holds your attention, and it's hard enough to get to in its own right that it can keep you from exploring further. But I was honestly curious about the lake, and also a little worried that someone would eventually ask me about it, based on the assumption that I've been kicking around the area for two decades and must know it like the proverbial back of my hand. I'd have to admit the truth, they'd say something like, "Oh, so in all that time you never actually went *all the way back in there*," and that would sting.

The three of us hiked in from the end of the four-wheel-drive road and, although we had a destination in mind, we couldn't help stopping here and there along the creek to catch, admire and release a few trout. I directed Larry to some good spots I'd discovered the year before, and in fifteen minutes he'd landed a couple of fourteen-inch cutthroats.

"Jeeze," he said, "I didn't know they got this big up here."

I beamed, proud of myself, even though he'd have found the fish easily enough without my help, and A.K. mumbled, "Just keep it to yourself, okay?"

There was talk of keeping a few trout to eat, but it was early in the day and we had a long walk ahead of us. The fish might have gotten a little funky by the time we got them home, and there are few things worse than wild trout that could have been fresh, but aren't.

Then we found the little feeder creek that was supposed to come from the lake in question and started climbing. The directions were good so far; there was the old skid road, the ruined bridge and the advice, "It's the first big feeder you come to." The slope was steep, the air was thin. A.K. and I began to plod while Larry pulled out ahead and found some perfect, doorknob-sized Boletus mushrooms that he stuffed into his fly vest.

Not far past the mushrooms we came out of the tall, shady spruce/fir forest into the open. Larry charged ahead, but A.K. and I stopped there for a few minutes to reacclimate. To me, coming out of the dark timber at high altitude is like walking out of a movie matinee into a hard, bright summer afternoon. The eyes squint, vision swims and you stoop a little so as not to bump your head on the sky.

After some more hard going we did, in fact, come to a lake, but it was too shallow, too small, obviously fishless and couldn't have been *the* lake.

We rested for a few minutes, then consulted the compass and map. We should have done this earlier, but the guy with the decade-old fishing report was the one who'd said to follow that particular feeder creek and we'd trusted his memory. He'd been wrong, which cast something of a shadow on the whole enterprise.

None of us are great at orienteering, but it became clear that we were too far east, although it wasn't clear *how* far. So we worked our way roughly west along the rock shelves, boulder fields and miniature knee- to chest-high spruce groves, finally coming to a pair of large pools on a feeder creek that weren't on the map and, a hundred feet farther up, a pair of lakes that were.

Okay, now we knew where we were. The shapes and placement of the lakes and the prominent landmarks were unmistakable. Where we needed to be was a mile or so farther south by southwest and a few hundred feet higher. We looked in that direction and there stood an enormous, ominous-looking crag of rock, on the other side of which would be the lake we wanted.

Someone dug out a watch to check the time. It was too late to do anything but fish the lakes at hand for half an hour and then head out at a quick pace if we wanted to negotiate that four-wheel-drive road with any daylight left. That seemed like a good idea, since we'd wrecked a tire on the way in and were running on the spare. We were using Larry's Suburbillac, an ingenious homemade Suburban/Cadillac/pop-up camper hybrid that I won't try to describe here. It's a solid vehicle, but too odd-looking to instill a lot of confidence in skeptical passengers.

We fished the larger of the two lakes for a while, mostly as an exercise. There were no rises, no fish cruising the shallows. In terms of vegetation, aquatic insects and trout, it looked as sterile as a stone toilet bowl. Still, after all that walking it was fun to stand and make long, straight casts out onto the pretty water.

These sparse, high lakes can and do winterkill, leaving them with no life that would interest a guy who'd carried a fly rod six or seven miles and two thousand feet up. Then again, bodies of water just like this have been known to look fishless, but hold a handful of five-pound cutthroats that you might locate after two days of watching and random casting, but not in half an hour. So if someone asks me if there are trout in Such-and-Such Lake, I'll have to answer, in all honesty, "I don't know, I didn't see any." But, I can add silently, I *did* go look.

We were at roughly 11,000 feet, where the air is cool, thin and dizzyingly clear, even to westerners. The larger of the two lakes was set smack against the base of a nameless (by the map) 12,400-foot peak on the Continental Divide with other sharp summits reaching past 13,000 visible along the ridge to the north and west. Looking down valley to the northeast, we could see the nearly flat-topped, almost vertical escarpment that forms the north wall of the gorge. This is a natural barrier to the elk herds that move down and east in the fall so that, although the little valley is rich in other kinds of game, elk are rare.

Fooling around with maps of the area, I once determined that from almost any good, high vantage point in the upper valley one can see something like ninety square miles of rock, tundra, forests, lakes and trout streams. On site, it doesn't seem anywhere near that big.

The lake itself was clear at the shallow end, but the deep hole on the far side was a milky blue-green color from the little glacier to the south. Patches of the nearer snowfields had a slight pinkish cast caused by a kind of wind-borne snow mold. This stuff is said to taste like watermelon, but it's also supposed to be either a neurotoxin or a psychedelic, depending on which survivor you talk to.

This is the area that lies between timberline (above which trees won't grow tall and straight) and treeline (above which trees won't grow at all). It's called *krummholz:* a German word meaning "crooked wood."

Some of the small, gnarled trees here are ancient, though how ancient I can only guess. The oldest known individual living things on the planet are some bristlecone pines living in California in terrain something like this. They're said to be well over four thousand years of age. A local botanist says that in this area krummholz spruce several hundred years old may have a trunk diameter of only four inches, and there are old trees here that are more than a foot across at the base.

It's trees like this that inspired the art of bonsai growing in China and Japan. The bonsai masterpieces (outrageous, shallowly potted trees, some of which are hundreds of years old) symbolize great strength, wiry toughness, stillness, patience, eccentricity, adaptation, harmonious balance, goofiness and the venerable wisdom that can come from old age: all the attributes enlightened humans can take from wildness if they're smart enough to pay attention.

Of course they also symbolize how an honest love of nature can turn on itself. According to bonsai grower Peter Chin, many mountainous areas of Japan were stripped of their beautiful, naturally dwarfed trees by bonsai collectors long ago. To see them now you have to go to the cities. And this from a culture that has always based its art and philosophy on a close harmony with the natural world.

It's interesting that, because we Americans have loved nature less and for a shorter time, these lovely little trees (which are, after all, too small for lumber) still grow in our mountains. In this kind of terrain you see examples of two classic bonsai styles—*kengai* (cascade) and *fukinagashi* (windswept). Digging one to transplant would be three times harder than grunting up there to fish, and it's illegal anyway.

No trout were going to come from the lake in front of us, that much was clear, and as we were reeling in and heading back to where we'd piled our day packs, A.K. said, "It's yet another success. We said we were going fishing and that's what we did."

A thousand feet below, down in the tall, straight trees, we could see a small, nameless lake where I'd caught cutthroat trout as long as sixteen inches that year, although we wouldn't have time to fish for them now. From that vantage point we could also pick out the easy, more or less direct route to the lake we'd set out for that morning, and we filed that for future reference.

The sun was far to the west, a little over an hour from dusk. The shadows across the valley behind us were long and pointed—olive and honey-colored on the bare rocks, almost black down in the trees and dull silver on the lower lake. The peaks on the far ridge were starting to get an amber glow. All in all, it was a far better place to be than a bar or a gas station when a flopped expedition begins to take on that aimless feeling.

It was going to be a long, fast walk out, so we broke down our rods, shouldered our packs and had that brief consultation that becomes standard with middle-aged outdoorsmen who have come to know of each other's old injuries:

"How's your back?"

"Fine, how's your foot?"

"Okay, how's your knee?"

"Sore, but it's all downhill from here."

CHAPTER

2

Quitting Early

*T*he deal was this: Most of the river was private through this stretch, or, I should say, the surrounding land was private, since Montana's enlightened Stream Access Law allows you to walk and fish on any river as long as you stay below the high-water line.

Still, some of this water would have involved a really long, hard hike from the nearest public access except that one landowner allows fishermen to park and get in on his land for a fee of three dollars. You have to know where the turnoff is, but once you get down to the river there's a large, hand-painted sign that explains the procedure in detail, complete with some interesting spelling errors.

You get an envelope from an old, tin tackle box on a stump, stick three dollars in it, write your license number on the outside and put it in the slot on a large, handmade strong-box that's too big and heavy to steal.

There's no one around, it's an honor system, but before you even think of not doing it, you come to the part of the instructions saying that nonpayers will be banned. Actually it says, "NONE PAYERS WILL BE BAND," which somehow makes the point with even more authority.

There were some other fishermen rigging up there, and one of them came over and asked me if it was true what he'd heard about the old man who owned the place: that he'd drive down from the hills in the evening, check the en-velopes against the license plates and go after cheaters with a shotgun.

"You bet," I said, although I'd never met the old man or even heard the story before. Everywhere you go in the Rocky Mountain West you'll hear tales of crazy old landowners with guns. More of them are true than you might suspect.

My partner and I had floated a different stretch of the same river with a guide that morning. We'd caught lots of trout and then had a great, leisurely meal at a little roadhouse nearby where it was okay to wear waders inside but, "please, no cleats." Before our guide headed back to town, he told us about the strongbox, the three dollars and all; said we should fish there as long as we were this close and asked me not to write about where it was. So I haven't. Okay, Tom?

He said, "You want to fish river-left this evening and river-right if you go back there in the morning." River-left is to your left as you look downstream, which is how Mackenzie boat guides view the world. It would also be the shady bank at that time of day.

You had your choice of sides because there was a rickety old one-lane wooden bridge down there. The river was way too wide, deep and fast to wade across.

Lunch was long and slow, as I said, but we were still at the bridge with our three dollars paid by early afternoon. Our guide had blasted back to town in what seemed like a big hurry. Some of these guys tow their Mackenzie boats faster than I'd drive a Porsche on those twisty, two-lane roads, but you hardly ever see them in a ditch, so they must know what they're doing.

This was in mid-August. The day was hot and bright, and it was going to be quite a few hours before evening when things should pick up. So we rigged up slowly to kill time: stretching leaders, checking perfectly good knots, adjusting reel drags that didn't need adjusting, carefully smoothing every last wrinkle out of the wader socks and drinking our canteens dry; hydrating, so we wouldn't have to carry water.

We even stopped and talked to another fisherman who was mad because he hadn't been able to get any good pancakes. He'd eaten breakfast in a dozen cafés and restaurants around there, but the pancakes were always too thick and fluffy. "Now any good pancake," he said, "is thin and firm, right?"

We listened to this guy for longer than we normally would have, but even at that, we were on the river by three o'clock and it would probably be seven or later before anything really happened.

The fishing was refreshingly slow-paced after the frantic morning in the Mack boat. We split up and worked the pocket water near shore, pretty much ignoring the great, roaring main channel out in the middle. I was using a size sixteen dry caddis fly with a little Hares Ear nymph on a short dropper, a rig I like because you seem to be casting a dry fly like a proper sporting gentleman, even though you're hooking most of your trout on the nymph.

I also like it because it goes against the still popular myth that the only way to catch trout in these big, western rivers is to dredge the bottom with a huge weighted stonefly.

The fishing was slow, but it felt good to be wading in cold water under a hot sun, and now and then—maybe once every half hour—you'd hook a nice, fat rainbow that just couldn't wait for the evening hatch. It was dreamy enough to let you stop and look at the birds and maybe scan the hillsides for game, but you'd get just enough strikes to keep your mind from wandering to far-off things like home, work and the future. This is probably how a grazing deer feels: happily lazy, but still alert and in the moment.

Things did pick up a little toward evening. A few caddis flies began to come off and some trout started rising. When I finally broke the nymph off on a fish, I clipped the rest of the dropper off and fished with the dry fly alone. When I lost the little Elk Hair Caddis to another trout, I tied a fresh fly onto a new, slightly heavier tippet, squared my shoulders, readjusted my hat and got serious for a while.

This is exactly how a summer day on a big, western river is supposed to go: hot fishing in the morning, petering off to a midday during which you can either pound up the odd trout if you want to or take a nap, then slipping into an evening rise that will likely last until past dark.

By the time the sun was completely off the river, I'd landed half a dozen good trout on the fresh caddis fly, including two rainbows that would have gone around sixteen inches. I'd started the morning with a couple of good fish on a dry fly, so this seemed to be an appropriate place to quit. When I released that last big trout I remember thinking the first one I'd caught that day had been thirteen or fourteen hours before and that I'd lost track of them in between. I also remember being a little tired.

Sure, the fish would keep feeding and there'd be enough light to see my caddis fly for another half hour or so. For that matter, with stars and a quarter moon, a guy could tie on a #10 Royal Wulff and go on for half the night, but toward the end of a long day that's gone well I now often ask myself things like, Just how many fish do you have to catch?

No, I'm not always this laid back, but we'd been out for several days, so the initial adrenaline rush had subsided. I've always enjoyed that moment on a trip when the long haul comes into view—plenty of water to fish, plenty of time—and it no longer feels like a suicide mission.

I got up on a faint fisherman's trail winding through the sage and headed back. When I passed my partner I yelled down to him, "I'll see you at the truck."

"They're really rising down here," he said.

Back at the parking lot I set up the camp stove on the tailgate and made coffee. There'd been six or eight trucks and jeeps there when we went out, now there were three. Right next to me the guy who'd asked me about the landowner there hours before was pulling off his neoprene waders and wringing out his wet long johns and socks. He sniffed his underwear tentatively and said, half to me, half to himself, "Can't tell if this is river water or condensation."

He seemed pensive, as though he was coming to the realization many of us have reached over the last few years, namely that neoprenes—expensive waders that make you wet whether they leak or not—are probably an elaborate practical joke.

"Got time for some coffee?" I asked.

"I'll have a beer," he said, reaching for his cooler, "but I sure as hell have time. The guy I'm with will probably be out there till midnight."

I said, "Yeah, my partner will be out late, too, if only because he knows I quit early."

The guy laughed knowingly at that, and then we ran through the usual fisherman's business. First things first: How'd you do today? (We'd both lost count of trout caught and were satisfied.) Where else have you been in the last few days? How was the fishing? What flies did you use? How do you like that rod? And, by the way, what's your name?

Shortly after dark two guys came off the water, derigged quickly and without much comment and drove off in the third pickup. Half a mile down the dirt track they turned left onto the county road, in the direction of that little roadhouse. I caught myself wondering what time they stopped serving burgers there and fought the impulse to look at my watch.

Checking the time when the time doesn't matter always makes me feel compulsive.

The river had gotten louder—as rivers do on those clear, western nights—and we watched what we could see of it for a while without talking. What we could see was a wide black stripe in a bumpy gray landscape.

There are times when I really enjoy that: coming back a little early, getting out of the waders, brewing coffee, unwinding and knowing that my friend is still out there in the dark somewhere, probably—presumably—landing a few more trout. It's like figuring the bats must be out because of the time of day and the season, even though you can't actually see them.

I knew what he'd say when he finally dragged in. He'd have hammered them, big ones, starting ten minutes after I left. (That might sound suspicious, but it would be true—the big trout really do move after dark, and the guys who stay late on the water usually get some.) He'd tell me this in a slightly accusatory tone because my quitting early would have offended him in some way. In the final analysis, he thinks I lack a certain grim determination when it comes to trout fishing.

And he's right, I do. In fact, it took me a long time to get to where I could fish as if it mattered, but not as if I was at war with the trout. I had to work at it at first, but now I prefer it that way.

So, he can't understand why I'd quit when there was even one more trout to be stuck and I can't understand why he can never quite get enough, but I guess it's one of those things that, in the long course of a friendship, seems to matter less and less. I mean, no one understands everything, right?

And it could be a lot worse. Over the years I've fished with frustrated drill sergeants who absolutely have to be in charge of everything; phony experts who always have to be right; competitors who keep score so they can win and you can lose; headhunters whose biggest trout has to be longer than yours for reasons that seem suspiciously Freudian and so on. In the grand scheme of things, someone who makes you wait at the truck for an hour or so is nothing.

The other man and I were still watching the river. I'd finished my coffee and accepted one of his cold beers, which tasted so wonderful I almost fell off the tailgate. My friend out on the water had taught me that years ago: When you're tired, have a cup of coffee first so you can stay awake to enjoy the beer. The night had turned cold and I'd put on a sweater.

I said, "This guy you're fishing with, have you known him long?"

"Oh, God," he said, "I've known him for years. He can be an asshole at times, but we get along."

3

Fool Hens

J ust over twenty years ago, not long after I'd moved to
Colorado from the Midwest, an old guy who lived up in the
mountains told me that porcupines were great survival food.
They don't taste very good (they're strong and greasy) and
they are, as you'd expect, a little ticklish to clean, but a person lost and alone without tools or weapons can bag one
with a rock. One thing I'd noticed right off about the Rocky
Mountains was that there was always one of those handy.

Fantastic, I thought. This was exactly the kind of thing I'd
come west to learn.

Second only to the porcupine, this guy said, was the blue
grouse. You needed a firearm of some kind (or at least a bow
or slingshot), but the blues, when you found them, would just
sit in trees looking at you stupidly and you could pick them

off easily. Sometimes they wouldn't even seem to mind the shot or a fallen comrade and you could knock off a couple. (You always start with the birds on the lower branches, the guy said.) And they tasted a lot better than porcupine, too.

This guy referred to blue grouse as fool hens, which I later learned is what most natives out here call them.

I may not have known much when I was in my early twenties, but I'd been brought up right and did know that grouse are properly shot on the wing with light double-barrel shotguns, preferably over dogs. I didn't say anything to the old guy, though, because I understood that I was talking survival (not sport) with a by God, authentic Colorado mountain man, or at least that's how I saw it then. I was, however, happy to learn that there were grouse in the woods.

In fact, there are lots of them, each different species neatly adapted to its own type of habitat to the apparent end that there should be grouse wherever possible.

Most of the grouse are described in the books as locally common with some seasonal movement, which, as far as I can tell, means either they're there or they're not. So western grouse hunters do a lot of walking and the kind of bird they're after determines the countryside they hike through.

Ptarmigan live at or above treeline, in the boulder fields dotted with gnarled, stunted tree islands and on up into the bare, exposed, jagged alpine tundra. The country is high (usually well above ten thousand feet), open, enormous, vertical, dramatic, at least chilly in the fall, if not downright cold, and always subject to storms.

A geologist friend tells me the rocks here are the oldest in the Rockies, pushed up from far below by the forces of plate tectonics, but in another way this is geologically new country. The peaks are sharp and fresh, not yet polished by the elements. Rocks regularly break off and rattle down the scree slopes (that's the distant clacking sound you keep hearing), and the boulders you walk through look freshly cleaved with sharp, clean edges, many so new that lichens haven't taken hold yet.

You can walk many miles here looking for a few spooky, well-camouflaged birds, and in some places you had to walk miles to get there in the first place, all uphill, of course. The air is thin, the slopes steep and the footing in these loose, young mountains can be uncertain. Rock-hopping with a shotgun and backpack requires balance, foresight and good depth perception. In most places, if you lose your balance you won't fall far, but you'll land hard on sharp stuff. You learn to go at your best, safe pace, even if the guy you're with is dancing out ahead like a goat.

Grouse plumage is cryptic, as the ornithologists say—that is, they take on the coloration of their environment—and ptarmigan are the best. In winter they turn pure white, like a snowshoe hare. In hunting season they're the overall golden tan color of, let's say, clover honey spread on whole wheat toast, laced with irregular patches of chocolate and black on their backs—like lichen-covered rocks—and they're white underneath. The white underparts break up whatever you might see of the bird silhouette and, since they reflect light from below, they don't throw shadows, which is kind of eerie.

Ptarmigan don't so much run and freeze through the boulder fields, it's more like they dissolve and reform. Even when they move, they look less like grouse and more like that swimming vision you can get from high altitude and more exertion than you're used to.

Ptarmigan back and flank feathers make good hackles for certain nymphs and soft hackled wet flies, and those mottled, honey and brown feathers are the perfect legs for golden stonefly nymphs.

I think about trout flies here because cutthroats are sometimes found in the small, cold lakes around treeline, and the short ptarmigan season in September runs right through some of the last and the best of the high lake fishing. Since both of these involve going a long way at some expense in physical effort, I tend to fall into the cast and blast mode, clumsily lugging a fly rod and shotgun along with all the other stuff I need for a day in the high mountains.

I say "clumsily" because I don't have one of those efficient little pack rods that break down into many pieces for easy carrying, although every time I do this I swear I'll buy one the minute I get back.

The cast and blast, fish and fowl trip doesn't always work, but it's glorious when it does. The last time out, Larry, Steve Peterson, Dutch the pointer and I hiked up into a high cirque above treeline where ptarmigan and cutthroats were said to live.

To make a long story short, the ptarmigan were there and it was amazing that we found them: a single, large flock dodging like hallucinations through vast boulder fields. The bag limit is three each. We got five among us.

Then we went to look at the lakes, but the wind was cold, stinging and howling way too hard for fly casting. So we split up to take different routes down, agreeing to meet at the outlet of the lowest lake. I came down the feeder creek and caught three small cutthroats right at the inlet. This was only five hundred feet farther down the slope, but that made a lot of difference. It was still cool and breezy, but manageable.

These trout were lying in the open in a clear, slow current and they came up easily to a #16 Adams dry fly. A ptarmigan and Hares Ear soft hackle would have been a more poetic pattern, but that didn't occur to me until days later.

I cleaned the fish, put them in plastic bags and stuffed them into the back of my shooting vest next to my birds. As I headed down through the trees to meet up with Steve and Larry, I started watching the ground. It was a little late in the season, but I thought there might still be a few Boletus mushrooms around (ideal in ptarmigan paprika), and then it occurred to me that between here and the trailhead an enterprising hunter/gatherer could, with a little luck, get into a blue grouse or two and maybe a few brook trout.

Then I saw the error in that and unloaded the shotgun. I've always thought the sight of the interesting but drab birds next to the bright, gorgeous trout implied some subtle comment.

Something like, "The only way you could spoil this for yourself now is by getting greedy."

Sage grouse live at the other end of things, in the sagebrush
shrublands variously called the upper Sonoran or high plains
desert. Where I've hunted them in northwestern Colorado
the terrain comes in swales and gorges separated by flat-
topped low hills from the summits of which you can see
enormous tracts of land. From vantage points like these you
can easily overlook a town of two hundred people unless it's
dark and there are lights on.

Sage is the predominant vegetation here, grayish blue,
tough, leathery-leaved, rough-barked aromatic stuff (though
not the spice you cook with), thicker in the shallow swales,
thinner on the low hills. On some of the ridges there will be
scattered stands of dark green dwarf junipers. The soil is usually a sandy gray color, poor in quality by farming or grazing standards and littered everywhere with the old bones of
cattle, antelope and assorted smaller critters.

It's said that one way to tell the difference between a tree
and a shrub is that you can walk under a tree, but you have
to walk *around* a shrub. Sage grouse are almost always found
near water where the vegetation is thickest, so you walk
through—or around, I should say—the thickest sage, salt-
bush, greasewood and shadescale, leaving weaving tracks in
the powdery soil that resemble those of a drunk.

This is agoraphobic country, the kind that caused the
prairie madness in early settlers. Too much exposure to too
much great, open space causes certain people to shrink, become transparent and eventually begin to dissolve altogether.

I'm one of those people, but I find that *some* exposure to
vastness is cleansing. A couple of days is good. After that I'm
longing for the shelter of trees.

Last fall DeWitt Daggett and I were out on the northwestern high plains looking for sage grouse. The procedure here
is to drive the endless dirt roads until you find a seep or stock

tank—any water at all. Then you hunt the immediate area, flushing the birds if they're there and then moving on.

This is virtually all public land in one way or another, so at dusk you simply pull off to the side of the road and camp. Traffic won't break the mood out here. The nearest town is thirty miles away, and it's a crossroads with a café, gas station and liquor store. The one rule is: Don't roll your sleeping bag out near a fence because antelope jumping over it at night could land on you with their sharp little hooves.

DeWitt and I camped on a low ridge for the view. It was just getting to be dusk by the time we'd gathered enough dead sage for a hot little fire and had the red beans and tortillas going. We'd been out for several days, shooting blue grouse in the Elkhead Mountains and then heading out to the plains to look for some of the big sage grouse, so our camps had become quick and minimal.

DeWitt is a publisher of audiotapes now, but he has a practical science background. In the rambling conversation around the fire the figure of a billion came up somehow, and I confessed that I was now lost. I said, "I can relate to a hundred, a thousand or maybe even ten thousand, but a billion means nothing to me."

DeWitt sprang to his feet and said, "Well, let's see if we can engineer an example."

Using the last of the natural light, we paced off two ten-yard squares, counted the number of sage plants in each one and took an average. I don't remember the actual figures, but it was roughly *x* number of plants per square yard, then a look at the topo map to figure how many square miles of land we could see from our vantage point.

I stood on the top of the ridge with a can of beer turning slowly round and round to get a feel for this enormous place while DeWitt scribbled the math on a scrap of paper. The sage was like a broken bluish haze from horizon to horizon.

Then DeWitt came up beside me and said, "This is just an informed guess, but I don't think we can see a billion sage plants from here."

I thought I felt my shoes lift off the ground for a second (gravity must have been suspended momentarily as the enormity of that sank in) and then DeWitt said, "I think the beans are done."

I haven't had much experience with sharp-tailed grouse, but I've gone to some lengths to hunt them a few times, if only so I can say I've shot and eaten every grouse species in Colorado and tied trout flies with their feathers.

Sharp-tails live in open grasslands and mountain meadows. This is dry, rolling country with low hills rising away from scrubby stream beds clogged with willow and scrub oak. The meadows are often a uniform golden brown in the fall, with rock ledges at the ridge tops and random outcrops here and there looking like wrecked ships.

As with the other grouse, you can walk a long way looking for a few sharp-tails but, as luck would have it, you can swing along pretty well out there, always watching for mats of cactus and ancient discarded tangles of barbed wire.

The last time I hunted them DeWitt, Larry, Steve, Ed and I spent a day at it and got one bird. We'd been hunting blues in the higher mountains, but there were some huge grassy meadows nearby that were known to hold sharp-tails and we had Dutch the pointer along.

The blues had given Dutch a hard time. The woods were dry—bad for scenting—and the birds were few and far between, which can cause a young pointer to either lose interest or forget what he's doing and begin to think he's just out for a walk.

We drove down from our campsite in the pine woods and walked the meadows. We walked quickly, five abreast, to cover ground, and Dutch bravely busted his little hump to work in front of the whole group.

It must have been five hours before we saw that single grouse. Like a young pointer myself, I had all but forgotten what we were doing. I knew we were walking hard across open, grassy country, getting pretty tired in the process, but feeling well-worked and nice and loose. I guess I was busy experiencing the emptiness: bright blue-and-white sky, wheat-colored grass, cool air. I was carrying the shotgun loosely at my side with very close to nothing on my mind.

I was on the far left end of the line of hunters. When Dutch flushed the grouse, it went straight away, and as I raised the shotgun the bird flared to the left and swung around behind me. It was a fast passing shot over my left shoulder and I must say I dropped the grouse neatly. This was the only sharp-tail I saw that season, and I had inadvertently followed the two best pieces of advice I've ever gotten about wing shooting, namely, "Mount the gun like you mean it" and "Don't think."

This is all fine, but for me it always comes back to blue grouse: my favorite, familiar upland game bird. You find them roughly in the cozy forests that lie between the sprawling, open high plains and the dizzying, open alpine tundra. The grouse that live out where there are no trees to hop up into are more likely to flush (ptarmigan won't always fly, but at least they'll run) and are therefore more stylish.

But I like the forest, so the forest grouse were the first ones that, in my haphazard, unsystematic way, I set out to learn about when I first moved here.

At first it seemed that most Rocky Mountain hunters didn't think much of blue grouse except as a menu item. Almost everyone I talked to admitted to having shot some, but most had done it with big game rifles while hunting deer and elk or with .22 pistols in the interest of camp meat, and they all acted a little sheepish about it. After hearing that story often enough I developed the commonly held opinion that blues *never* fly and that anyone who ever bagged one probably did it in a manner not befitting a gentleman.

The first ones I ever saw—on a hike in springtime— seemed to bear that out by just sitting in a ponderosa pine and looking at me. They were big, handsome birds. If only they hadn't acted like barnyard chickens. The next day I told a friend that I'd seen a couple of fool hens up at the mouth of Skunk Canyon. It's a derisive term, but it does have a certain ring to it when you're trying to fit into a new part of the country.

The first ones I ever shot also just sat there looking at me. I was rabbit hunting, blue grouse season was open, and there were three of them in a pine tree. The daily limit just happens to be three and it's legal to shoot them with all manner of artillery, including the .22 rifle I was carrying. It was all too perfect to resist, and I got two before the third one flushed. Sure enough, you do feel a little sheepish about this, even though everyone does it.

The birds were great roasted, though—all grouse are delicious—and they are great in grouse paprika, boned and stuffed a la Steve Peterson or just about any other way you can think of. I fell into the common misconception that the two best things you could say about blue grouse were that you couldn't actually bludgeon them to death on the ground and that they tasted better than porcupine.

But then I began to hear rumors to the effect that there were, in fact, some hunters around who took these birds seriously. There weren't many of them—a Division of Wildlife biologist told me in the early eighties he thought there might be a few hundred honest blue grouse hunters in the state, tops—but they were mostly guys who carried twenty-gauge doubles and hunted with pointers or Labs. Pointers are said, by the owners of pointers, to be the best because, with their tendency to freeze, blues hold well for a point. The Lab faction says you need a flushing dog, and a big, strong one at that because mountainous blue grouse country can take it out of a dog.

Be that as it may, the word was these grouse hunters mostly shot the birds out of the air, although some did carry .22 pistols, just in case.

That same biologist also told me he couldn't understand

why people didn't hunt blues as avidly as they did sage or sharp-tailed grouse. "They flush as often as not," he said, "and when they do they're as impressive and hard to hit as any game bird."

And they're a big bird. When you first catch sight of one (you're excited and the exact range may not be clear in your mind) you can blow a second or two thinking it's a small wild turkey. And they are *so* good to eat that you won't waste them on just any old dinner guest. A blue grouse is often saved for serious game feasts followed by fine port or a seduction.

By then I had wandered around in the Rocky Mountains long enough to have come upon a number of blues and I had to agree with the biologist that if they stood around like chickens half the time, they flushed thunderously and thrillingly the other half. And, as a second biologist said, "For every dumb one you see in a tree, you probably walked by a dozen smart ones on the ground." That's the number-one reason for using a dog.

The first few times I was properly armed with a shotgun and fired at the flushing birds, I found them to be like geese, that is, a big target that's faster and harder to hit than you think.

I also noticed that they were not all that easy to find. They're often so hard, in fact, that many hunters consider just locating the birds to be the true sport in blue grouse hunting. As a general rule, they like ridge tops, old burns and sometimes the edges of clear cuts. In early fall they're often at lower altitudes in aspen/sage/serviceberry/chokecherry country, although they may have moved uphill by the time the season starts. In practice, they're where you find them, usually near food.

They like conifer needles, the leaves of certain wild shrubs and also the flowers and berries. Sometimes they'll eat bugs, and they're said to have a sweet tooth for grasshoppers.

Blues tend to spend the warmer months at lower altitudes, and then migrate upslope in the winter. During hunting season they are often on the move. In winter they grow feathery snowshoes on their feet so they can get around and have been known to burrow under the snow to stay warm. Through the colder months they exist almost entirely on Douglas fir needles or, in a pinch, those of lodgepole pine. For some reason, they prefer the young needles from older trees.

On the lower end, their range overlaps that of the sage and sharp-tailed grouse. At the higher altitudes, blues are often found near ptarmigan habitat. Bagging all four species in a single trip is a grand slam. It's also a hell of a walk, not to mention a stroke of luck.

For a long time I wondered why they call them "blue" grouse, because the ones I'd seen were all a regulation game bird mottled brownish tan with chocolate, brown and black-marked flank feathers perfect for legs on dark stonefly nymph patterns. But then I saw my first male. He was bigger than the females and he was a dusky bluish gray on the breast: what a fly tier would call a medium blue dun. This stately bird stood proudly on a log about twenty-five yards away, apparently ignoring me, although he'd have flushed if I'd walked up on him. I was hunting snowshoe hares with a small-bore rifle. Grouse season had been over for a couple of weeks.

I think it was inevitable that I would become a genuine blue grouse hunter. At first I just figured that a blue-collar hunter makes the best sport possible out of what's at hand, but these things take on a life of their own. These birds are *grouse*, after all, and I am a grouse *hunter*. Given that, it is impossible to remain casual about it, and if most people wanted to think of them as fool hens, that only made them more endearing.

I learned that blues tend to frequent the same places year after year, based, of course, on food availability and weather patterns. Still, if you see them on a certain ridge in the last week of September one season, there's a good chance they'll be around there next year, too. Like a true blue grouse hunter, I became very closed-mouthed about my few dependable spots.

I learned that it was better to hunt them early in the year when they were still able to feed on berries. That puts them on the ground, and when they're underfoot they often flush beautifully. A diet of berries also gives the meat a luscious, not quite sweet, fruity flavor.

Blues aren't terribly hard to hit when they flush from the ground (a dove or quail hunter will tell you they're a piece of cake), although that's not by any means to say that you can't miss. On a ridge, however, they'll typically swing downhill, presenting a shot that often baffles me. They'll do the same thing coming out of a tree.

The first season I got fairly serious about this, I had a day where four birds flushed from trees, all flying downhill. I shot and missed all four times, and this after putting in three days and many miles uphill and down looking for them. I thought something that still comes to mind ocassionally, but that I haven't said out loud since I was ten years old: "It's too hard, I can't do it, it ain't fair!" Then later, driving home, I thought, these are big, handsome, good-tasting game birds that are hard to find and that you can't always hit. You wanted sport, so quit complaining.

You must do this, too, right? I can't be the only hunter who talks to himself.

So the blue grouse had become a respectable game bird. I stopped calling them fool hens and started thinking about a sweet little twenty-gauge double with an English-style straight stock—the classic English grouse gun. Snazzy shotguns can be more expensive than bamboo fly rods, but the same vision leads you to them: the idea that the tool should be as elegant as the creature it's used to bag. I got the shotgun, and then my old shooting vest started looking seedy. You know how it is.

Now I'd rather kill blue grouse than pheasants or the ruffed grouse I grew up on, nostalgia notwithstanding, or any of the other grouse hereabouts. Everyone has his bird, and this is mine.

And a funny thing has happened over the years: It seems that the more desperately I want them to fly, the more often they do. Maybe the places I thought were my secrets are actually heavily hunted and the birds are spooky, although it's rare for me to run into another grouse hunter. Maybe it's magic. Or maybe they can just smell the adrenaline that's generated by paying a lot of money for a shotgun.

I *do* still find blue grouse sitting in trees from time to time, but I no longer look down on that. These are wild birds and that's just how they are sometimes. I've seen ruffed grouse do the same thing, and I've heard wild tom turkeys gobble back at a car horn. It's just a matter of how you look at it. As I once heard a man say about his country relatives, "They're either ignorant and simple-minded or refreshingly uncomplicated. Take your pick."

When blues are sitting in a tree, the time-honored method of flushing them is to throw sticks at them. This is a skill in itself. When you're alone, lobbing a stick accurately and then getting your shotgun to port arms before the stick hits takes some practice. When you're with a partner, you take turns with the stick. Your friend says, "Ready?" and you say, "Okay, pull!"

Every season does present opportunities to shoot blues out of trees, and it can be a strong temptation, especially after a number of long, grouseless days. The gourmet in you wants the meat, the fly tier wants the feathers and the sportsman wants to take the game in a skillful, honorable way. It's a quandary, but it's probably useful to be presented with a value judgment that you must make fresh each time. It's a kind of ethical calisthenics.

Some hunters turn the old survival rule around. "Shoot the top one first," they say. "When he falls, he might flush the rest." The one thing you can be sure of is, when you show up with a limit of blues someone will say, "Shot 'em out of a tree, huh?" and you really want to be able to say, "Nope. On the wing. All of 'em."

This can become the kind of technical point that requires a finely honed sense of sporting ethics to appreciate. A few years ago a friend and I had a single bird sitting in a tree—the classic fool hen situation. Taking turns, we had each thrown several dozen sticks and rocks at the thing, but the most he'd do was duck. We were getting a little fed up with this, and my friend's poor springer spaniel was going nuts.

Finally, when it was my turn with the gun, my partner clipped the grouse with what would have been a good piece of campfire wood, and the bird hopped from one limb to another, at which point I harvested him, as they say.

"At least you shot him off a different branch," my friend said.

"Branch, hell," I said. "That bird was in the air."

CHAPTER

4

Bugs

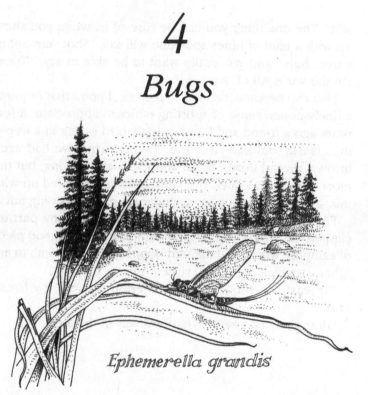

Ephemerella grandis

Some years ago I was fishing the Green Drake mayfly hatch on Idaho's Henry's Fork with a couple of friends; it was the first time I'd ever attended one of these famous hatches on what people still insist on calling a "world-class fishery."

Well, maybe that's not entirely true. Back home in Colorado I'd fished hatches that had been written about in books and magazines on rivers people might have heard of, but your local water is different somehow. You don't have to buy a nonresident license and half the time you end up back in your own bed the same night, which makes it all seem strangely ordinary.

I guess it's just that I'd heard a lot about the Green Drake hatch on the Henry's Fork, but I'd never driven all the way up there to see it and, since this was known as a place where the really serious fishermen went, the trip felt a little like a pilgrimage.

The first day we stopped in at Mike Lawson's fly shop and I overheard a guide referring to this event as the "Gortex hatch," an allusion to all the spiffy fly fishers in town, half of whom looked like models from one of the more expensive catalogs. (The guide didn't mind that my friends and I were standing right there because we clearly didn't fit into the snappy sportsman category.)

Some of these guys had come from faraway places like Pennsylvania and New York, and they were not only well-dressed, they also seemed to be awfully knowledgeable about this and other hatches. There was a subtle academic atmosphere in and around Last Chance, Idaho. Over breakfast at the café you'd hear as much Latin as you would English.

It was a little intimidating, but if I didn't exactly fit in here, I felt I could at least hold my own in a pinch. I knew, for instance, that the Green Drake mayfly in question was the *Ephemerella grandis*—not to be confused with the almost identical *E. doddsi* or the similar but smaller *E. flavilinea.*

I'd done some homework on this hatch because I understood that bugs are the key to fly-fishing. Or, to be more correct, you might say "insects." Then again, allowing that a trout's diet could include some critters that are not technically in the class Insecta (like scuds and such), maybe you'd want to say "food organisms." This is how it begins: You start to get a burr under your saddle about accuracy.

We'd tied some flies for the trip—standard, by-the-book drake patterns with collar hackles and split wings—but that year everyone on the Fork was using the newer, fancier Para-drake, the one with the bullet-headed deer hair body, parachute hackle and extended abdomen. So we bought some of those for what, at the time, was the most I'd ever paid for store-bought flies.

The first thing I did when I got on the water was to whip

out my ten-cent aquarium net and catch one of the fabled *Ephemerellas* because that's what a properly scientific fly fisher does, especially when there are other fishermen watching. It was a pretty bug all right; beautiful, in fact. At first glance it's just a large, grayish-green mayfly, but then you notice that the soft-looking underside of the abdomen is a pale olive, while the back is hard and gray, with fine green lines between the segments. The shell-like, gray armor extends up the back in overlapping plates to the head. The tibia of the legs are pale green, but the femurs are an iron gray. The wings are slate-colored and darkly veined, but there's a small green patch at the base of each costal margin.

Not knowing what else to do with it, I compared the bug to the Para-drake. Considering that no trout fly exactly copies the real creature, this imitation looked okay (maybe a little too fat and too green), but out on the current when the drift was right it looked great: I think "perky" was the accepted term.

I'll admit that there was a certain feeling of power in knowing the Latin name for the bugs on the water. Never mind that I knew only because I'd been told by people who *really* knew, there was still this vague sense of mastery.

But then there's always someone around who doesn't seem to care about any of that and who's happily catching fish anyway, which is puzzling as hell to the novice entomologist. That week on the Henry's Fork I kept running into this old guy dressed in coveralls and a T-shirt. He was catching a lot more trout than I was, so I finally waded over and asked him what he was using.

"Green fly," he said. "These bugs are green, so you gotta have a green fly."

Right. That's pretty much what the fishermen back at the café were saying, only he said it in English.

My friends and I stayed there for most of a week, and we all caught trout. On the days when the sky was that bright, pure western blue, the hatch was thin and didn't last too long. On the gray, low-ceiling days, the flies poured off the river by the thousands from nine in the morning until midafternoon. We did well overall, and during the best parts of the best days the fish were almost easy to catch.

Between the peak times for the Green Drakes there were usually some *Ephemerella infrequens* or *inermis* (large and small Pale Morning Duns) on the water, and we spent a couple of nights downstream fishing to an *Ephemera simulans* (Brown Drake) hatch. We bought Green and Brown Drake flies at Lawson's (same pattern, different size and color) and we used our own Pale Morning Duns because those little Henry's Fork bugs were pretty much like the ones we had back home.

We did try to use the scientific names for a while, but we soon slipped back into the comfortable—and traditional—procedure of calling the bugs by the names of the flies used to imitate them. I don't know about the others, but I began to think that the Latin sounded a little hollow coming from me because I didn't really know what I was talking about. That first morning when I marched into the fly shop and asked what fly pattern was producing the best on the *Ephemerella grandis* hatch, it was just a pretentious way of saying, "Gimme a dozen of whatever's workin'."

I will say that knowing about the bugs can be extremely helpful at times. There's some real hard-nosed fishing stuff there that will sometimes cause you to catch trout when you otherwise wouldn't, or catch more of them when you'd only have caught a few.

Understanding just the basic lifecycles and typical behavior of the various bugs—which is both the first and last step for many of us—will tell you that if mayflies, caddis flies or midges are hatching, there are emerging nymphs or pupae just beneath them under the surface, but that when it's stoneflies, mating caddis or mayfly spinners on the water, there are no hidden emergers.

Or let's say there's a mayfly hatching and the trout aren't

taking the fly pattern that seems to imitate the dun. If you know what the bug is, you'll know what that particular emerging nymph looks like, what color it is and how it acts, which means you won't have to guess which nymph pattern to tie on or how to fish it.

If it's one of the *Ephemerellas* known as Green Drakes, you'll even know that the bug usually sheds its nymphal husk deep in the water and swims to the surface as a winged fly, so the floating nymph pattern you'd use for another mayfly probably won't work. What works is something that looks a lot like an old-style wet fly, only bigger and greener than most.

If you know beforehand that the hatch is an *Ephemera simulans* mayfly, you'll not only buy or tie up Brown Drake dry flies, you'll also know that the hatch will probably be in the evening, that there's a simultaneous spinner fall that you had better have flies for and that the nymphs have prominent gills. You may want to painstakingly tie individual feather tip gills on the abdomens of all your nymphs or just tease out the dubbing on a Hares Ear pattern with your pocketknife. Your response is a matter of personal style. The point is, you know something useful.

If you do much fly-fishing you'll eventually absorb a cursory knowledge of the bugs just from listening to people and reading the odd book, but in my experience genuine angling entomologists are few and far between, and those who haven't written a book are extremely rare. The precious few I've met seem to fit a certain profile. They probably started out doing what I still do, that is, getting the species designation from someone at the local fly shop and then looking up some particulars in one of the bug books, maybe learning something helpful in the process. At first they did that just to get a leg up on the hatch and catch more trout, and, like most of us with a little knowledge, they were at least tempted to drop enough terminology into their conversations to impress their buddies.

But eventually they became honestly fascinated by the

loveliness and complexity of what happens on trout streams and began to engage in some real study and observation. That might have cut into their fishing time a little at first, but they didn't care about that because they'd been grabbed by a healthy curiosity about the environments where they spend so much time. If their accumulated knowledge finally gave them an advantage over the trout, they accepted that fact with some grace and used it, but their real advantage is over other fishermen. An authentic entomologist can have as much fun looking at bugs as you or I have catching fish.

And if the hatch of the moment is a size eighteen Blue Quill Dun, then that's how they'll describe it. They won't look you in the eye and call it a *Baetis spinosus* sudimago by way of a gut check.

I kept studying bugs for a while because that's what one did if one wanted to become serious about fly-fishing—and seriousness, in a sort of Zen sense, is what we all secretly aspire to—but I also kept running into these archetypal old guys who were catching lots of big fish on the apparently simple-minded premise that if the bugs on the water were, say, small and dark, you had to use a small, dark fly. One of them even told me, pointedly, that learning more about bugs than the trout know is a waste of time.

So I never became a real angling entomologist. For one thing, I have reservations about science as the One True Way to understand reality. Luckily, there are other good vantage points. If there weren't, many of us would have to go through life hopelessly ignorant. I remember this exchange from a PBS science program:

Earnest interviewer: "Can you put that in layman's terms?"

Rumpled physicist: "No."

To put it another way, an ichthyologist knows about trout and an entomologist knows about bugs, but it's the fly tier who knows how to fool a trout into thinking something is a bug when it's not.

I decided I was more comfortable with fly-fishing as a folk art rather than a science and, to be honest, I realized I wanted to know about bugs for the wrong reasons. That is, it was really enough for me that the bugs were there, the trout ate them and there were fly patterns that imitated them. As for the rest, I guess I just suffered for a while under the delusion that you can somehow bludgeon trout into submission if you just have enough facts, and if that doesn't work you can at least intimidate other fishermen.

Maybe this reveals a deep character flaw (other fishermen get good at this without turning into creeps) or maybe it is just a stage you go through on the way to deciding what kind of outdoorsman you're going to be. Whatever, during my short entomological phase, I saw that I was like the guy who takes up the guitar not because he loves music, but because he thinks it will attract women.

I do own five books on trout stream insects, and I've actually read two of them—the last one, published in 1975, was drier and more detailed than the first, which was published in 1955. Now and then, if someone who actually knows can tell me the species of bug that might be hatching, I'll look it up to see about recommended patterns, hatch times and fishing tactics, but I usually don't care that the nymph has eight posterio-lateral spines on the abdomen or that the median vein on the hind wing of the dun is distinctly forked at slightly less than halfway to its base. Maybe I should care, but I just don't.

If I now toss around terms like *Baetis* or *Trike* (short for *Tricorythodes*) it's only because that stuff is common knowledge, and on those trips where I slip and begin dropping what to me are largely useless, often inaccurate bits of taxonomy, one of my friends usually shuts me down.

Once, on a drive through Montana, a friend and I stopped for gas. It was nighttime, and the lighted gas pumps were covered with mayflies from a nearby trout stream. I said, "Hey, look at this!"

My partner—a notorious deflater of egos—peered at the

bugs and said, "Yeah, *Parallelia flavahoovias,* right?"

That's a point. If you were a consummate phony with an ear for dead languages, you could make this stuff up and sound pretty good to a gullible greenhorn. And I guess I *had* been spouting a little amateur entomology.

For all practical purposes, the flies were Red Quill spinners, about a size sixteen. Whatever species of mayfly they represented, we knew they'd be forming up into a mating flight over the riffles in the evenings and that the trout would feed on them in the first slower water downstream. We could also safely figure that riffles near the gas station would be a good bet.

We were on our way somewhere else to catch other trout, but if we'd stayed there until the next evening we'd have known what to do, and that was comforting.

5

Texas

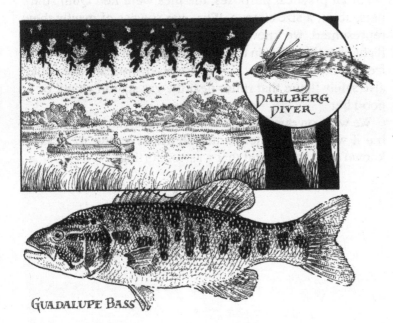

GUADALUPE BASS

*T*he Texas hill country north of San Antonio struck me as wildly foreign and strangely familiar at the same time. The rolling topography forested in live oak, pin oak, walnut, pecan and such reminded me of the Midwest where I was born, as did the humidity and the small, old towns built around shady courthouse squares, but of course there are differences. Try to picture rural Ohio but with armadillos, ringtails, rattlesnakes, cactus, great Mexican food and hard-scrabble goat ranches instead of farms.

And then there's *poco tiempo*: the slow pace, of which Texan English is one example. It's a lovely language to hear spoken, and after a few days of it you come to realize that you'd drawl too if you had plenty of time to speak your piece and could assume your listeners were too polite to interrupt. Pause to search for the right word, and everyone waits patiently. It's amazing. You find yourself saying pretty much what you meant to say instead of just blurting something out.

Ed Engle and I drove down there in April to do some "real" bass fishing, as opposed to whatever kind of bass fishing it is we do back home in Colorado. The possibility of bigger fish was part of it, but more than that we wanted to catch bass in a place where they belong—as opposed to a place like Colorado where they've been introduced—in the company of people who grew up there and really know how to do it.

This is important because to catch a certain kind of fish you must come to understand them, and that understanding becomes part of the character of a place. That's why fishermen are almost as interesting as the fish themselves.

We were in Ed's old Datsun pickup with my new Mansfield canoe strapped on top. This truck doesn't have a proper boat rack on it, so we had jury-rigged one with foam blocks and lots of rope. If we hadn't had to stop to retie the canoe every hundred miles or so, we might have cut a few hours off the trip. As it was, it took the better part of two days.

Ed and I aren't kids anymore, but we still believe in the hip romance of long road trips—you know, the boredom, risk, sense of purpose and the distance from all that stuff that, before you left, seemed too damned important.

The first night we slept in a park somewhere near Big Spring, Texas. We'd spent an hour in town asking people where we could camp and no one seemed to know what we were talking about.

"You mean park a camper?"

"No, we mean 'camp,' you know, sleep on the ground."

We were a little road-burned and I suggested getting a room, which we both usually consider to be the same as giving up, or at least giving in to lazy, middle-class comfort. But Ed held out for a quick, cheap camp. Our road trips have always been low-budget by necessity, and at this stage of the game a room just seems like a needless extravagance. And, as Ed the pragmatist says, "You should always scrimp early on a trip because you never know what you'll run into later."

Finally a woman at a gas station said it would be all right if we slept in the park just down the road. It wasn't clear whether it was all right officially or just all right with her, but it was dark, we were tired and we didn't pursue it.

It took about ten minutes to toss out the sleeping bags and set up the camp stove. Then I started supper while Ed drove back into town to call home. Seems his wife, Monica, was having some trouble at work serious enough that she might lose the job. Ed had offered to cancel the trip so he could be there during the crisis, but Monica had said, no, go, staying won't make any difference. Bless her heart. I've always liked Monica.

I was sitting at a picnic table under a street light surrounded by a thousand bugs, drinking a Lone Star beer and trying to keep at least the larger insects out of the stew. I've made some of those calls myself—the ones where you feel like you really should be home, even though you probably couldn't be much help, but instead you're on a trip, supposedly having fun, although you're not having as much fun as you might ordinarily because you really should be home. You feel slightly irresponsible, but you know in your heart that life is short and responsibility is overrated.

I could picture it: Ed calling home from an outside pay phone to see about the trouble, the trucks on the highway drowning out parts of the conversation. First she'd ask, "Where are you calling from?" and Ed would say, "Big Spring." That probably wouldn't mean anything, but she'd try to picture it anyway. Was it a nice little town or a neon shithole along the highway?

All the calls I've made like that seemed crucial at the time, although now I can't remember what a single one of them was about. All I remember is the feeling. It's not loneliness; more like just the experience of distance.

Ed was back in fifteen minutes. He got a beer from the cooler and said, "It's okay, at least for the time being. *Now* I'm glad I came." That's about as specific as Ed ever gets about things like this. He's a bit of a cynic (he once told me his only retirement plan was to have a massive heart attack) but he's not a whiner, so it's: "Well, there's a little trouble, but when isn't there?" and then some time later, "Oh, that. I guess it turned out okay."

It's not that Ed won't bitch if you get him started, but about personal matters he exhibits a kind of restraint I've always admired: a sort of things-are-a-mess-but-I'm-okay attitude that makes him more likely to argue than complain.

We made Mason, Texas, by late afternoon the next day, and checked into the motel where we were supposed to meet our unofficial guides, Bud Priddy and Joe Robinson. The drive seemed to go quickly. The conversation was more spirited because we were getting closer to actually going fishing and because Ed had a load off his mind. And then there was a lift, literally and figuratively, as we drove up out of the scrubby plains into the forested hills around Mason County.

Bud showed up in time for supper—burritos at a little café on the corner—and Joe arrived some time after dark. It was a hot night, so we sat in the air-conditioned room to discuss our strategy. The first order of business was to float the Llano River in canoes for two days, camping overnight on an island. That's permissible. "Islands are considered no man's land," Bud said.

Ed and I were concerned about what was permissible because there is almost no public land or water in Texas. Everything is so uniformly private—and trespassing is so universally frowned upon—that most land isn't even posted. The assumption is that you will exhibit the proper respect, and if you don't you'll learn damned quick and in no uncertain terms. This made us a little nervous, coming from

Colorado where there's more public than private land to wander around on.

So in our midwestern Germanic way, Ed and I wanted to know the rules. Bud said, "Well, there's things that'll get you yelled at and things that won't." Joe added, "It's best not to go acting like a hippie *in front of people*."

Officially, you can put your canoe in and take it out at road crossings on navigable rivers. In between, you'll probably be okay if you conduct yourself like a gentleman. You'll naturally get out of the canoe from time to time to wade, cast from the bank, have lunch and relieve yourself, and all of that *may* be illegal. If you want to do this yourself, don't just bring a copy of this book. Contact the State of Texas Parks and Wildlife Department.

These lush, pretty, spring-fed hill country rivers are perfect for a canoe paddled by people who are less than experts: mostly slow flowing and lazy, but with enough rocks and rapids to make things interesting. Ed and I were using my new Mansfield canoe, a sweet little boat with thin cedar strut construction inside and an equally thin fiberglass shell. It's pretty and delicate looking, and when we lifted it off the top of the truck Joe said, "Nice boat. I hope you don't bust it up in here."

I thought he was giving us some of that good-natured grief, but when I looked at his eyes I realized he was honestly wishing us well. He really hoped we wouldn't bust it up.

These streams are not only pretty, they're also rich in fish: several species of sunfish (called "perch" locally), catfish big enough for head mounts, carp, alligator gar and some largemouth bass, but the definitive fish is the Guadalupe bass. These are small, stream-dwelling bass native only to a few rivers in Texas.

Guadalupe bass are somewhat troutlike in their habits, even to their tendency to feed daintily on mayflies below riffles, and local fly fishermen like to call them "Texas brook trout." They even look a little like trout in the water. The coloration varies, but many Guadalupe bass have distinct spots and bronzish-green backs; actually more like a cutthroat than a brookie.

The only catch is that they seldom grow to more than two pounds, so many bass fishermen overlook them and, as near as I can tell, the trout fishermen who would appreciate them don't usually *go* to Texas.

Fly-fishing is considered a minor angling method in Texas, and fly-fishing for small stream fish with light tackle is a downright rarefied sport. Before this was over we'd spend four days on rivers, and in that time we'd see one other boat, from which no one was fishing.

So there was that cockeyed familiarity again. The Llano was wider and slower than most Rocky Mountain streams, but there were rock cliffs and it was flowing water with bright, spotted fish, and so completely recognizable. But then when you got out to wade and fish you didn't need waders because the water was warm, and you usually fished something like a deer hair frog instead of a mayfly—although you *could* fish a mayfly during a hatch and do well.

The banks were forested with deciduous trees filled with cardinals and, unless you count the odd trotline set for catfish, there were no signs of civilization. If I wasn't casting a little cork or deer hair froggie along the banks and picking up fish, I was paddling with long, slow strokes trying to keep Ed in the best casting position. If you're fond of canoes, one is about as much fun as the other. The newness of the place sank in quickly and I became pretty happy.

We took turns paddling and fishing and tried to look around as much as possible, knowing that you'll never see enough of a new river in just a couple of days. I saw a snake that could have been a cottonmouth and a mature white-tailed deer no bigger than a Great Dane. The deer are tiny here, stunted because there are so many of them.

We each caught our first Guadalupe bass, first yellow-bellied perch, first long ear. You couldn't tell what kind of fish you had by the strike, but once hooked the largemouth bass would often jump, Guadalupe bass would jump higher and the panfish would plane heavily with their flat sides against the current.

Sometimes we'd beach the canoe to admire and photograph these fish, and then there'd be a strange bird we had to get a look at. I saw a little green kingfisher: another first.

Often the two canoes were far apart, but sometimes you'd catch bits of conversation. Once, after an hour of virtual silence, I heard a thump and Joe's slow voice saying, "Bud, I believe that bass just took a bite out of your boat."

The first night we camped on an island of bleached round river stones that would not take a tent peg. Bud cooked steaks and beans and made biscuits in a Dutch oven while Ed and I went through the guidebook trying to identify, from memory, some of the unfamiliar birds we'd seen. We turned the canoes over to drain. Mine had taken a few scratches, but we hadn't busted it up.

The island is accessible by car over a narrow bridge, and just as we were all crawling into our tents a pickup with two young couples pulled in. They saw our camp, talked it over for a minute and left. In the polite way Texans have, Joe suggested that they'd driven out there to "look at the moon" and required a little more privacy.

A few days later we were in south Texas looking for the entrance to a private fishing camp. In between there had been a party at a Mexican restaurant in San Antonio with great food, lots of beer, many wild fishing stories and an awful mariachi band. I'm as multicultural as the next guy, but I draw the line at mariachi bands with no sense of rhythm and two flat trumpets. One of the guys at our table went over and tipped the band leader. When he came back I asked, "You like that?" and he said, "Hell no, that's how you make them go away."

Joe had gone home and we'd picked up a man named

Tommy and his huge, apparently oceangoing, metal flake red bass boat with white Naugahyde swivel seats and chrome steering wheel. There were no dingleberries only because there was no place to hang them. This thing was towed, at great speed, by one of those enormous pickups with the four wheels in back.

The camp consisted of one big building—which was mostly kitchen—that you might call the main lodge, surrounded by several trailers, outbuildings and a collection of possibly abandoned trucks. There was a small airstrip off to the side with a limp orange wind sock hanging from a pole and cracks in the paving through which weeds were growing. As we pulled up, a flock of maybe twenty wild turkeys darted off into the mesquite and cactus.

People in Texas sometimes use a kind of enviable economy in their conversation. Bud could have warned me specifically about rattlesnakes, water moccasins, scorpions, poisonous spiders, wild boars, cats claw bushes, killer bees and such, but instead he just said, as we were getting out of the car, "Now, be careful. Everything down here will either sting you or bite you."

Ed now refers to that first afternoon as the Comanche Tank Disaster. (There are no bass ponds in Texas, but there are plenty of "tanks.") While Bud and I were getting the aluminum john boat into the water, Tommy backed his trailer way too far and too fast out into the tank and got both the trailer and the truck stuck in the deep, clinging mud.

Bud told me to get into the john boat, cranked up the outboard and said he thought the fishing would be best way over there on the other side of the six-hundred-acre lake. As we pulled away, Tommy was gunning the pickup. You could see the rear wheels sinking deeply into the mud, the dual exhausts blowing big bubbles in the muddy water.

I got most of the rest of it secondhand from Ed. Tommy fought the truck and trailer until they were both stuck up to the axles, but the trailer still wasn't deep enough to float the bass boat and it was too heavy to push off. Tommy tried, and he might have done it. He was about seven feet tall, weighed several hundred pounds, and looked strong, but that was offset by many old injuries from a few seasons of playing professional football, as well as numerous other accidents before and since.

Once Tommy was out deer hunting at this very camp. He was riding a dirt bike with a scoped .270 slung over his shoulder when he spotted a big rattlesnake and decided to run over it. (Rattlers are killed on sight in Texas.) But the snake got caught in the front tire, flipped up into Tommy's lap and the whole assembly—bike, snake, rifle and rider—did half a dozen forward somersaults. Tommy was unhappy about that because he "busted the damn gun."

Ed suggested calling a wrecker to pull the truck out of the tank (there was a phone in the pickup), but Tommy said, "They'd never find us out here," which seemed true enough.

Sometime during the struggle Ed's graphite rod got broken, he lost track of his Hardy reel, and then Tommy called someone on the car phone, said, "Hi. Oh, we're stuck in the lake, what're you up to?" and chatted for half an hour.

Then they decided to walk back to the camp for help, took a short cut and got lost.

Bud and I had a nice time catching some bass and watching the pelicans. Later, when Ed accused me of abandoning him, I thought of several excuses, but finally just said, "You're right, I'm sorry."

Then Ed said, in an admiring tone, "You've always been good at sidestepping the weird shit."

Over the next few days we fished the big Comanche Tank and several smaller ones where fly-fishing was a little more reasonable, places like the Frog Tank, Rock Tank and a few others the names of which I either didn't catch or wasn't told. We were in the company of half a dozen middle-aged men who, apparently, had all played high-school football together. Football is a big deal in Texas. You can drive through many small towns without learning their names, but you'll by God know they're the home of the Cougars or the Trojans or whatever.

One of these guys took us aside and said that, although Tommy seemed big and dangerous, he was really just accident prone, but otherwise gentle as a lamb. "Just give him plenty of room," the man said.

The standard tactic in these tanks was to fish a floating bug with the diving fly routine. You start by cutting off half of the sinking portion of a sink-tip fly line and throwing it away. Then, on the part that's left, you tie on a short, stout leader— maybe four feet of fifteen- or twenty-pound monofilament— and attach a bass bug to the business end with a Duncan Loop, a knot that lets the fly wiggle around, even on a stiff leader.

Bud's flies of choice are Dahlberg Diver–style deer hair bugs. The standard froggie is good, but Bud also has some patterns of his own design, including an injured baitfish and a neat little baby catfish with rubber whiskers. Bud ties some of the best-looking deer hair bugs I've ever seen. They're right up there with the ones tied by Dave Whitlock and Jimmy Nix: trim but buggy, tails perfectly matched, deer hair spun tight as cork.

Anyway, you cast the bug up against the bank, a weed bed or flooded stump. When the sinking tip of the line has bellied out under the surface of the water, you give it a good pull and the floating deer hair bug dives with a beautiful wiggling, swimming motion, kicking its feather legs behind it. I tried other flies, but it only works right with a Dahlberg Diver. I don't know how Larry Dahlberg figured this out, but it was a stroke of genius.

Sometimes the bass do hit like outdoor writers say they do—"like a freight train" is what you usually hear—but more often the take is so subtle you can think the fly has just bumped a weed or a waterlogged stick. Consequently, you set up on everything, and you set up hard, pulling line with your left hand and raising the rod tip with your right. "The harder the better," Bud said. "You want to cross his eyes."

We caught a lot of what I think of as big largemouth bass, but of course the locals outfished us, which is only right and proper. Most of these guys were Ugly Stick and rubber worm fishers, and they were good. Some of them, when they saw that Bud, Ed and I were fly-fishing, dug into their incredible piles of gear, got out their own fly rods, to be polite, and outfished us *that* way.

The often-written-about style of bass bugging, where you fish a floating deer hair bug on a floating line, letting it sit perfectly still on the surface for two, three minutes between gentle twitches, is not much thought of here. "That was invented by some goddamn outdoor writer from up north," Bud said. "These fish are aggressive and you gotta go after 'em aggressively."

He seemed to be right about that, but then this was the way I knew to fish for bass, and in a tank that was so choked with weeds they said it would be unfishable in another couple of weeks, I tried it. I cast a big Near Enough deer hair froggie to the edge of a five-foot-wide pothole of open water, let it sit there for two, three, maybe four minutes and then gave it a twitch.

The fly went down in a rise that looked like a toilet flushing. That's what bass fishers say. It's not the prettiest analogy in angling, but, I'm sorry, that's exactly what it looks like.

I was fishing a stiff, nine-foot, nine-weight rod and had already learned that if you gave a fish even a foot or two of line in these overgrown tanks you'd lose him in the weeds. So the fights were short and brutal. You'd grab the rod in both hands and haul, figuring you had spare rods back in the car, so you could break one, which would at least make for a good story. The bass would either throw the hook or come to the apron of the belly boat still thrashing. That day I got a case of tendonitis in my right elbow that lasted most of the season.

I think that bass weighed eight pounds, so figure seven. I held it up for Bud at a distance and he later said, "Now that was a *big* ol' bass." He was probably being kind. Usually the technical term "big ol' bass" refers to something in the ten-pound class.

That was the prettiest of all the tanks we fished. It was set in flat mesquite country with an enormous horizon and was full of tough weeds, bleached flooded timber and water moccasins they said you should watch out for because they like to crawl up on your belly boat. There were big white-winged whistling ducks that made an eerie, piping call that sounded like the first few notes of a sad folk song. Tommy said that if you got up on the dam and looked west over the tops of the mesquite bushes you could see Mexico. "And if you see dark-haired people running through the bushes," he added, "don't wave."

That night we ate home-cooked tacos at another camp that seemed abandoned, except that the electricity was still on. It was just dark and a storm was coming in from the southwest, so we stood at the open door for a while and watched the lightning. A guy who had made a comment about animal rights nuts two days ago picked up a gallon tub of guacamole dip and said, "Just think how many guacamoles had to die to make this."

The conversations in these fishing camps had less to do with fishing than I'm used to. These men were there to catch bass, but it was generally known where the fish were and how to catch them, so there just didn't seem to be a lot to discuss. Instead there was a lot of catching up. Those who hadn't played football together were distantly related or had once worked for or worked with or been the neighbor of a cousin or great-uncle or had shot deer on the same ranch as boys or *something*. When two strangers meet in Texas they pick each other's pasts apart until they find that connection, a whole universe of discourse opens up, and then they're buddies, if not actual relatives.

Once that's done, conversations take place in which little

is apparently said. One night the name of a girl everyone had known in high school came up. A quiet smile went around the room that I thought I recognized as the prelude to an off-color story, but instead someone said, "Well, she was a pretty girl and she's grown into a handsome married woman." Everyone agreed. "Yes sir, a *hand*some married woman."

One of the best parts of this leg of the trip was all the fish we ate. These tanks are extremely rich in food organisms and the climate is such that bass will spawn several times in a season, so the prevailing management philosophy is that they need to be harvested heavily so they won't overpopulate. "Now kill all the little bass you catch," they kept saying.

"What's 'little'?" I'd ask.

"Oh, say five pounds."

"Back home we'd think about *mounting* a five-pound bass," I said.

"Yeah, I know."

Tommy turned out to be the best cook. He didn't exactly teach me how to make mustard beer battered fish—when I asked him how he did it after the fact he said he couldn't remember—but I watched him do it a few times and picked it up. You mix equal parts mustard and yellow cornmeal, add a dash of baking powder and maybe some hickory salt or whatever else is lying around in the spice department and enough beer to make a thin paste. Then batter the fish and deep fry them in hot Crisco until they're just brown. And watch out for the spitting grease.

I never did land the ten-pound bass on a fly rod—which you can do in south Texas—but I had one on. At least that's what a gentleman named Dan said from the seat next to me in the big red bass boat one day. I was fishing some kind of streamer on a sink-tip line and had gotten a little lazy, as you can do on a hot day, fishing from a plush seat, roll casting with your right hand and holding a cold Lone Star in your left.

The fish hit, I struck and had him on for about as long as it took for him to come to the surface, jump and throw the hook. "That would have gone about ten," Dan said casually. "You shoulda set up harder."

I was trying to fix in my mind that fleeting glimpse of the biggest largemouth bass I'd ever seen alive and I almost said, "How the hell am I supposed to set up harder with a beer in my hand?" but of course the answer was obvious. You *can* fish and drink at the same time, but you can't do both well.

Later I told Ed about the big bass that had gotten off. He said, "Well, that's another one you can think about for the rest of your life."

A day or two later, Bud, Ed and I were back in the hill country, staying at a campground on the Nueces (pronounced "new aces") River. We were a few miles from Camp Wood, the little town where Bud, who now lives in San Antonio, was born. Ed and I were beginning to show signs that the trip was winding down—wondering what was happening at home, talking about work. If we'd stuck to the original plan, we'd have been in northern New Mexico by then, but this was one of those trips that takes on a life of its own. When Bud suggested canoeing one more river, we'd gotten a second wind and called home to say we'd be a little late.

Ed said, "Well, one of us is still employed," meaning Monica. Ed makes a living as a writer and fishing guide, but he wisely doesn't think of either as "employment."

We were a man short for the float the next day—you need a fisherman *and* a paddler per canoe—so we spent a few hours locating Bud's friend Don who, Bud said, "needed to go fishing." Don was a tall, wiry man with a handlebar mustache and one of those silver belt buckles the size of a saucer. He had apparently done many things in life, judging by his stories, but was now happy to be an ostrich rancher. He told us about ostriches in some detail in camp that night, as huge Hexagenia mayflies from the river collected on the picnic table and flying beetles the size of golf balls buzzed the lantern.

The Llano River had been clear, as someone said, "In that pea green way those warm rivers have," but the Nueces was as limpid as any trout stream I've ever seen. Glancing over the gunnels of the canoe in a deep hole, you could count the scales on a bluegill at ten feet.

Bud said the river was fishing a little slow. The water did seem a bit cool and, as clear as it was, it was running a little high. The weather had been chilly for spring in Texas—in the eighties—and there'd been a couple of horrendous rains. In fact, we'd talked about floating the Guadalupe River, but it was blown out by high water.

The Nueces *was* slow in the morning, but it was a bright, almost hot day and by noon the water had warmed and we started getting into fish. Sometimes we'd stop and wade, but more often we'd drift along a shady bank with one man paddling and the other casting. The river was slow enough in most places that if you hit a good bank you could paddle back upstream and drift down again.

We portaged around a few rapids on the Nueces, but I had already put some scratches on my no-longer-new canoe on the Llano, so I had gotten a little braver by then.

Maybe the fishing *was* a little slow, but then Bud has fished these rivers off and on all his life, so he has a different perspective. You have to understand that when a local fisherman tells you how a river usually is, he's describing the best day anyone ever had there. It seemed fine to me and, it being toward the end of the trip and all, I'd have been happy enough just to float and look around, experiencing that edgy sadness you feel when it's almost over, but you still have a hard, two-day drive ahead of you. We did catch fish, but I considered them a bonus.

I guess I had finally achieved the regional pace. I didn't really notice that until I got back home, decompressed for a day, and then forged ahead at what I thought was my normal speed, which is none too fast anyway. Down at the café someone asked, "Are you still tired from your trip?" and I said, "Why, no, darlin', I'm just relaxed," remembering too late that "darlin'" is politically incorrect in Colorado.

I also found that I wasn't bragging. When asked if I got into fish, I allowed as how some folks had been nice enough to show me how to do it and, yes, I did catch a few.

For a couple of days there I was even hesitant to criticize people, tending to say either nice things or nothing at all, as in, "Oh, I don't think he's incompetent, he's probably just in the wrong line of work." It wore off eventually, but for a week or so I was actually acting like a gentleman.

6

The Curse

A.K. and I have been fishing together for I don't know how long now, and early on in our loose partnership a seemingly odd karmic undertone began to make itself known: For some reason, when one of us does well, the other does poorly, or at least not *as* well.

If one of us catches lots of fish, the other catches only a few or, rarely, none. If A.K. gets into big fish one day, I typically get into the little ones. If we're fishing a warm water pond, one of us will catch only bluegills and pumpkinseeds while the other will get all the bass. It doesn't exactly alternate from day to day, but it does seem to even out over time.

Of course it doesn't always happen that way, which makes

it seem even stranger. There have been a few notable times when we both caught lots of big fish or both got completely skunked, but those days seemed weird, and were only exceptions that proved the rule.

We don't talk about this much anymore, but when we do, we refer to it as The Curse.

For a while I thought it was just us. Years ago we decided not to compete with each other on the stream. This wasn't something we had to hash out; it just happened, we noticed it, and agreed it was for the best. After all, most competition isn't about what it *appears* to be about, and two people bickering about who's the better fisherman are often getting at something much deeper and nastier than that.

So, since neither one of us had an ax to grind, we became friends, but I think the normal parrying and testing still goes on at another, more subtle level, and I once thought The Curse was some kind of spooky subconscious thing caused by suppressed male aggressiveness—or whatever the latest New Age term is for macho.

But then I started hearing the same kind of stories about other fishing partnerships, and some of these guys were real fish-counters, so they had the actual figures to back up their claims. They didn't usually get dramatic about it, they just said things like, "We were fishing the same hatch with the same flies, but it was definitely Mike's day. Seems like that happens a lot—one way or the other."

Eventually, to make life easier, I filed this under the growing category of interesting but inexplicable phenomena or "things for which even elegant explanations are meaningless." I started this file way back in college when I met a philosophy student who made a good case that buses didn't really exist, but still wouldn't step in front of one on a ten-dollar bet.

Early last spring, A.K. and I went down to the South Platte River near the town of Deckers, Colorado, to see about the

Blue-winged Olive hatch. It was a little bit early, but we'd heard that the mayflies were a week or two ahead of schedule and figured it was worth a try. We watched the weather reports for a few days waiting for one of those gray, gloomy days when the hatch usually comes off the best and timed the trip around what should have been a falling barometer.

It turned out that the television weatherman and the newspaper were both wrong—as they often are in mountainous country—and we arrived on the river at 9:30 in the morning on a bright, sunny, bluebird day. But the hatch turned out to be a good one anyway. The little flies weren't "boiling out of the riffles," as someone told us they'd been doing the day before, nor was the water "fuzzy with mayfly wings," but some flies hatched and some trout ate them, which is all you can ask for.

In fact, I've come to prefer hatches like that. There are enough mayflies on the water to get the trout interested, but not so many that your own little trout fly gets lost in the crowd.

The hatch started early—about 10:00—and, with a few dead spots, lasted until almost 5:00 that afternoon. I caught fish in the morning, broke around noon, found a pod of spawners and caught a great big one on a streamer, then went back to the dry flies. I can't say how many trout I caught, but I'd lost count by the middle of the day.

A.K., on the other hand, was having a pretty slow time. He was getting some strikes, but he seemed to be having a hard time hooking the fish.

He thought he'd figured it out when he checked his hook and found that he'd ticked his back cast on a rock and broken the point off, but when he changed to a good fly the fish still managed to elude him. It was one of those days when something—no telling what—was out of sync.

Finally he said to me, "They seem to be striking short," and I said, "Funny, I haven't noticed that."

A.K. did manage to land a few trout, but not many, and

on the ride home that evening he said to me, alluding to The Curse, "This was your fault."

And then, sure enough, it happened in reverse the next time. A.K. and I went back a few days later and met Ed on the river. It was another sunny day that was supposed to have been cloudy and, once again, the bugs came off unexpectedly well, except that this time they started later in the morning.

While we were waiting for the hatch to begin, I waded up into the shallow riffle where I'd landed that big spawning rainbow last time and caught another one just like it, only a little bit bigger. Ed waded over and took a photo of the fish. It was a large one, as I said, and the first trout of the day between us. I thought maybe it was going to be okay.

But then when the hatch came on and the trout started rising nicely, I found that I couldn't catch the fish, even though Ed and A.K. seemed to be doing well enough. I was using the right pattern—a #20 Blue-winged Olive parachute—and I was getting some strikes, but I just couldn't hook the fish.

I started setting up more quickly on the strikes—a sign of panic I exhibit automatically when I'm missing them, even though I know that's usually wrong. (As an afterthought I checked the hook, which was fine.) Then I started taking deep breaths and trying hard to slow down, you know, going for that imperceptible hesitation that's too long if you actually hesitate. I must have been on the right track because I felt a few fish and even had one or two on for a second or two before they threw the hook. I began to get that helpless feeling that there's one, single way to do it right hidden somewhere in a thousand easy mistakes.

Naturally, A.K. was hauling them in like a commercial fisherman.

Finally I said to him, "They seem to be striking short today," and he said, "Oh?" as he released a fat, fourteen-inch rainbow.

I did finally manage to land a handful of trout, two or three as I remember. A.K. and Ed, trying to be kind, allowed as how they'd done okay, although I had personally seen A.K. land maybe fifteen or twenty trout.

I guess I kind of expected this; what I didn't expect was that I'd break my bamboo fly rod.

There's no amusing story here, the rod just snapped cleanly in half below the ferrule while I was casting. I wanted to believe that I'd just thrown off my tip, but I'd heard a crack and, although I'd never broken a rod before, I knew what that had to mean.

Naturally, there was a photographer present. The guy had just wandered downstream wearing waders, carrying a camera and a small net, but no rod. He was catching mayflies and taking pictures of them. He saw me break the rod and watched me splash out to retrieve the tip, but when I glared at him he politely turned away. All I could think of was, any competent photographer would be tempted to capture a moment like that on film, and if this guy did I was going to have to throw his camera into the river.

The next day I took the rod down to Mike Clark, who'd made it for me almost ten years ago, to see if he could fix it. When I laid it on his workbench he said, as if he'd just found his favorite dog hit by a truck, "Aw, it's number thirty-three." (The serial number is actually 833, which, in Mike's system, means it was the third rod he made in 1983.)

He said he could repair the rod easily enough if I didn't mind it being about an inch shorter in the butt section, which wouldn't noticeably change the action. I said that would be fine.

As for the cause, we both knew that I had dropped the rod into its aluminum case too hard a number of times, damaging the joint between the bamboo and the female ferrule, which is precisely where it broke. Bamboo may be magic, but it still obeys the laws of physics. All Mike said about that was that it was a nice clean break. It almost sounded like a compliment. I expected a lecture on the proper treatment of a fine fly rod, but Mike just muttered something about pearls before swine and said he wouldn't charge me for the repair.

Luckily, Ed had a spare graphite rod along that day and he let me finish the afternoon with it. I didn't catch any more fish, but my heart wasn't really in it either, so at least I had an excuse.

On the drive home A.K. was jubilant about all the fish he'd caught, but he got serious just long enough to say he was sorry about my rod.

On our last trip to the Platte we were pushing our luck a little. It was the third week in February. The flow was decent for that time of year—about ninety cubic feet per second—but it was too early for the first mayflies, too early for the scuds, and reports said the usual late winter midge hatches hadn't really started yet. The day before, I'd called Ray Sapp at the Colorado Angler fly shop—a guy who's more likely to catch fish on the Platte than most—and asked him how the river had been fishing. "Weird," he said, which was not encouraging.

The February midging can be wonderful when it happens, but you have to be philosophical about it because there tend to be more slow days than good ones. You'll often spend eight or nine chilly hours on the river and maybe tease up a trout or two at best while getting your dues paid.

This is a safe trip, though. That is, if you get into fish at a difficult and spooky time of year, you've done something that at least approaches being extraordinary, and if you don't, that's pretty much what you expected, so you can congratulate yourself for being right.

And anyway, in late winter it seems only proper that you haunt the river for a while before things really start to happen. If nothing else, this qualifies you as a genuine local, so when some tourist turns to you on a pretty summer evening and asks, "Is it always this good?" you can say, "Nope."

This last time, we drove to Deckers, where the river was full of the previous night's glaze of bankside and bottom ice, now broken off, largely turned to slush and filling the main currents. Ten minutes down the road at Trumbull it was the same, or maybe a little worse.

Trumbull, a real town of maybe twenty cabins, seemed entirely deserted, as it often does in the winter. The only signs of life were a handsome black Lab and a dopey-looking basset on patrol. They stood in the middle of the road and watched us approach in the pickup as if they'd never seen a motorized vehicle before.

This ice floe, locally known as the slush hatch, only happens on mornings that are warmer and brighter than usual, and it makes the water unfishable. Trout won't rise through slush (bugs probably won't hatch through it, either), and even if fish are feeding under the surface, you can't get a nymph down to them. There's nothing to do but wait. Usually the river flushes itself clear by late morning. In the meantime it looks lonely and uninviting.

We drove back up to the Deckers bridge because the ice clears sooner upstream than down. There were a few other fishermen around, either sitting in their cars or rigging up slowly to kill time. The bar and restaurant at Deckers wasn't open yet, but the little worms and cold beer store was, and we got some fresh coffee there.

When the ice finally cleared, we got in at a favorite pool not far upstream from the bridge and started to fish. There were no rises and no flashes of trout feeding underwater, so this felt like the beginning of one of those long hauls where you cast and cast on automatic pilot, waiting for something to happen, living with the idea that it probably won't.

I don't mean to imply that we were depressed or anything. This is just a kind of fly-fishing—the kind where the odds are against you—and it's actually one of the better ways to spend a winter day.

I tied on a #20 South Platte Brassie, twisted some lead wire onto my leader to sink it and started fishing in a deep hole. I hooked and landed three trout on three successive casts, each one a bigger surprise than the last. A.K. was amazed. So was I, although I tried not to let on.

I was fishing the same rod I'd broken there almost a year before, which I now think of fondly as Old Number Thirty-three. Mike's repair was flawless, the rod does in fact cast just the same as it always did, and I've come to see that missing inch of bamboo as a barely perceptible, but honorable, scar. It's still one of my favorite rods, and I might even like it more now than I did before.

Over the next half hour or so I caught four or five more trout from that same hole, and then it went dead, as if someone had flipped the proverbial switch. A.K. had missed a couple of strikes, but he didn't land any fish.

For the rest of the day we went through the obligatory motions. We drove back to a place just below Trumbull to check on another favorite pool and found a guy fishing in it. I walked past him twice, saying hello both times, and A.K. sat on the bank near him for a while making a big show of rebuilding his leader. We gave the guy every opportunity to leave or say, "Come on, there's room for all of us," but he didn't, so we fished some other water and then drove back upstream.

By late afternoon it had turned cold and cars full of fishermen began passing us as they headed north up to the main highway and home. I started thinking in terms of packing it in, and I think A.K. was also leaning in that direction. But then there was a short flurry of activity, just a few trout rising to a few tiny midge flies in two pools. A.K. missed two strikes and I caught one small brown trout on a dry fly. Then A.K. said something about hamburgers and one beer before the drive home and that was the end of it.

There's a specific etiquette to this. The guy who didn't catch fish must not whine or complain or offer excuses, and the guy who *did* land a few (whether it was through luck or skill) is not allowed to either preen or engage in false modesty. I've been on both sides of this often, and I don't know which is harder.

When we walked into the Deckers Bar we went straight to the wood stove to warm our hands. A blond woman turned around on her stool and said, "It's not that cold out, is it?"

"It is when you've been standing in the river fishing all day," I said.

"Jeeze," she said, "that's nuts. You guys must be from Texas or something."

There was a moment of silence during which any of the four other people in the little tavern who were Texans could have spoken up, then the woman said, a little shyly, "Well, *ah'm* from Texas."

She said she hadn't been to Deckers in many years, but had spent some great summers there as a little girl playing, climbing the hills and "terrorizing the fishermen." She'd been sitting there all afternoon playing ballads on the jukebox and talking about the old days with the bartender, who I think would be a little too young to remember.

I almost asked the woman about the two old mounted trout above the bar. Over the years—out of idle writer's curiosity—I've asked dozens of patrons and a handful of bartenders in this place about those fish, and have always gotten the same answer. It's believed they were caught from the very river you can see from all but two or three stools in that bar, but no one knows when or by whom.

These elderly stuffed fish are yellowed now, with slack jaws and curling fins, but once they were big, lovely, twenty-inch rainbows. Now they're just proof that trout have lived here for a long, long time, and that some people, at least, have been able to catch them. I almost asked the woman about them because she'd spent part of her childhood there and might know some history, but I stopped myself in time. Having talked with these nice Texas ladies before, I knew what her answer would be. She'd say, "Stranger, how old do you think I *am?*"

After we'd ordered our burgers and beers, the woman said, "Well, did you guys catch any fish?"

A.K. nodded toward me and said, "*He* did," and then he grinned. This was the properly gracious thing to say, but the smile was a little too wide. He was thinking, "Next time it's my turn."

In the Woods

Most stories about big game hunting are deceptive to the point of being untrue. That is, there's usually much more action in the story than there was on the actual hunt. It's not as bad now as it used to be, though. If you're old enough, you'll remember the lurid illustrations on the covers of outdoor magazines showing a hunter about to be devoured, gored or stomped by a different game species every month. The animal is only a few steps away—in full charge, drooling horribly or blowing snot—and the hunter, though surprised and off balance, is either chambering a cartridge or drawing a large Bowie knife. Things look grim, but there's the off chance the guy will come out of it alive.

A friend of mine refers to this as the "wild animals are trying to kill you" school of pulp art. Even when I was young and impressionable, I knew it was crap.

The fact is, a hunting trip is sometimes punctuated by a fabulous success, a horrendous failure or even something as unlikely as a misfire, but mainly it's days of standing, walking or sitting quietly, doing nothing obvious, in a state of mind that borders on meditation. This is how it's done, but it's not the stuff of thrilling narratives.

You'll usually see the species of game you're after, although often it's out of range, running, screened off from a clear shot by trees, or it's the right species, but the wrong sex: does instead of bucks.

In this last case you kick yourself for not having applied for a doe, or "antlerless deer," tag before the deadline four months ago. Maybe you spaced it out because it's hard for you to stop in June, when the fishing is just getting hot, to think about the October deer hunt. Or maybe you just couldn't get straight about *where* you were going to hunt and, since limited licenses here are for specific game management units, you had to let it slide.

Or maybe every few seasons you can't quite bring yourself to go through filling out an application form and entering a computerized drawing—always calculating the preference points you've accumulated from previous drawings or the ones you might get from this one—just in order to hunt one of the People's deer on the People's land. Putting together a good application now can be like figuring out your income tax and, in certain frames of mind, it's just as insulting.

But that's not your problem now. Now you're in the woods carrying an antlered license bought at the last minute from a hardware store, going to great lengths to blend into the environment; to be there, but not there, in what you know to be the finest hunting tradition. This takes either concentration or the thoughtless lack of it, and it's not something many of us get much practice at. Fishing takes patience and focused attention, but it's not the same as deer hunting. Neither is grouse shooting, or hiking, or bird watching, or mushroom gathering or politics or any of the other things you can practice until skill comes out your ears. I know some very good deer hunters, but I don't know how they got that way doing it for one week out of every year.

Sometimes in the spring or summer, when I'm just out for a walk or the fishing is slow, I'll spot a deer and try to sneak up on it, but something is missing. My ears aren't ringing with adrenaline, and the deer, though alert and suspicious, seems to understand that it's the off season and I'm just fooling around, which is true enough. I know that if this was October and I had a rifle under my arm, it would all be different.

I do a lot of what they call "stillhunting" because even now, in my mid-forties, I often lack the patience to sit absolutely motionless on a stand for hours on end.

Stillhunting is not exactly what it sounds like: You don't just sit still, you walk through the woods very slowly and as silently as you can (that is, with great stillness), taking a few cautious steps, then stopping to look and listen to everything around you.

No, that doesn't describe it properly. You move in deliberate slow motion, like in tai chi. Imagine that someone is watching you: In the space of five minutes you've gone twenty yards, but they never actually saw you do it. Okay, maybe not, but *imagine* that.

No, don't. Imagination is distracting. Get it into your head that you must see and hear everything, but disturb nothing. To stillhunt properly is to stand perfectly still while walking.

It's amazing how the distance you travel in even a single slow step can change your whole perspective. I don't know how an entire 250-pound mule deer buck can hide behind an aspen tree no bigger around than your arm, but I know he can—I've seen it.

You've just stood there for five minutes checking out every trunk, branch, twig and needle in the woods, then you take one step and there's the deer, looking right into your eyes, both ears trained on you like radar dishes. You're not acting like a normal human, so he doesn't exactly know what you are, although he's beginning to suspect something.

The trick now is to cock the rifle and raise it to your shoulder slowly and gracefully enough that you can get off your shot before the animal vanishes. A place to rest the rifle would be nice, but, although you're in a thick forest, there is no tree handy at the moment.

I've found it can be helpful in this situation to sink down on one knee or, better yet, drop slowly to a full sit. Not only is this a better shooting position, but I believe the deer thinks you're lying down, which, to him, is a curiously nonaggressive gesture. It puzzles him—sometimes he'll even take a cautious step in your direction to see what you're doing.

But that's a whole other story. That's the drama and excitement that, as I said, is rare. Your main occupations are slowing your pace, reducing noise and motion to a minimum and picking the forest apart piece by piece with your eyes and ears. You're not expecting to see a whole deer standing there like a field guide illustration, you're tuned for a glimpse of a white butt, an ear, a brownish-bone-colored antler, the line of a gray-brown back that looks like all the other rocks and logs, except that this one has no snow on it.

That's what you're looking for, although mostly you see birds, squirrels, hares, porcupines, maybe a fox or coyote, and as the days go by, if you're doing it right, you begin to appreciate what the woods are really like, that is, what they're like when you're not there.

Some years the forest may be lousy with coyotes. You'll

hear them at night—sometimes a long-eared or great horned owl will answer their calls—and after the first good snow you'll see their busy tracks everywhere. I'm told that coyotes are much in evidence during the hunting seasons because they're cruising around feeding on the entrails left by hunters who have field-dressed their deer and elk. You'll see ravens doing that, too, but you may never actually see the coyotes.

There may be blue grouse around, and you'll naturally consider shooting them for camp meat, although you should resist that because the report of a big-bore rifle—or even the crack of a .22 pistol—will blow a two-hour stalk. If you want grouse, you should *hunt* grouse. Now you're hunting deer.

Okay, so where are they? That's the big question. I've met hunters who seem to know, but each one of them has a slightly different theory. Some like to hunt hard in the evenings and early mornings when deer are moving between the places where they feed and the spots where they bed down. The mule deer we hunt in the western mountains aren't as habitual as whitetails, but if they're feeding in a certain meadow, there will be more or less logical routes to it along a ridge or through a saddle.

This will be stand hunting. You find a spot where you're fairly well hidden, but downwind and with a good view, and then just sit there doing your best to become a rock or stump. I don't much care for this, as I mentioned, but the rule of thumb is, when the deer are sitting still, you move, and when the deer are supposed to be moving, you sit still.

Often you'll see more deer during the season than at any other time because there are lots of people in the woods pushing them around, sometimes without knowing it. In that sense, it can be better to have loud, dumb hunters out there with you than good, quiet ones, although I don't know anyone who would consciously make that choice. In some cases where animal rights nuts have gone out in season banging pans and blowing whistles to scare the game, hunters have worked around them, using them as beaters. Or so I've heard. If you didn't care how you got your deer, I suppose it could work.

Over the years, what you think you know about deer is colored by having other humans in the woods. I once hunted in some special muzzleloading deer seasons not far from home. I liked the antique strangeness of the old rifles, the fact that you had just the one shot with at least a couple of minutes' reloading time, but mostly I was tempted by the limited number of hunters out early in the fall, before the regular rifle seasons.

I'll be hunting in something resembling natural conditions, I thought, with the deer doing what they normally do instead of being pushed around by crowds of other hunters. Then, after a few days out without seeing any animals, I was thinking, Okay, but what *do* they do when no one is around?

I finally did shoot a deer with a muzzleloader, but it was during a regular season. That fall I hung the .50-caliber cap lock rifle on the wall—where it looks real pretty—and got what some friends enjoyed calling a "real gun": a .30-06 with a scope. I realized that handguns, bows and muzzleloaders are for hunters who are so skilled they must always impose greater restrictions on themselves to keep things fair. I'm not that good.

The satisfaction of deer hunting comes not so much from killing something as from being in the woods in a fundamental way, that is, as a participant rather than an observer. The same is true of small game hunting, fishing, or mushroom gathering, but a deer is a large piece of meat and to hunt one is to intend to cause what seems like a big death. Even if you're only thinking of what you may have to drag back to the road, it seems pretty serious. That's why I've never shot an elk. They're not only more difficult to get than deer, they're just too damn big.

Interestingly, the most practical state of mind for deer hunting is one of calm receptiveness, or about as far from blood-thirsty as you can get. You enter a stand of spruce and fir that looks and feels like an abandoned railroad terminal on a cloudy day: an apparently gloomy place that's cool in warm weather and sheltered from wind and snow when it's nasty.

A patch of this dark timber looks quiet and brooding from the outside, but if you sit absolutely still in there, or stillhunt through it for, let's say, two hours, you'll find that the trees are full of small, drab-colored birds, and that in breezes so slight you can't feel them the trunks of the trees creak and squeal like the doors of crypts in 1930s horror movies. It can take half of those two hours just to reorient your flawed human sense of what "silence" means.

Pinecones sometimes drop of their own accord, making thumps on the spongy ground that sound like hoofbeats, or rather, a single hoofbeat. This can leave you holding your breath, waiting for the other shoe to drop.

Little pine squirrels that you weren't aware of will suddenly break into a startled chatter, and this can be loud enough to stop your heart. The same little guys crashing around in dry leaves can make a racket like a bear rolling a log.

If the wind picks up a bit, there will be a shower of dead, rusty-brown needles that sounds like rain. Rain itself sounds like gravel being thrown against a blanket. Dry snow hisses, and wet snow sizzles like frying bacon.

Of course you can't be still forever—at least I can't—and eventually you'll begin to think you should hike another mile along the ridge and try it there, or go have lunch, or you'll just decide to break the silence on general principles. With those first few careless steps the rustle of your clothing is deafening. You walk twenty yards, step out into a grove of aspen and it's like someone switched on the lights. You've stepped back into your skin, and it will take a few more minutes to get used to it.

• • •

For the last several seasons, DeWitt, Ed and I have hunted deer in a rough part of a somewhat obscure big game unit on Colorado's West Slope, one of those places where doe tags go begging because the area is too rugged and not glamorous enough for many hunters.

There are some elk and plenty of deer here (including some big, handsome bucks) but they're widely scattered through steep, rough country, some of which is wilderness area where vehicles of any kind are forbidden. In short, you have to work hard for your animal—both before and after shooting it—so there aren't too many other hunters around. And what hunters there are tend to concentrate in the easier terrain, thus running many of the animals into the harder country where *we* hunt. Yes, we do feel sort of cagey about this.

And it doesn't hurt that DeWitt and his wife, Julia, have a snug little cabin up there. Having a warm, dry place to sleep on the deer hunt is downright luxurious.

Last year the party consisted of me, Ed, DeWitt and Julia. Actually, Julia only came up for a few days because she was busy with work and a graduate degree. Still, she didn't want to miss the hunting.

I enjoy hunting with Julia because she's good company, she's a good shot (she carries her father's old .30-06) and she shatters stereotypes, which is always fun. When we mentioned to a group of hunters who were staying nearby that DeWitt's wife would be arriving a day or two later, one of them asked, innocently, if she was coming up to do the cooking. The three of us glanced at one another, imagining what would have happened if this guy had asked Julia that.

The hunting conditions were tricky that year. There was no snow down for tracking and the country was dry, with lots of brittle aspen leaves and crackly pine needles on the ground, so stalking quietly was almost impossible.

I tend to start off sharper some years than others, and this time it took me a while to get into the proper head. I spent most of opening day wandering around the steep aspen benches and lodgepole pine woods where I'd shot my deer the season before. I tried to stillhunt, but several times I caught myself crunching loudly through the dry leaves and duff at a sauntering, game-scaring pace. We'd come up a day early and taken the obligatory hike to look things over—either to scout for sign and plan strategy or, as DeWitt says, to say hello to the country before you get down to business—but I still hadn't relaxed into the place yet.

I tried sitting a few times along wide, well-used game trails, but I was convinced that the deer weren't moving in the daylight, so I couldn't muster even the little bit of patience I have access to.

That evening I did take a stand at a good-looking spot. Two game trails converged in a saddle leading down to a grassy meadow. There were fresh scat and tracks showing that deer had fed there recently, and this was the only logical, easy way for them to come down off the mountain on that side. It was a perfect spot, but the only way to hunt it was to pick a place, become motionless and stay that way.

So I brought a book. This is a trick Julia uses and I thought I'd try it. We're both restless hunters who have a hell of a time sitting in one place quietly for, say, an hour and a half waiting for a deer to come along. Julia said that a book keeps her quiet and in one place long enough. Two years ago she shot a deer with a paperback novel open on the rock beside her without even losing her place.

Naturally, there are pitfalls here. I hunkered down about an hour and a half from dusk with some short stories by Raymond Carver. I got a little too engrossed in a piece entitled "Where I'm Calling From," and when I finally thought to look up the doe had already gotten way too close: no more than thirty feet away. Just that little movement of my head spooked her.

The story, like most of the others in the book, was about how heavy drinking can ruin a marriage.

Ed refuses to read on a stand, even though he's at least as

restless as I am. He feels that trying to fool yourself like that is futile because you're always in on the joke from the beginning, not to mention that flipping a page is like waving a flag. Instead he quiets himself by practicing meditation, or what he calls, "that old Zen stuff from the sixties."

Of course there's a pitfall there as well, which I pointed out to Ed. You'll see deer if they're there to be seen, but if you're meditating properly you may also come to realize that shooting one and not shooting one amount to about the same thing in the grand scheme. This can cost you your predatory edge.

As it turned out, we hunted up the deer we got by stalking them in daylight under what to me are the most difficult conditions. DeWitt's big buck was lying in some dark timber below a quartzite ridge. My doe was bedded down in tall grass on the edge of a broken aspen grove. I believe neither of these deer knew a hunter was there or that things were about to go wrong for them.

When I shot the doe I felt the usual jarring mix of emotions: a combination of something like surprise and elation, followed by a moment of sadness and, let's say, gratitude. Then I went to find DeWitt because it was a big one and I couldn't drag it all the way out by myself.

I like hunting with this group in part because we can talk about things like the sadness and the gratitude without feeling self-conscious. In the company of some hunters, that stuff goes over poorly.

Usually by the time someone shoots a deer we've been out long enough to have exhausted the latest media crisis. That year it was the idiocy with Clarence Thomas, Anita Hill and the U.S. Senate. Julia brings a refreshing perspective to these things because she doesn't pay much attention to the Big News, preferring to busy herself with more immediate puzzles that actually have solutions. When she walks in on the conversation and asks, "Now who are Clarence and

Anita?" you see the simplicity of it. You say, "They are two people in Washington, D.C., who both may be lying."

"Oh," she says, "what else is new?"

Then there's time to talk casually about the inseparability of life and death, joy and sorrow, skill and luck, hard work and good food and so on. We fry thin slices of the current fresh deer liver with onions. This is a casual, little, old ritual having to do with pride and thanks, and it's the only time liver ever tastes good to me. Then we drink some wine (De-Witt is in charge of selecting the wine) and Ed says to me, "Maybe you'd do better on a stand if you read something more cheerful than Raymond Carver."

Another thing I like about this group is our feeling of community. When we started hunting together a few years ago we agreed, in one of the shortest important discussions I've ever been part of, to split up whatever we got so that everyone would come home with at least some meat. It was just an obvious, practical thing to do, but I've come to really like the sense of community that's formed around it. I'm hunting for everyone, and they're all hunting for me.

Sometimes at a game dinner someone will ask, "Now did you shoot this venison yourself?" and I've noticed it's as pleasant to say, "No, it was a gift from some friends," as to be able to say, "Yes, I did."

You'll sometimes run into hunters (older ones, for the most part) who say they no longer care if they get a deer or not, that they just enjoy the hunt, and that, in fact, killing an animal is when the fun stops and the hard work begins.

It *is* hard work, and I know it's possible to get enough of that, and if you're hunting to prove something, I suppose it's possible to get it proved, finally, and then just want to hang around camp doing the cooking and splitting wood.

For my part, I still want to get one, that's why I'm out there, although I have gotten to the point where it's okay if I don't.

Not entirely acceptable, mind you, but okay. That's another way of saying, *I wanna get one.*

And I guess I also enjoy that poignant mix of emotions. If I try to live by a single principle, it's, "Do no unnecessary harm." This principle actually comes into play more often when I'm contemplating punishing someone or exacting revenge. If I take an insult too seriously, I have to wonder if maybe the insult wasn't accurate, or consider that I'm getting arrogant, as in "who is *he* to say that to *me*?" In other words, before I say something like, "Now listen, you asshole . . ." I am forced to think, Is this necessary?

When it comes to shooting one deer a year for food, I've already decided that it's the correct thing to do: a matter of necessary or at least useful harm. The chore at hand is to do it right, which is what separates sport from mere food gathering—that and the fact that I wouldn't live as well without deer meat in the freezer, but I *would* live.

So what I want is a clean, humane, one-shot kill, and I won't fire at an animal if I don't think I can manage that. Mostly this is a matter of understanding your limitations and being properly humble. I'm a decent rifle shot out to about 100 yards, which means if I see an animal at 250, that's not my deer—and you don't want to shoot one that is not, somehow, yours. Consequently, I hunt dark timber and broken woods where the skills I have are right for the habitat.

If I get a deer early in the season I'll still stay on for a while. Technically, that's so I'll be there to help the others haul out and skin *their* deer, but really it's because I don't want to leave yet. It's such a great place to be: The country is pretty, the cabin snug and comfortable, the talk good.

Sometimes I'll have an elk license, even though I have little interest in killing an elk or, maybe more to the point, in quartering one and hauling it out of the woods. More likely I'll bring a shotgun and wander around the woods with it on the pretext of hunting grouse. There's a pretty good trout stream not twenty feet out the back door of the cabin, but I never bring a fly rod because this is a hunting trip.

In seasons when I don't get one early, I find I become more instead of less patient as the days go by—at least up to a point. This is not exactly resignation, it's just that I know I'm doing what I'm supposed to as well as I can, and I also know that desperation is not a productive attitude.

Maybe later in the week, with the season beginning to wind down, I'll drive the ten miles or so to the nearest little store for provisions and gossip. You know this place: one gas pump outside; deer antlers nailed above the door; one small, unpainted room containing stale bread and single-serving cans of pork and beans at prices three times what they'd be in the nearest town.

There's an excited, slightly paramilitary atmosphere in the store, and some other hunters are hanging around in their orange hats and vests, some of which are newer and brighter than mine. It occurs to me now and then that if I hadn't grown up dressing like this every fall, I might feel a little bit ridiculous.

These guys have three elk and a deer hanging in camp and they feel pretty good about it. Not crazy or anything, just good—satisfied.

One of them asks me, "Have you killed anything yet?"

"No," I say, "but it's sure nice to be out in the woods."

They don't reply to that. They just look at me as if I was the quarterback of the Denver Broncos and I'd just said, "Sure, we lost the Super Bowl, but what the hell, it's only a game."

8

Scotland

*F*or once it was exactly as I'd pictured it, which is something a fisherman doesn't get to say very often. There were real castles and slate-roofed stone cottages scattered around a green river valley, ghillies in knee-high breeches and leather vests, a water bailiff in a deerstalker cap who slept days and only ventured out in the gloaming when poachers were about. Hundreds of pheasants strolled the fields and roosted in the oak forests where the deer live, waiting for the driven shoots in the fall.

We dressed in jackets and ties for dinner, drank the good whiskey they don't export to America and, of course, our party of five fished hard for six days and caught one fish among us.

We were fly-fishing for Atlantic salmon on a private river in Scotland in late June—a good river at a pretty good time of year, by all accounts—but this was what everyone had told me to expect. "Even if you do everything right, you might not catch one. *You've got to understand that*," they said, or words to that effect.

The thing about Atlantic salmon is, once they've run out of the sea and into their home rivers to spawn, they don't feed. As always, there's a logical reason for that. If these big salmon came into the rivers hungry, they'd eat up all the salmon parr from the previous year's spawn and wipe out the whole next generation of fish. Perfectly logical, when you think about it.

So a salmon comes into a river carrying enough nutrients in its tissues to last it many months, its digestive system ceases to work and physical changes occur in the fish's hypothalamus that bring on what Lee Wulff called "a loss of appetite or nausea." This is not the moodiness you sometimes see in trout; these fish really don't eat, so they're really not supposed to bite.

This is something a fisherman has to think hard about and get firmly in mind.

Hugh Falkus, in his inch-and-a-half-thick, three-pound *Salmon Fishing: A Practical Guide*, says, "What is surprising is not that salmon are hard to catch, but that any are caught at all." Every salmon-fishing book I've ever peeked into has said something like that, usually right near the beginning so you won't get the wrong idea. This has been known to work, but you've gotta understand that it's not *supposed* to work, okay?

I'd never fished for Atlantic salmon before and in the end it was the very unlikelihood of catching one—the exciting weirdness of that—that finally attracted me to it, or at least that's what I thought. Looking back on it now, I realize I didn't believe I'd actually get skunked. I thought I'd experience the epitome of sport everyone talks about, work hard, confront frustration and otherwise take my lumps, but I also thought I'd eventually catch a fish.

I should have known better, because the sport is lousy with stories not just of blank days but of entire blank seasons. A man in Scotland told me he'd caught five salmon the first time he'd fished for them (that's unheard of and it cost him a fortune in scotch at the pub afterward) and then he didn't catch another fish for three years.

Once a story like that is told among salmon anglers, everyone else trots out *their* story. It's a form of competition, the winner being the guy who went the longest without a fish, but still didn't give up.

When I said okay, sure, it's just that I couldn't remember the last time I'd fished for six days straight without so much as a strike, I was told, "A bad week is nothing, lad, nothing a'tall."

This river had been held privately for the last six hundred years—the whole river, not just a piece of it—but an English company had recently bought the fishing rights from the estate and was offering them for sale on a time-share basis: one week in perpetuity for seventy thousand pounds, or about twice that many American dollars. There were six of us altogether: five American writers—Tom, Scott, Don, Clive and me—plus Laine, Clive's photographer (although Laine might have said that Clive was *his* writer). Some of us were magazine staffers, some were on assignment and others were freelancing, but that was the story: time shares on a salmon river in Scotland, a cultural hybrid of an idea that was supposed to make Americans dive for their checkbooks.

Since only five rods were allowed on a beat, Laine couldn't fish, but he said he wouldn't have even if he could. He thought fishing was insane. He hated the boredom, couldn't stand getting wet or cold and didn't care much for fish anyway, except maybe kippers. Turning to Clive he said, "Remember when I covered that sea trout story with you? Night after miserable night in the freezing rain, in a leaky boat, not even the paltry excitement of catching a fish, and having to put up with you the whole time."

But, he added to the rest of us, as a professional photographer he could, and would, take pictures of anything, and they'd be damned good, too.

We began downstream at the Downie beat. Our ghillie, Matthew, put me on The Breaches pool and asked to see my flies. I had a single box of brand-new wets: Copper Killers, Thunder and Lightnings, Undertakers and General Practitioners that a man who'd fished Scotland had recommended, plus a brace each of Jock Scotts and Green Highlanders for local color.

"Did you tie these?" asked Matthew.

"No, I bought them."

"In America?"

"Yeah, from a place called Hunter's."

"Well," he said, "they're terribly pretty," as if prettiness was a nice enough touch, but it wasn't going to make any difference.

He broke off my tippet and retied it—because no guide anywhere likes *your* knots—then selected a small General Practitioner on a double hook and tied that on for me, too. There's no reason in the world for an Atlantic salmon in a river to bite any fly, but among the people who fish for them this way there's still something that clicks, making one pattern look better than another.

Laine was photographing all this: the American fisherman being instructed by the Scottish ghillie with Croiche Wood as a backdrop and good morning light. He hated to get wet, but to achieve the right angle he had waded into the river up to his shins in tennis shoes.

There are subtleties to Atlantic salmon fishing (there must be, there have been so many thick, ponderous books written about it), but when you don't know what you're doing, you do what you're told. In this case, you "work the water."

You start at the top of a pool, make a quartering down-stream cast, fish it out, take a step downstream and do it again. The fly is fished on an across and downstream swing, so you end up covering the entire pool in what would look, in an illustration, like a series of sickle-moon-shaped stripes about two feet apart.

At the bottom of the pool you get out, walk back to the top and start again. You're fishing with a floating line, so your unweighted wet fly swims very shallowly, within an inch or two of the surface. Of course the salmon usually lie much deeper than that so, as unlikely as these fish are to bite in the first place, they have to make the full commitment and move for the fly. It seems like an outside chance, but that's how a gentleman fishes.

I asked if maybe a guy shouldn't concentrate on places where salmon would likely be lying. "Yes," said the ghillie, "that would be all right."

"So where do you suppose that would be?" I asked.

"Oh," he said, making a gesture that seemed to include the whole pool, "all through there."

You think the ghillie should have more to tell you about this, but he doesn't, or at least you assume he doesn't be-cause you don't see much of him. I had assumed the ghillie was there to be helpful, like an American guide, but then I was from out of town.

I fished down the pool, letting the fly hang in the current for a minute or so at the end of each swing because some-times a salmon chases it and hits it when it stops. I fished through the pool maybe five times. On the third or fourth pass two men on horseback trotted into a clearing on the far bank and sat watching me. I waved, but they didn't wave back. That was the most exciting thing that happened all morning.

A friend of mine said he'd been salmon fishing once and had actually enjoyed the mindless, repetitive nature of it. He didn't mention whether he'd caught a fish or not, which means he didn't. He also said he can spot the Atlantic salmon story in which the writer got skunked by the first paragraph. "It's all about the castles, cottages, ghillies and deer forests," he said.

We were staying at the Cruvies House, a large cottage on the river at the bottom of the Falls beat, complete with a tile-floored fishermen's changing room and a heated drying closet for waders and rain gear. The river side of the dining room had a line of French doors looking out on the cruvies themselves—a set of V-shaped stone dams with cribs used for netting salmon in the old days. The old days in this case dated back to the 1400s.

Lunch was served at the hut on whatever beat we happened to be fishing, but we ate breakfast and dinner in that room overlooking the river, usually with Dick, who was president of the company that owned the fishing rights.

Dick was charming, quick with a joke, always in charge in an evenhanded, British way and, he said, a student of all things American, even to doing most of his riding on a western saddle. He gently instructed us in the ways of salmon fishing—more the etiquette than the technique, although some of us were weak on both—and occasionally corrected our speech.

When the subject of priests came up, someone asked, "What do you mean by a 'priest'?"

Tom said, "In this context, it's a little weighted club you use to bonk a salmon on the head to kill it."

"I wouldn't put it quite that way," Dick said.

"Why not?"

"Because here 'bonking' means 'screwing.'"

He also tried to explain cricket, but gave it up when I said I didn't even understand baseball.

These dinners were at least three courses, prepared and served by Jane, who is probably the best fancy meat and potatoes cook I've ever met. She was self-employed, working sometimes for Dick and sometimes for other parties of salmon fishers who rented cottages in the valley. She was the best cook in the county, she said, and these rich folk, being used to the best of everything, often bid against each other for her services.

One day I got to talking with one of these guys, a wealthy sport who was a tenant on half a dozen of the country's best salmon and sea trout rivers, and who seemed to stop fishing only long enough to do a little driven grouse and pheasant shooting. He seemed like a nice man—if nothing else, he was spending his money right—but he also gave off a certain air that's hard to describe: almost as if he thought he could have you beheaded if the mood struck him. Anyway, he'd told Dick he wanted to meet some of these American writers who were such hard-core fishermen they weren't even stopping for tea.

He asked me about the Frying Pan River in Colorado, which he'd heard about.

"Now, when you go over there and camp for a week," he said, "do you bring your own cook from home or do you engage someone locally?"

I had to tell him that, as far as I knew, there was no one like Jane in Colorado. He winced slightly when he heard the name. She was cooking for us that week, which apparently meant he and his party were getting by on cold porridge, stale bread and cheap wine in bottles with screw caps.

I liked Jane immediately—we all did—and not just for the great food she put out. She was a genuine wild Highlander who pointedly took no crap from anyone, addressed no one as "mister," liked to refer to us as boys, her boss included—although she was younger than most of us—did not engage in false modesty and managed the kind of dignity that allowed her to serve meals without seeming like a waitress. She made you want to hang out in the kitchen, even though (or maybe because) that seemed to be frowned upon.

Jane could do a great impression of a midwestern American accent, complete with appropriate dialogue ("Hey, Bob, get a load of this here church"). She said, "You can always spot Americans by their wide arses and small heads." She also happened to be pretty: willowy, but not anorectic-looking like a model.

I noticed right off that Scott was hanging out in the kitchen more than the rest of us, but I thought maybe he just had a domestic streak and was pumping her for recipes.

I think that cottage is the most comfortable place I've ever stayed while fishing. We each had our own big, homey, high-ceilinged room with a huge bed, down comforters and a private bath (with English plumbing, but then nothing's perfect). My room looked out on the river, and since the nights were only chilly, I slept with the windows open. We put in long days fishing, drank some and ate large meals, but I still think it was the river that put me away each night. The sound of it hissing through the cruvies had the same effect as morphine.

Laine seemed happy enough for a day or two. We fished methodically and he took pictures. Fishermen casting, or wading, or tying on a fly while standing conveniently in front of an ancient churchyard. He'd pose you carefully one minute and then tell you to just do whatever it was you were doing the next.

At first he'd be saying, "Yes! Great! Perfect!" all the time he was shooting, but then he started muttering things like, "No," "No good," or "Nope, not weird enough."

"Not weird enough?" I asked.

"Any idiot can take a picture of a man fishing," he said. "Anyway, the magazine likes weird photos. That's why they hired me. And by the way," he added, "is someone going to catch a fish soon?"

Don did catch a fish the next day when we rotated up to the Falls beat. It was about eleven o'clock in the evening, just dusk that far north, and he was casting to a salmon that had boiled several times more or less in the same spot. Tom said, "Now that's a taking fish," and Don had started down the bank saying, "Let's see."

A "taker" is the salmon everyone is looking for. It's the one fish in God knows how many that, for reasons of its own, will take your fly. This may have to do with habit or the memory of feeding, aggression, curiosity, playfulness, the fish's freshness from the sea, time of day, time of the most recent tide, weather, water conditions, fly pattern, a defective hypothalamus or some combination thereof. It's a mystery but, since it ultimately has to do with sex, the odd moodiness of it also seems vaguely familiar. One thing is clear: A taking fish is defined after the fact. As Matthew told me, "A taker is the one you caught, if you catch one."

"How do you know that's a taker?" I asked Tom.

"Just a guess," he said.

And then Don caught the fish, a lovely fourteen pounder. It was what they call a "bright fish," fresh from the ocean with sea lice still on it and shiny as a chrome bumper. We all ran down to watch him land it and take some photos, even though the light was almost gone. All of us except Scott, that is. He hadn't come out with us after dinner. In fact, it seemed as if he vanished about the time Jane went home.

Come to think of it, Laine wasn't there either. Earlier that day he'd begun mumbling about taking a different approach and needing some props. No one had seen him since.

It turns out that Laine had driven into the nearest town and, after hours of haggling, had rented an ornate old grandfather clock from the suspicious owner of an antique shop. When we came in that night it was lying in pieces in the front hall.

"What's it for?" Dick asked at breakfast the next day.

"I don't know exactly," Laine said, "but, you know, it's about time shares, so I felt I needed a large clock."

Dick nodded thoughtfully. There *was* a certain logic to it.

We were late getting on the water that day because it took an hour or more to drag out Don's salmon and pose it and him in every way any of us could think of. Then someone else would have to pose with it so Don could get some shots. After all, it was his fish. And then you'd have to do everything both with and without the ghillie, who would have been happy to get done with this foolishness and get on the water. "This is a good deal of excitement over one fish," he said.

Laine followed us around for another day and a half, taking candid shots, posing each of us in turn at the scenic Back of the Castle Pool, fooling with fill-in flashes and reflectors and generally waiting for someone else to catch a fish.

It seemed as if all of us fishermen were waiting for the same thing. That's what it feels like: the repetitive, almost hypnotic cast, drift, step; cast, drift, step. You're not so much fishing as you are waiting for a fish.

Of course as writers we had other things to think about. Presumably Don had at least the germ of his story, but what about the rest of us? Fishing with fishing writers is strange enough anyway, but when almost everyone is getting skunked and searching for a new angle, the conversation can get pretty weird. You'll make some idle comment like, "Well, it's a pretty spot anyway, with those castle towers poking up above the trees," and someone will say, "Yeah, man, there's your lead."

Scott seemed to be sublimely above all this, taking the lack of fish philosophically, but he *was* under some strain. In the evenings he'd say he was bushed and was going to turn in early. Then in the morning we'd come down to find him in the kitchen chatting quietly with Jane as she cooked breakfast. But it was all just a little bit *too* discreet, and peeking into his room was too much of a temptation for some of us. Sure enough, the bed hadn't been slept in, not that it was any of our business, of course.

Then later, out on the river, Scott would turn up missing

again, only to be found curled up in the tall grass sleeping like a baby. When he'd get caught at it he'd say something like, "Gee, this salmon fishing is more strenuous than I thought."

One day Laine and some of the others decided to photograph one of the great lunches we were having catered at the fishing huts. (The angle everyone seemed to be working on now had more to do with cuisine than fishing.) We hauled the table outside—for natural light and the river as a background—and Laine, Tom and Don began arranging food, wine, wicker picnic baskets, two-handed fly rods and Dick into the perfect *Gourmet Magazine*-style composition.

Of course no two photographers think alike, so there was some disagreement about what should go where. I didn't have an opinion, so I was standing off to the side, out of the way. Scott sidled up beside me and asked, quietly, "Ever hear the expression, 'high-speed goat fuck'?"

I said, "No, but I like it."

Someone commented that the only thing missing was a salmon, at which point Matthew jumped into his little pickup with the dog kennels in the back and roared off down a dirt road. I thought he'd gone to the cottage to get Don's fish, but instead he came back in ten minutes with a nice grilse (young salmon) of about seven or eight pounds. The fish was so fresh that, although he'd killed it, it was still twitching.

Someone said, "Perfect!" but I thought, Wait a minute, if the ghillie knows where a fish can be caught that easily, shouldn't he be putting one of us on it? One of us like me, maybe?

It was just an idle thought. The grilse did complete the photograph and Dick, who'd been standing at the head of the table holding a glass of wine and wearing a frozen smile, seemed relieved to finally hear the shutters clicking.

"May I drink this now?" he asked.

• • •

On the fifth day we trudged back to the hut on the Home beat for lunch and Dick, who looked a little confused, said that before we sat down to eat, Laine would like to see us all up at the cruvies, in waders, with our rods.

We drove up to the house, and when we got out of the van I heard bagpipes. They were faint, but unmistakable.

"Scott," I said, "do you hear pipes?"

"Yeah, I do," he answered sleepily, "but I wasn't gonna say anything."

It seems that the same day Laine had rented the clock, he'd also engaged the services of a piper; an authentic Highlander in a kilt, bearskin hat, dagger in his boot, the whole catastrophe. By the time we arrived Laine had the clock sitting in a shallow riffle out in the river with a battery of lights and reflectors trained on it. Don's salmon had been resurrected and was lying on the bank. It was a couple of days old now; its eyes were glazed, its jaw was locked open and it was starting to look pretty dead.

The piper was standing back in the trees to keep out of the light drizzle. He was playing his heart out because, as near as he could figure, that's what he'd been hired to do.

I've always loved the sound of bagpipes—played well, they make me want to either cry or fight—but I noticed Matthew cringing every time the guy launched into another tune.

"Don't you like this stuff?" I asked.

"Well," he said, "a little of it goes a long way, doesn't it?"

I thought, of course: punk rock, spiked hair, pale girls dressed in leather. Our immediate surroundings notwithstanding, this is still the twentieth century.

Over the next two hours, in a steady light rain, Laine posed every possible combination of one grandfather clock, one piper, one dead fish, five fishermen and one bored ghillie with a long-handled landing net. He was the only one not wearing rain gear and he was soaked to the skin.

"This is it!" he kept shouting. "Time! Salmon! Scotland!" Then he'd rush to adjust some small detail. "What time should the clock say?" he asked of no one in particular. I guess we were watching genius at work.

Dick was a little puzzled by all this, but he wasn't shocked. Over the last few days you could see him slowly getting used to us. We asked some impertinent questions, but then we were writers. Sometimes our language was a little rough, especially after a few drinks, and we seemed to prefer the company of the help instead of the rich sports, but then we were Americans.

I didn't think Dick cared about Scott "taking up with the cook," as he put it, until we rotated back up to the Falls beat on the last day and Scott wasn't there because he'd disappeared with Jane again. Dick didn't say much, but he was clearly scandalized, so I asked, "Does this really bother you?"

"Who's bonking who isn't my business," he said, "but one simply *does not* give up a salmon beat."

As near as I can tell from the little bit of reading I've done, fly-fishing for Atlantic salmon is based on the premise that anything that can happen will, eventually. There are many theories on when, where and on what fly pattern salmon will bite, but, by all accounts, no theory produces fish often enough to be proven true.

Even the experts speak in italics. There *should* be a fresh run off this last tide; this fly *should* work in this pool, if only because it has, off and on, for generations. When salmon aren't caught—which is most of the time—these people take a kind of sly comfort in the fact that, given the circumstances, you really ought not to be able to catch them at all. Meanwhile, the accommodations are posh, the food is good, the booze flows freely and there's the general feeling that things are as they should be.

This would seem like an expensive snipe hunt except that you see fish. Some are boiling and porpoising, others are jumping to dislodge sea lice. Jumpers won't bite, they said, and that was the only statement about salmon I heard that wasn't followed by several contradictory footnotes.

You put yourself through this because some fishermen say catching an Atlantic salmon on a fly is as good as sex, even though you know in your heart it isn't. I agree with a friend of mine who says that if fishing is really like sex, then he's doing one of them wrong. Still, there do seem to be similarities.

For one thing—as the salmon fishers tell it—either you catch a fish way too soon, before you're fully able to appreciate it, or you have to wait much longer than you think you should have to, so that when you finally hook and land one the elation is tempered by a profound sense of relief.

And, of course, repeated failures don't lead you to the logical conclusion; they only whet your appetite.

Back at the cottage in the evenings, the more experienced salmon fishers—Clive, Dick and Tom—would hold forth. The river flowed by just outside the French doors. It was clear but, because all its water had first filtered through peat in the Highlands, it was slightly whiskey-colored in the deep pools. The way to catch salmon, they said, is to keep your fly in the river and be of good cheer. They didn't seem to understand it either, but they still appeared to possess a kind of wisdom.

It reminded me of when I was a kid and some grown man would decide to take me aside and give me the kindly lecture on women. He'd fall into this vague, humorous mode, trying not to let on that, although he had considerably more experience than I did, he still didn't know what the hell he was talking about.

Apparently, the genuine salmon fisher takes pride in his acquired tastes, strength of character, fine sense of irony and apparent craziness, which he and a few other aficionados know isn't really craziness but, well, something else entirely. As a trout fisherman, I used to think I understood that, but salmon types look down on us trouters as dilettantes. I mean, we catch what I now think of as quite a few fish. Small ones by comparison, but fish nonetheless.

• • •

We fished for six days and took Sunday off, not because we were tired or discouraged, but because it's illegal to fish for salmon on Sunday. I asked why, but no one knew. It's just always been that way. We took the rented van and, with Dick as guide, drove up into the Highlands to look around. All of us except Scott, of course. By now, no one had to wonder where Scott had gone.

I kept dozing off in the backseat. When you've fished long and hard and it's become obvious that you're not going to catch anything, it's a relief to finally stop and let it all sink in. As it sank in, I tended to lose consciousness.

On the flight over, Tom had gone into that old salmon-fishing refrain: *You've gotta understand you might not catch one*, and I'd said, maybe a little impatiently, that I understood that. "You understand it intellectually," he said, "but if you really *don't* catch one, there's a hump you'll have to get over."

Right. I could see that now. You have to learn to see yourself not catching fish as if from a great theoretical height.

I also realized that I liked it and that I'd probably do it again, and then again if I had to, until I finally hooked and landed one of the damned things. To prove something, to be able to say I'd done it and because I knew it would be beautiful somehow; not like sex, of course, but in a way so weird that that's the only fair comparison. I also knew that this is how a life can be ruined by sport, and just as I was dozing off I had a vision of myself on a street corner with a tin cup and a sign reading, "NEVER COULD CATCH AN ATLANTIC SALMON ON A FLY ROD—PLEASE HELP."

The next morning, Dick drove Don and me to the airport at Inverness. Clive and Laine had left early, and Tom was staying on for a day and then heading to Russia, where there were bigger, dumber salmon that hadn't seen six hundred years' worth of flies. We could only guess at Scott's whereabouts. He hadn't been seen for at least a day and a half.

Dick was in a good mood. He said he'd enjoyed having us. "There was a lot of laughter this week," he said, "much more than usual. To be honest, some of the people who fish here are a little stuffy."

Then he asked, "Do you think we'll see Scott at the airport?"

There was some shrugging and throat clearing, and I thought, Would *I* be at the airport?

Dick drove on quietly for a minute and then said, "Well, if he turns up in the next few days, I'll see if I can find a little job for him."

(Author's note: Five months later, in Virginia City, Montana, Scott and Jane were married.)

CHAPTER

9

The Storm

*I*t was a good spring to be self-employed and a fisherman. From early April all the way into June the weather had been flipping back and forth more wildly than usual, even for Colorado—warmer when it got warm, bitter when it got cold, snowing when it should have just rained—but if you averaged it out it still amounted to what you'd expect: Things were waking up and, when you could catch it right, the fishing was good. But if you wanted to fish in the proper conditions, you had to be in a position to drop everything and go when things fell into place. At those times when things weren't as right as you thought, it was good if that wasn't your only day off.

The rocky weather muddied the trout streams early, broke some freshly leafed-out cottonwood trees with wet snow, pleased some farmers, worried some ranchers and brought complaints from spring turkey hunters, as well as the usual pissing and moaning from big-haired local television news-casters who can't understand that the American West is not the Bahamas.

Local bass fishers weren't whining because it's undigni-fied, but they did say the largemouths never really got on the spawning beds "in a meaningful way."

That's where it stood when Steve, Larry and I went to a private bass pond out east to try to re-create an earlier per-formance. We'd fished there a week before, dodged the weather successfully for a few hours and caught some good-sized fish before getting rained out. These bass were in ex-ceptionally fine shape—chunky and heavy—and we thought maybe the aborted spawn had saved them from getting beat up and then having to recover. In the long run, there'd be a missing generation of bass in the waters where they manage to reproduce naturally, while in the short run the fish were fatter and prettier than usual. In the interest of playing the ball where it lay, we thought we'd try them again, even though the odds are against pulling it off that well twice in a row.

On the long drive out to the pond, things seemed to be shap-ing up into a nice enough spring day. The air was warm and there were scattered puffy white cumulus clouds against a blue sky so perfect it looked like the underside of the uni-verse. Driving east, away from the foothills and out toward the Plains, the country always strikes me as enormous, but in that first bass-fishing weather it seems bigger yet, as if doors you'd forgotten you'd closed had been flung open. The conversation was louder than usual, both from happi-ness and because the windows in the pickup were rolled down.

The big, dark thunderstorm to the south looked as if it would blow past us by quite a few miles. Judging by the an-gle of the gray veil of rain trailing behind it, we figured it was going roughly west and a little north, while we were going east and a little south. There was no telling how far away it was without knowing its size, but I claimed—based on its purplish-black, almost eggplant color—that it was a great big one and, therefore, many miles off. With the air of a man who has just heard what he wanted to hear, whether he's completely convinced or not, Steve said, "No question about it," and quickly moved to a different subject: canoes, I think.

But by the time we got to the pond the storm had changed direction (or we'd guessed wrong in the first place), and it looked as if it was wheeling toward us. We stood watching it for a few minutes and agreed that we'd just get clipped by the extreme eastern edge of it—a cool, twenty-minute squall at the worst.

A breeze was already ruffling the pond, and it seemed the smartest thing to do would be to cast streamer flies from the bank, working the rough water in the shallows where fish might come in to see what was being stirred up. Little fish to eat the bugs, big fish to eat the little fish—the old by-the-book theory that works more often than most. We were still in sunlight, but the sky was troubled and the bright air felt chilly and damp. This was no time to launch Steve's and Larry's belly boats, let alone my fragile little canvas canoe.

By the time we had our rods strung up, the wind had gotten a little too strong for fly-casting. Steve tried, but no. When you have to hold your hat on your head with one hand and dodge your streamer fly, it's too windy. But the weather wasn't threatening enough yet to drive all three of us into the cramped cab of the pickup, so we took a walk. It was something to do, it would be bracing and we wouldn't get so far from the truck that we couldn't make it back in one good dash.

This pond lies in a low spot in an expanse of classic western high plains country. At first glance it's dry, open, rolling and scrubby—dramatic and severe—but of course it's populated by most of what are now the appropriate creatures, native and otherwise, many of which are attracted to the scattered, cottonwood-lined ponds. This is where you see herons, ducks, geese, pelicans and ibis and where the white-tailed deer you never see in daylight seem to grow up out of the ground at dusk.

This is settled, owned country where it's almost impossible to step off the road bed without permission and not be trespassing, but it's also pleasantly empty: few buildings, few paved roads, a couple of scattered oil wells. The fabled Rocky Mountains are back on the western horizon looking lower and closer than they really are.

This is not great pheasant country, but we saw two and heard at least another cock. The cackle of a cock pheasant sounds like the squeak of an oil well in need of lubrication and also the sound a loose, rusty barbed-wire fence makes in a gusty wind, but you do learn to tell the difference after a while.

As we strolled past a windbreak of trees, a mourning dove flapped off across the ground doing the injured-bird distraction routine, and we were able to find the nest. There were two young doves in it, just starting to get flight feathers.

There were all the usual magpies, cowbirds, blackbirds, starlings and such. And there was a western tanager and also a blue grosbeak, which was a new bird for me, one I'd always wanted to see.

I've always liked the way birds chatter when weather is moving in. They're like humans then, pointing out the obvious, having conversations like, "Hey, look." "Yeah, I see." Not long ago I read that the Tlingit Eskimos in Alaska think owls say, "Get under trees," when a storm is coming, and whenever they say that a storm *does* come.

The wind was really up by then and we decided to head back to the truck, which was the only real shelter in sight. For a while the sky had been blue with lit-up clouds almost yellow above the purple underside of the storm, but suddenly it was gray and somber, with just a line of bright weather to the north. I was carrying my hat because it wouldn't stay on my head, and I could feel a few raindrops on my bald spot.

Back at the pickup we ran into a pair of big peacocks. They came out of the trees to meet us, clearly used to people, but then realized we weren't who they thought we were and shied off a little. We knew the guy who owned this spread raised some exotic birds, but we didn't expect to see them two miles from the house.

We stood by the truck watching the edge of the storm slide in toward us. At a distance it looked almost stationary, but right above us the disk of cloud was scudding by pretty quickly. The tall, slate-gray part of the storm went right to the ground about two miles off in solid curtains of rain. On the edges we could see either filmy rain squalls or the beginnings of funnels, we couldn't be sure which.

The center of the storm was full of lightning, and we counted the seconds between the flash and the crack to see how far away it was. Not far. We noticed that the peacocks had hunkered down under the truck, so we decided to get into the cab ourselves. We were starting to get wet and the temperature seemed to have dropped by about twenty degrees.

It was a wonderful storm: The sky was dark, the rain was in nearly rhythmic, pulsing sheets that laid the cattails down flat. The pickup was broadside to the wind and it was high profile, a big, square '78 Ford with a topper on the bed and a canoe on top of that. It caught the air like a sail and rocked on its springs, making a sound like, oddly enough, a cock pheasant. To the south and west was a purple wall, but what we could see of the sky behind us to the north was clear, so we were just into the edge of this thing.

At the height of it there was some small but dangerously driving hail. Larry pointed at the roof of the cab and asked me if I was worried about my canvas canoe up there. I said, "Maybe a little, but I'm not gonna go out there and do anything about it."

"Yeah," he said, "that's probably wise. I was just asking."

We had a good time sitting in the truck for about forty-five minutes, not talking much because of the din of wind, rain, hail and thunder; just taking the occasional small nip from the flask of Southern Comfort and now and then yelling, "ISN'T THIS GREAT?" or "SON-OF-A-BITCH," or "IT'S GETTING KINDA COLD, ISN'T IT?" It occurred to me that this is something you have to look for in fishing partners: the quality of uncomplaining acceptance, or at least the ability to have a decent time even when things aren't going too well. To put it another way, you don't want to be trapped in a storm with a whiner.

Then I thought I saw something on the water, a funny movement, a shape that wasn't waves: something. I turned on the windshield wipers, which helped only a little. We were parked facing the pond, maybe ten feet from the bank.

I said, "Are there fish rising out there?"

Steve said, "No."

Larry leaned forward, squinting, and said, "I think I see what you see, but I don't know what it is."

I turned the wipers to high and we all leaned up over the dashboard. Yes, it was hard to see, but there appeared to be greenish-bronze shapes moving at the surface. Not logs, not weeds, too substantial to be water shaped by the wind, too green to be carp (and there are no carp in there that I know of), too big to be panfish. I opened the door and leaned out. Before I could even focus I was soaked all down the right side, but I could just make it out.

"God damn it," I said, "there are bass rising right in front of us."

Larry opened his door, leaned out for a second, then slammed it closed again and said, "Yeah, maybe."

Steve sat between us holding the Southern Comfort and said, "No."

"Get out and look," I said.

"No."

• • •

We got on the water when it was all but over. The storm had bashed off to the northwest and the thunder had gone from loud cracks to dull, retreating rolls. Gusts of cool wind were blowing themselves out in the trees. The pond was nearly still and the sun was back out, even though a thin drizzle was still sifting down from a great height. The peacocks seemed blissfully unconcerned. They were high-stepping through puddles of clay-colored water and pecking at seeds and bugs. The air was sweet and magical, and I thought of a line written years ago by my old, mad poet friend Marc Campbell: "Peacocks strolled beside the lake/Like illuminated manuscripts."

I launched my canoe while Steve and Larry were getting into waders and flippers and skidding their float tubes down to the water through the dripping grass. The canoe's caned seat was wet from splattered rain, but there was no hail damage to the leathery hull.

I made a quick, ten-minute tour of the pond just to feel the little boat glide, passing Steve and Larry twice as they paddled their tubes over to the good bank. I like belly boats when I'm in one, but when I'm next to them in a canoe I feel like a swan.

Then I tied off to a bleached stick and flipped a little cork popper into the flooded timber. After a few casts I had a big bluegill and then, out of thicker cover, I got a heavy, fifteen-inch bass. I held him in the water for a few seconds before letting him go and thought, That's what I saw boiling around in the shallows during the storm; same shape, same color, only bigger than anything I've ever seen or caught here before.

It wasn't what you'd call useless information, just too small a piece to too large a puzzle, like when, once every two or three generations, it rains frogs. Okay, but if you *want* frogs, there are better ways to get them than standing in the backyard with a bucket. A friend tells me that trying to figure out things like this is like teaching a pig to sing. It may be interesting, but in the end it's a waste of time and it annoys the pig.

We all caught some fish, but the storm had cooled things off, so there wasn't the usual flurry of feeding right at dusk. We fished until dark anyway, going the last half hour or so without a strike. The pond was like a smooth disk by then, but rainwater was still dripping from the trees and spattering in the shallows near shore, making a narrow band of muddy water. Both the bluegills and the bass seemed to be cruising along the edge of it, right where the water cleared.

The closest town was closed up and pretty much deserted, but Larry said he knew of a good, cheap Mexican joint that might still be open. It was two blocks off the one-story main street, with a warehouse on one side and railroad tracks on the other.

"La-something," he said.

"Cocina?" I said. (Half of all Mexican restaurants in the west are known as "The Kitchen.")

"No," Larry said, "La-something else."

They had just closed when we walked in, but when all three of us looked pitiful the guy told us to sit down while he saw if he could still whip something up. When he came back with some beers, he nodded at the bass bug stuck in Larry's baseball cap and said, "You been fishing?"

"Yup."

"Where?"

We told him, vaguely: "A pond sort of near Such-and-Such."

"That tornado out there give you any trouble?" he asked.

"Not much," Larry answered.

"Well," the guy said, "we still got some enchiladas."

10

Getting Lost

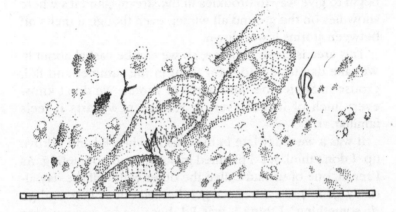

*E*d Engle and I were hunting snowshoe hares in a stretch
of northern Colorado not far from where I live that's a little
too low to be properly "in the mountains" the way tourists
mean that, but still a bit too high and rugged to be considered the foothills. It's not remote, but it's nicely in between,
so it doesn't get a lot of traffic.

Technically, this is where the foothills and montane forests
blend together at an altitude of around eight thousand feet,
with the mixed textures of juniper, red cedar, Douglas fir, aspen and ponderosa, lodgepole and limber pines. Not all together, of course, but shading together, with odd patches
and stands here and there. It's all thick, western woods. There
are no meadows, and even small clearings are rare.

This transition zone is one of the richest parts of the mountains around here and my friends and I are automatically
drawn to it. There are lots of different trees and shrubs, and

lots of wildlife. This is where the cottontail rabbits begin to thin out and the snowshoe hares take over. There are scattered but dependable pockets of blue grouse up there, deer, elk, plenty of coyotes and bobcats, the odd fox, two kinds of squirrel and so on.

This is roughly the altitude where brown and rainbow trout begin to give way to brookies in the streams, and it's where snow lies on the ground all winter, even though it melts off between storms lower down.

This area is close to home, so we can be casual about it. We take day trips into it for trout in the summer and fall, grouse in September and hares in winter. We don't know every inch of it, but even in strange new parts it feels familiar.

It was a weekday late in the season when Ed and I drove up. I don't think we'd planned in advance to go hunting. As I recall, one of us had called the other with half the day already gone and said, "Let's get the hell out of here and go *do* something." I think it was Ed, because he was working on a book that winter, and when he's deep into a big project, he sometimes explodes out the door with a firearm or fly rod, depending on the season.

This was a cold, heavily overcast day with a good base of snow down and a fresh cover falling lightly, straight down, without a breath of wind. This is perfect, of course, because every track you see that looks fresh *is* fresh.

This was an area we'd only started hunting that season, but it had turned out to hold lots of hares, so we'd been in there four or five times, not enough to really come to know the place, but enough to have become a little bit casual about where we were. You know how that is.

Ed had discovered this spot the summer before when he moved up from Colorado Springs to work for the Forest Service in the Boulder District. It's a sizable chunk of Forest land that, for one reason or another, most people don't understand to be public—including me until recently. When we took a mutual friend up there he said to me, "It's interesting that you've missed this for fifteen years or so and Ed found it in one summer."

"That's why I hang out with the guy," I said.

Ed and I left the pickup on the snowy dirt road, strapped on our snowshoes and waddled roughly south until the land began to fall off into the narrow east-west valley. Here we split up. Ed likes to hunt the aspen bottoms where the hares feed, while I prefer the ridge sides where the animals' forms are. A "form" is the somewhat sheltered spot where a hare will sit out the time he's not feeding. Usually it's next to a pile of rocks, a tree, a stump or something else that will break the wind.

My theory is that the hares eat in the mornings and evenings and often at night, even in winter. (Actually, it's not *my* theory, it's what the books say.) I think they then hop up onto the hillsides where they sit in form through most of the day, resting and digesting. At least that's how I hunt them, and it works as often as not.

Then again, the fact that Ed gets them down in the aspen bottoms means that this is somewhat short of the whole truth, not that the whole truth matters that much.

Anyway, I'll cruise a hillside not too far up from the brushy bottom where the tracks in the snow will be matted and crosshatched as if fifty animals had wandered through there the night before, although in fact, it was probably more like three or four. When I find a single track heading uphill in a more or less straight line, I follow it.

There's a certain logic to this. That is, there *will be* an animal at the end of the tracks; the trick is to pick out a fresh, readable trail and then be able to stay with it. On a calm, cold day after a fresh snow, it's not that hard, but all kinds of things can screw it up.

In fluffy powder, all tracks can look fuzzy and aged. A track left in wet snow that then freezes in a cold snap can be a week old and still look fresh. Wind can age a track in a matter of minutes, and so can falling snow, or old snow sifting down from the trees, or an hour of warm, high-altitude sunlight. A hare that's run from soft snow onto a crusty patch can seem to have taken flight, although if you look carefully you may find faint claw marks.

A snowshoe hare tracker pays closer attention to the condition of the snow than a skier, and he should also have a pretty good idea of what the weather was like yesterday and last night.

I've gotten fairly good at tracking, but there are still days when it baffles me, even though I may know, in an intellectual sense, what must have happened. I have learned to walk next to hare tracks instead of in them in case I have to go back and start all over again. To me it's like Spanish. Living here in the West for so long, I've picked it up a little bit, by which I mean I can order *huevos* and *cerveza*, and sometimes understand simple directions spoken slowly, but I can't read the poetry.

The tracking is the art, but the shooting can be pretty simple. If you've done it right—following the tracks with your eyes as far ahead as you can see, and then scanning the ground—you'll spot the hare sitting, and in thick woods the ranges are close.

I used to use a .22, but now, in the interests of class and sport, I carry a .36-caliber flintlock squirrel rifle, complete with fifty-five inches of tiger stripe maple stock. This thing is handsome, heavy and difficult to shoot, and there's some suspense inherent in the fact that sometimes it chooses not to go off. You'll never fully understand the meaning of the phrase "just a flash in the pan" until you've had your flintlock misfire on a hunt.

Anyway, the rifle saves me from having to admit that the shooting part of it doesn't require much skill.

Snowshoe hares really are amazing animals. Around here they live in the roughest country starting at, let's say, around seven thousand feet and ranging all the way up to the scrubby brush above timberline, although they seem to like forests best. They're active throughout the coldest months when they manage to scrabble out a living on twigs, buds and the bark of young aspens. They're also known to be fond of frozen meat and will gnaw on the carcasses of dead animals.

Because they live where the snow gets deep, they have evolved unusually large, fuzzy hind feet that act as snowshoes, hence the name. It's even been said that these hares gave the American Indians the idea for snowshoes, although that's probably just an informed guess.

In summer these animals are brown and look like oversized cottontails, but in winter they turn white for camouflage, and their primary survival tactic is to sit motionless while a predator just walks by. Their secondary tactic is speed, and they can really move. I've measured the tracks of running hares at as much as six feet apart.

The meat is excellent, although older animals can be a little tough and should be stewed or marinated. In many parts of Europe, wild hare is a delicacy, and it would be here, too, if we paid more attention to what we eat.

The glossy hair from the hind feet is used as wings on a trout fly called a Usual, and the under fir on the body is good dubbing for dry flies and nymphs. It's a pale tan color (only the guard hairs turn white), so it's good to dye or to blend with other colors for shading and texture.

Hares are everywhere in the right kind of habitat, but as white bunnies frozen on the snow, they're not easy to find. Once found, they can materialize, vanish or seem to fly low over the ground in a disturbingly ghostly way. They're great to watch, even while they're getting away.

I think the fascination I have with game animals, fish and birds is a kind of envy. They live in and with wild country in a way I can't with my technology, my need for comfort and my poor, slow, hairless body.

Here in Colorado, the daily bag limit on snowshoe hares is ten, but I can't remember ever getting more than three or four in a single trip, and one or two amounts to a good outing. In that way it's like fishing. It goes on and on—good, poor, occasionally fabulous—and some days it seems that this could last forever.

Not long ago a friend asked me if I wanted to go hunt bunnies with him in Wyoming. It seems he'd found this place where there were thousands of them. It was easy shooting, he said, and he and his friends had gotten thirty-five apiece on the last trip. (I didn't ask what the legal limit in Wyoming was, but I had to wonder.) Tales of slaughter can get to a hunter, but I said no. I told him that if I shot thirty-five of them, my freezer would be full and my personal bunny season would be over for the year. I'd rather get them a few at a time and keep hunting. It ends soon enough as it is.

So, Ed and I split up in the bottom to pursue our different theories. I'd hunted the two facing ridges a few times before so, just for a change, I decided to cross the valley, climb the next ridge and hunt the slope down on the far side. It would be a little piece of new country that I'd better see soon if I didn't want to wait until next fall. Sure, I could go up there after the small game season ended at the end of February and just take a walk, but I knew I wouldn't.

It took some doing to get where I wanted to be. It was steep going down and steep going up the far side. The snow was crusty under a thin cover of powder, so sometimes my snowshoes didn't bite and I'd slip. Of course a hare doesn't have this problem. In deep, soft snow he spreads his toes to gain surface area; on hard snow he brings them together; and on crust he digs in his claws. (You don't need to study bunny physiology to know this; you can see it clearly in the tracks.) Anyway, human-made snowshoes are neat and useful, but they're a poor approximation of the real thing.

On the top of the ridge—a place I'd never been before—the trees were shorter and the snow had been dusted off by the wind so that it was only an inch or two deep, polished hard and punctuated with bare, rocky spots.

Hares don't like it on the tops of ridges. There's nothing tender to feed on up there, and they like to be out of the wind when they're sitting in form. I also believe they use the deep snow on the slopes to get away from predators, skipping over the surface of it while the bobcat, fox or coyote that's after them bogs down.

I hurried over the top—snowshoes scraping on exposed rocks—and just before starting down into the deep, fluffy snow on the far side I heard the single, muffled crack of Ed's .22 rifle. So, he had a bunny. Ed is not the type to whang away at improvised targets while hunting. Nor is he the type to miss.

Once I was well down the far slope I turned to my left. That, I figured, would take me out the ridge more or less to the east. When it was time to come out, I'd simply climb the ridge again, drop over the other side into the familiar valley, and up the hill to the north would be the road. When I hit it, the truck would be to the left. Simple.

I hadn't shuffled twenty steps in that direction when I spotted a hare hunkered down stock still next to a fallen tree. Believing in his white camouflage right to the end, he just sat there and I shot him. Sometimes hunting is *not* a great drama.

I wondered if Ed had heard the shot. Possibly not. There was snow on the ground, snow in the air and a ridge top between us. And, for that matter, the muzzleloader makes a duller thump than the sharp crack of the .22.

It was late in the season, as I said, ten days until the end, in fact, and I had already eaten a number of snowshoe hares that winter. I wasn't exactly tired of them, but as I dressed this one out I thought maybe I'd make something special with him: roast him in sour cream and wine perhaps, or serve him fried with a goat cheese sauce. I've noticed that the fancy cooking starts late in the season.

A brace of bunnies would have been nice, but the hillside didn't produce. There were only a few old tracks fading in the fresh snow, and no other hares that I could find. Maybe there were no juicy young aspens down in the bottom on this side, or maybe the bottom was so far down there that the hares didn't climb this high on the ridge. I have come to think that the high ridges separate populations of snowshoe hares because the bunnies don't like to cross them, but I can't prove that.

I could have gone down the slope to see what was there, but it was getting a little too late for any more exploring. In fact, it was getting late enough to start thinking about heading back.

I'd gone about a mile to a mile and a half out the slope, so I figured I'd go over the top where I was, drop down into the valley, and then angle west and up on the far side. That way I'd cut either the road or my own tracks from where I came in.

So I did that: up the slope, across the windswept crest and then down the far side. I was swinging along—as well as one can swing along in snowshoes—supremely confident that I knew exactly where I was and where I was going.

About halfway down one of my snowshoe bindings came loose and I stopped to fix it. When I straightened up I looked over at the far ridge through the falling snow and it occurred to me that it was both lower and about three times farther away than it should have been.

Bummer.

I looked around. I don't know why, but I always look around at a time like that as if there's going to be a sign nailed to a tree saying "YOUR TRUCK IS THIS WAY," complete with an arrow.

If this sort of thing has ever happened to you, you know it represents a crucial moment. The difference between being lost and being just temporarily turned around is simply a matter of attitude. If you approach it as an interesting problem, you are momentarily disoriented. If you freak out, you're lost.

I figured a compass reading would be a good place to start, but after a few minutes of rummaging around I realized that the compass was in the pocket of the jeans I'd worn last time, and that said jeans were hanging over the back of a chair at home.

The check is in the mail; I'm from the government and I'm here to help you; the compass is in my other pants.

I had a pretty good idea of what I'd done. I must have walked to a point where the valley had swung south, making the ridge fall off to the east instead of continuing in that direction forever. Instead of making the 180-degree swing over the top, I'd made more of a 90-degree track, so I was going parallel to the road instead of toward it: east instead of north, looking across a wider valley at a hillside I'd never seen before.

That had to be it, right? I had never looked at a topographic map of the area so I couldn't be absolutely sure, and the sky was a uniform flat gray, so I couldn't locate the sun for a fix. But what else could have happened? All I'd have to do was follow the hillside around until the far ridge got closer and higher like it should be. That would head me west, and a right turn would point me north, toward the road.

That had to be it, but if it wasn't I'd be spending the night out. There was enough daylight left for one try, but not two. I wouldn't have died or anything. I'd spent two unplanned nights out in the woods in the past and hadn't died either time. I guess I had been a little worried and sleepless those nights, but in the end the worst part had been the embarrassment.

This time I even had a rabbit to eat, although it would be tough and dry, roasted over an open fire, no goat cheese sauce, no California cabernet.

The woods seemed profoundly quiet, although I could hear the almost imperceptible white noise of light snow sifting through pine needles.

Of course there was an easy way out of this. Behind me stretched my own snowshoe tracks that would lead nowhere but back to the truck. They were filling with snow, but that was happening slowly. Even dusted over, the trail was deep and wide enough to follow easily in the failing light.

So I backtracked. It added a mile or more to the hike, but

it was a sure thing. I found the road right at dark and Ed was waiting at the truck.

Ten days later, February 28, Steve and I went back to the same place one final time to observe the last day of the season. It was a low-key hunt, the most memorable part of which were some sets of tracks Steve called me over to look at. You could clearly see where a bobcat had chased a hare, at one point getting close enough to pull out a few tufts of his white fur amidst a jumble of footprints. The hare had finally gotten away, and the cat tracks seemed to just vanish in a grove of trees. We thought maybe he'd climbed one of them and we looked for him for a long time. We never saw him, but he could well have been up in there somewhere. These were tall spruce trees with their tight needles packed with snow. There could have been a bear up there and we wouldn't have seen it.

All this was very fresh, and we discussed the possibility of following the tracks of the escaped hare, but Steve said he thought maybe the bunny had paid his dues for today already and didn't deserve to be shot. That sounded reasonable. Maybe a small act of kindness is appropriate on the last day of the season.

Steve headed off to find another set of tracks, and I decided to go find the place where I'd gotten lost and turned back the last time. It took me less than a half hour to get there, and I walked right to it as if it was a familiar bus stop.

So, I had been right that day; I had known exactly where I was and had simply lost my nerve, opting against having faith in myself.

It was a rather pretty spot, actually: a pine-forested hillside with the trees spaced wide and parklike and a jumbled rock outcrop standing to what I now knew for sure was the west. But I didn't remember it as pretty when I was lost there. Then it was just a strange place, a single, useless coordinate, like one of those "you are here" markers without the rest of the map. If I was the lover of the outdoors I claim to be, I would have at least taken a second to think, "Well, wherever the hell I am, it's sort of a nice place."

Interesting. Something to think about during that long wait from the end of February until the fishing starts.

My old tracks were faint, but still readable. I could see where I'd come down the ridge, stopped to check the snowshoe binding, paced around in a tight circle a few times, and then started back along the old trail.

Funny, I don't remember pacing.

11

On the Ice

*I*t was novelist Jim Harrison who said that ice-fishing is "the moronic sport," and he lives in Michigan, so he should know. Still, that's not entirely fair, because it actually takes some skill, patience, understanding and fortitude to do it right. (An actual moron would catch a few fish, but not many.) But at the same time, every fisherman sort of knows what he means. There's something about sitting on a frozen, windswept lake staring down that eight-inch-diameter hole that looks—at least from a distance—like the primitive equivalent of watching television.

For a long time the ice-fishing I did was out of desperation. As a kid in Minnesota, I went because the men went and I naturally wanted to be a man, although a little ice-fishing got me to wondering if I really wanted to grow up so fast after all.

Here in Colorado I got back into it because it helped fill those long, dark months when nothing much else was going on outside. It didn't exactly cure the shack nasties, but after a day of ice-fishing, sitting around the house being bored didn't seem so bad after all.

Once I was ice-fishing a big, flatland reservoir for perch and walleyes. I had a small pile of fish lying on the ice and it wasn't so cold that I was quite miserable yet, but it was still one of those dank, leaden days when the chill really registers as the absence of something. You stand there with hands in pockets watching the two shades of gray where the sky and the horizon meet, and if you're not careful you'll start cataloging your regrets.

I'd spotted an odd-looking bump about a hundred yards farther out on the ice and finally, just for something to do, I wandered over to see what it was. It was a prairie dog, frozen dead in a posture I really don't care to describe. I can't begin to imagine what he was even doing out of his burrow on a day like that, let alone half a mile out on a frozen lake.

If you spend a lot of time outside, things like this are like strange little gifts, in this case a simple illustration, without editorial comment, labeled, "Mortality: for what it's worth." It was getting late anyway, so I got my fish and went home where it was bright and warm.

As I've gotten older I see that there's a positive, bioregional perspective to sports like this that most objective observers would think are no fun at all. Throughout much of the world, the lakes freeze in the winter, but fish can still be caught through holes in the ice if you possess the old knowledge. Once, knowing about things like that was crucial to survival and even now it seems more than just interesting. It is a thing to do in the place where I live, so it's compelling. And if it's sometimes desolate and uncomfortable, well, as Gary Snyder says, "Life in the wild is not just eating berries in the sunlight."

• • •

That's how I'd come to think of the sport when I fell in with a couple of guys who were serious ice fishers. That is, they fished year-round, but they seemed to prefer doing it through the ice. When they caught trout from pretty mountain lakes in the summer with fly rods, they said they learned things about the fish and the structure that came in handy later, when they could walk to wherever they wanted to be on the lake instead of just casting from shore. I know, that's hard to picture, but there *are* different ways of looking at things.

These men also fished for trout in a style that was unfamiliar to me at the time. Instead of sitting on an overturned bucket watching a bobber—a pose that can suggest either prayer or the contemplation of suicide—you lie face down on the ice with a blanket over your head, look through the hole and watch the fish.

It's not as bad as it sounds. For one thing, you lie on a foam pad, and my friends had even designed a pad with a hole in one end to fit over the hole in the ice, stubby wings of foam on either side for your elbows and attached hoods. You carry your pad rolled up under your arm or, if you're going some distance, strapped to the top flap of your pack like a sleeping bag. When you get where you want to be, you bore your hole, place the pad over it and point yourself into the wind to keep the hood from blowing off. You're dressed for serious cold weather and the hood cuts the breeze, so it can actually be pretty cozy in there.

But the best part is how well you can see. These guys fish in no more than ten feet of water—usually less—and when the conditions are right it's like looking into a well-lit aquarium. You can see everything: individual grains of gravel, nymphs and scuds crawling on the live green vegetation and, of course, the trout. This is the most visual kind of fishing I've ever done and, although fishermen always say this, you really can have a great time whether you catch anything or not.

The right conditions include clear water, a day at least

moderately bright and a windswept lake where most of the snow has been dusted off. Too much snow dampens the light and things can get pretty murky down there.

For a fly fisherman like me, the actual fishing tackle is disturbingly simple: a small spool of monofilament line, a pair of clippers and a handful of jigs. That's it. It all fits neatly into one coat pocket, leaving both hands free to lug the rolled-up pad and an auger.

Although I claim to admire sparseness, I don't think I'll ever get used to this. True, a real outdoorsman carries only the tools he needs and depends more on cunning than technology, but I can't get it out of my head that if you want to catch lots of fish, you should have lots of stuff, or at least a varnished bamboo spool for your hand line.

Once you're in place and your eyes have become accustomed to the light, you lower your jig until it's about a foot off the bottom. Then you wait for a fish. (That last sentence should probably be followed by five or six blank pages to illustrate the potential weight of it.)

I'm calling the things you use here "jigs" because that's how I know them—small, lead-headed lures with their single hooks riding up—but I understand that some purists insist on calling them "ice flies," which I have to admit sounds better to the ear of a fly caster. I guess I sometimes grasp at aesthetic straws here, if only because fishing without a rod seems as if it should be illegal. Whatever you call them, they are usually nonrepresentational, tending toward clunky and heavy on the bright colors. My friends said it was hard to find good ones.

So I got some standard one-thirty-second-ounce jig heads and tied some flies on them: Hares Ear soft hackles, Zug Bugs and Damsel nymphs with heads painted to match the bodies and two-tone enamel eyeballs. They looked good, more like something a trout should want to eat, and I gave a hand-

ful to each of my friends. They were duly impressed. "Yeah,"
the one guy said, "*that's* what I meant."

The flies caught fish—suddenly they did seem more like
flies—but I have to say they never quite replaced the black-
bodied Tube Jigs or White Walleys that are local favorites.
When the pretty ice flies were finally all gone, I didn't bother
to replace them because I didn't have to. By then I had also
learned that a proper ice fisher buys his few sparse items of
tackle at the hardware store like everyone else. In one sense,
style is just style, but it does grow out of actual conditions
so it shouldn't be ignored. When you're ice-fishing, there's
no reason to get classy, and a couple of reasons not to.

But if the gear isn't especially snazzy, there are still plenty
of elegant little tricks to it that unfold slowly, even in the
company of experts.

One November we hiked into a high-country lake not far
from here. It seemed way too early to ice-fish, but my friends
assured me this is how it's done.

"Look," one of them said, "you go way up high early because the ice is safe sooner up there and because if you wait
too long it will be two feet thick."

Sure, that's obvious once you think about it, and there was
also an undertone of experience to it, as if two-foot-thick ice
was more than just a sterile concept.

I showed up for the trip with the usual gear, including the
auger, which one of the guys pointed to and said, "Don't
bring that."

"Why not?"

"Because you won't want to carry it where we're going."

The day was bright, clear and crisp—good shirtsleeve
walking weather. We slogged up a steep hill from the trailhead (not on the trail, this was a shortcut) and worked our
way west along a dry, rocky ridge. I knew it would be colder
up high, but a safely frozen lake still seemed unlikely.

We cut a trail and followed it uphill through open pine,

then denser spruce and fir. It was chillier in the trees and we
hit the first snow at about nine thousand feet. It was just a
dusting on the ground at first, but it got deeper as we gained
altitude. When the snow was about ankle-deep, just enough
to drag each step a little, we stopped to rest and pull on
sweaters. Even with the uphill grind, it was getting brisk.

The last mile or so was agonizing. The snow had gotten
knee-deep, crusty on top, powdery underneath. We took
turns breaking trail to the top of a deeply forested ridge and
then started downhill to the north. We'd put on the waterproof wind suits to keep from getting wet.

The steep pitch down to the lake wasn't long, but this was
a north-facing slope and the snow was waist-deep in places.
I'm convinced it couldn't have been negotiated without the
help of gravity. Luckily, we could go back up though our own
trail.

The lake itself was small, maybe ten acres, and set in a
deep cirque. A little creek drainage fell off to the southeast,
and to the northwest was a looming, distinctively horseshoe-
shaped mountain. The mountain and the lake have the same
name, and it's one I promised not to divulge.

The rocks visible above timberline were all but dusted
bare, but down in the trees the snow was piled deep and
undisturbed except for the odd tracks of pine squirrels and
snowshoe hares. The lake, however, was swept down to clear,
gray-blue ice and when we stepped out onto it we could feel
the cold wind that must blow up there all winter long.

We chopped our holes with a short spud one of the guys
had carried in neatly sheathed in an old, three-piece aluminum rod case strapped to the side of his pack. As I
chipped away with the thing, he said to me, "Now when you
break through with that, *don't drop it*," and I thought I heard
the voice of experience in that, too.

The ice was perfect, four or five inches thick, hard as glass,
and the guy had been right. An auger would have come in
handy, but I was glad I hadn't tried to carry one in.

We only fished for about two hours. We weren't doing very

well and it was blisteringly cold up there. Even under the hood, packed in so many clothes I could hardly bend my elbows, I was beginning to shiver and the tips of my fingers were numb. The wind was a constant whistle and the edges of the hood popped like a flag. I began to long for the slog back up that snowy hill to the top of the ridge because I knew it would warm me up.

We only caught a handful of fish. I got one, a beautiful little ten-inch cutthroat with the greenest back and the reddest stripe I'd ever seen on a trout. When I hand-landed the fish through the hole, it felt warm.

As we were getting ready to leave, I made the mistake of taking my foot off my pad for a second. It sailed across the lake, piling up on the rocks on the far bank, and I had to waddle after it like a penguin. Coming back I thought, Someday I'll be telling someone how to do this; I'll say, "Don't drop the spud in the lake and hold on to your pad."

After we caught our breath at the top of the ridge, one of the guys said, "Sorry, it's usually a lot better than this."

I said it was fun and I had, after all, caught a fish. That's the polite response when a friend apologizes for the fishing, but it was true. I was in that state of grace that comes early in such things: still delighted that it even works, too new at it to think I could have done better.

It's not always that dramatic. Usually the hikes are shorter, and sometimes we fish within sight of the car because hardly anyone does this so there's no competition to speak of.

The small mountain trout lakes are always beautiful in winter in a forbidding kind of way, and at first it's always hard to imagine that anything is going on under there. But then you auger your hole and peer in and it's all still happening. Bugs crawl, trout cruise. They even work the shallow littoral zone just like in summer. It's the same element, just a little more inaccessible.

So there you are, face down, peering through your port-hole in the ice, waiting for a fish to come along. If you were fly-fishing, you could cruise the bank, casting in a pattern and watching the birds, or climb into a canoe and troll; if you were grouse hunting you could try another hillside; but drilling another hole is a big commitment. For one thing, it's too much like work. For another, the sand and grit that are always trapped in the ice of windy mountain lakes will quickly dull the blades on your auger, although if you have an allen wrench and a stone, you can remove and sharpen them.

It's permissible to twitch your jig from time to time to attract the attention of fish—a sharp, upward bump of about two inches followed by a slow sink is good—but it's best to go easy on that. Even under the ice, trout are touchy, skittish fish, and too much action on the lure will spook them, especially if they're close to it.

If you jerk the lure and spook a trout that's close, but still out of sight, you'll know it. Sometimes there's just a momentary current caused by the trout wheeling and swimming off, enough to move the jig a few degrees to the side and then let it fall back. A larger fish might stir up a little silt off the bottom, and the effects of a really big trout bolting look like those atomic bomb test films. First all the weeds lean in one direction, and then a blast of mud blows through. That was a six-pound trout that will probably not come back.

You're not supposed to talk while you're under the hood, on the premise that the fish can hear you, but at a time like that it's permissible to shout a muffled obscenity.

Sometimes a trout will sail into your cone of vision, casually inhale the jig and keep going—an easy strike—but more often the fish will materialize a few inches from the lure and hover there studying the thing, paddling his pectoral fins in a thoughtful way. He may eat it then, or he may swim off, only to come back a minute later to glare at the jig again from another angle.

At times like this you really want to give a little twitch to that jig—just to be doing *something*—but of course that's the one thing you shouldn't do. The trout seems very close; in some cases it may be only an arm's length away. You're looking down on its dark back, but you can easily count the spots and see the red stripe on the side of a rainbow or the orange flanks on a brook trout.

You feel like a voyeur. You notice that you've been holding your breath. Naturally, the bigger the fish the more unbearable the suspense.

When you hook a fish, you throw the hood off and lurch to your knees to play it. For a few seconds you're blinded by the sudden light and disoriented by being back in the air again. You had begun to feel as if you were really underwater with the trout. The hand line is clumsy, easily fumbled or fouled. All in all, there can be a good deal of confusion.

But it can be a long time between fish, and the excitement is mostly cerebral. From a distance, someone fishing this way looks like a frozen corpse, especially when, as often happens on these windy lakes, a little powdery snow has drifted up around him.

A season or two ago a carload of tourists in Rocky Mountain National Park spotted one of my friends fishing like this. They drove right down to the ranger station and reported a body on the ice with its head covered by a blanket. Clearly a mob-style execution—one of the things they'd come all the way out here to get away from.

CHAPTER

12

Alaska

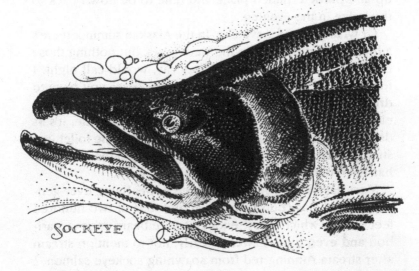

SOCKEYE

*T*he backcountry of Alaska is a perfect silence broken by the sound of motors: generators, outboards and especially the droning of float planes. Up there the single-engine plane is the equivalent of the pickup truck. Once you're away from the state's handful of roads—in the bush where the fishing is really good—a plane is your only way of getting anywhere, not to mention getting back.

I was in Alaska not too long ago with my friends DeWitt Daggett and Dan Heiner. DeWitt is a publisher and Dan is the managing field editor of an outdoor magazine (which means he manages to get into the field as much as possible). I'd never been to Alaska before and DeWitt had just moved to Anchorage, so this was a first good look around for both of us. Dan was the local boy with all the connections.

We fished from three different lodges—technically, two lodges and a hotel—and spent a lot of time in the air, which is standard procedure. There would be the flight in and then, most days, weather permitting, we'd fly out to this or that river in the morning to be left with a guide and maybe an inflatable raft or a boat stashed on site. Then we'd be picked up at a predetermined place and time to be flown back to the lodge in the evening.

Or what passes for evening. In the Alaskan summer there's a little bit of duskiness in the wee hours, but nothing those of us from "down below," as they say, would call night. I found that if you really want to see darkness you have to drink three or four beers just before going to bed at around eleven o'clock. When you get up to pee about one, it's as dark as it gets, but not so dark you can't find the toilet in a strange cabin. That's important, since by then the generator has been turned off and the lights don't work.

Most days we spent two or three hours flying over genuinely trackless country, often at altitudes of two hundred feet or less, which is low enough to see bears, moose, caribou and even tundra swans clearly, not to mention stream after stream running red from spawning sockeye salmon. I must have asked a dozen people why the salmon turn red in the rivers, and the only one who knew was a native guy. "It's so the bears can see 'em," he said.

We often had the rivers we'd chosen entirely to ourselves, and that sense of loneliness was enhanced by the knowledge that now and then the plane doesn't show up to take you back to the nice, cozy lodge. This doesn't happen often (it never happened to us) but there *is* weather to consider, or engine trouble, and every now and then a pilot will get sick or even just forget he was supposed to pick you up, only to slap his forehead in a bar two days later, turn to the guy on the next stool and say, "Oh, shit." Fishermen are seldom lost forever, but they've been known to get stranded for a while.

At the time it seemed like an outrageous odyssey, but back

in Anchorage I found that we'd only gone a couple of inches down the Alaska Peninsula on a map of the state that would cover the average kitchen table. I went out on the front porch and tried to extrapolate the feeling of vastness from our own little trip to all the rest of that game- and fish-infested, largely roadless open land as an exercise in meditation. I sat there through two cans of beer and couldn't do it, but I did remember something Wallace Stegner had said on an audiotape DeWitt's company produced: something about how you don't even have to go into the wilderness to get its benefits; just knowing it's out there is a great comfort.

When we boarded the Alaska Airlines flight from Anchorage to Iliamna, the stewardess got on the intercom and said, "Fasten your seat belts and, yes, the reds are running." That was welcome news because I was psyched to catch salmon, as was everyone else on the plane. There were sixty-some passengers and exactly that many rod cases. No briefcases, no lap-top computers. We were there in late July so any salmon caught would probably be sockeyes, aka "reds." These are a marginal fly rod fish, many people said, but that hardly mattered.

For one thing, I'd spent a week fishing for Atlantic salmon in Scotland that same summer and had gotten skunked. I wasn't exactly looking for revenge—although going after, but not catching, a certain kind of fish does give you a long-lasting itch—there was just the idea of those millions of big fish that live somewhere out at sea and then run up into the rivers once a year, past orcas and seals and bears, to spawn and then die. When you come from a place where there are fewer fish and they pretty much stay put, that's romantic stuff.

And then there was the book tour I'd just finished. It was a mercifully short one, three cities in three days, but it was hell nonetheless. I'd be up too early to get breakfast, and with only one or two cups of coffee under my belt I'd be talking to a motor-mouth morning disc jockey who'd never fished and didn't seem to have read the book.

Then it was more or less constant media for the next six or seven hours. I'd appear on the noontime television talk show as a five-minute segment right after how to buy the perfect gift and just before household tips from kids. The interviewer had fished once as a kid, but he also didn't seem to have read the book. He'd read the press release, though.

"It says here that you're 'the undisputed bard of fly-fishing.'"

After a pause that's too long for television I said, "Yeah, I read that, too."

Despite my anarchistic tendencies, I was intimidated, so I lacked the courage to say, "Look, it's just some bullshit cooked up by the publisher, okay?" Back home some friends had started calling me the undisputed bard of fly-fishing, and then laughing hysterically.

Then came the reading/book signing. It's July in the Northwest, so it's warm and humid anyway. Then I get up on the podium in this stuffy room and they turn a battery of lights on me. These are the same lights they use to keep hamburgers hot in fast-food restaurants.

I'm thinking, If I'm gonna suffer this much, maybe I should get into something that really pays. I'm also thinking, In another fourteen hours I'll be in Alaska where I will burn this sport coat on DeWitt's front lawn. There are shuffling noises coming from the small crowd because I'm thinking instead of talking.

I got into salmon on our first day on the water. I was a little short on sleep and felt jet-lagged, even though I'd only crossed one time zone between Seattle and Anchorage. I guess it was the flying. I'm not as terrified of flying as I once was because I do more of it now. Then again, I can't shake the feeling that every time I fly and live I've used up a bit more luck.

We'd flown into the mouth of the Tazamina River and then motored upstream a mile or so. The water was full of sockeyes, but that didn't seem to interest anyone much except me. Dan, DeWitt and the guide were calmly speculating on where the rainbows and grayling might be, while I kept leaning over the gunnels saying, "Jesus Christ, look at all the salmon. Stop the god damn boat!" Most of the fish were nice and silvery, still fresh from the sea.

When we finally beached on a sand bar the guide got the other two guys going with streamers and then led me to a huge pod of sockeyes. He told me to rig a pink Polar Shrimp with split shot, as if I were fishing for trout with a nymph. One thing about the Alaskans: Unlike the Scots, they fish for salmon as if they actually want to catch them, with sink-tip lines and lead.

When the guide saw that I was rigging up an old Payne nine-and-a-half-foot light salmon rod with a brand-new Peerless #6 reel, he said he'd never seen one of those and asked to try it.

"Shoot," he said, "this is a little heavy, but it casts real nice."

There were fifty salmon in a pool not ten feet from where I was standing. "I'm glad you like the rod," I said, "but give it back."

I had a fish on for a minute or two and lost him. Then I got a good hookup, but the fish was snagged in the back. It weighed six or seven pounds and took longer to land than it should have.

I thought, Yeah, I've heard about this. There are those who say the plankton-eating sockeyes don't take flies and the best you can do is foul hook them, and there are others who say they do too take flies if you do it right. The rules say the fish is a keeper if it's hooked somewhere in the face, ahead of the gill covers.

If I remember right, I landed seven salmon that afternoon, four of which were hooked in or so close to the mouth that I'd say they either ate or tried to eat the fly. And that's as far as I care to delve into that controversy. I will say that when a sockeye is hooked near the front it fights real good, especially on a bamboo rod.

Those first few days we fished from the Iliaska Lodge, owned by Ted and Mary Gerkin. There's a long story here, and if you'd like to hear it you should read Ted's book, *Gamble at Iliamna,* because he tells it much better than I could. Anyway, it was here that I began to understand how sockeye salmon were viewed by Alaskan fly fishers.

The sockeyes, along with the kings, silvers, chums and pinks, form the basis for the entire ecology of these watersheds. The numbers of fish in these runs are astonishing: 6 million in this drainage, 19 million in that one, and there are hundreds of drainages.

Salmon often run all the way up into the smaller rivers and creeks, many of which are connected by large lakes. There are resident grayling and some Dolly Vardens in these streams, but the big rainbow trout and arctic char are only in the flowing water in significant numbers when they follow the salmon runs up out of the lakes. Sometimes a fisherman will say that Such-and-Such River isn't good for big rainbows yet because the salmon aren't in. If you're new at this you'll have to ask him what the hell he's talking about.

The trout, char and grayling feed on salmon eggs that are dribbled by the ripe hen salmon as they run up the rivers and then later on the ones that wash out of the spawning redds. This sounds like an incidental dietary footnote until you multiply the salmon by millions and get tons of protein from stray eggs alone.

The fish are really onto these things. It's said that big rainbows will swim over and nudge ripe hen salmon to dislodge eggs. Every guide and bush pilot I talked to claims to have seen that.

Still later, after the spawn when the salmon all die, these same game fish feed on bits of rotted salmon meat dislodged by the current. It's hard to picture, but in this scheme the pretty rainbow trout, char and grayling fall into the same ecological niche as maggots and vultures.

The standard flies are salmon egg patterns and sickly beige-colored "flesh flies," tied from rabbit fur. Naturally, these are fished on a dead drift. This may not be what you'd call classy stuff, but it does match the hatch perfectly.

The dying and dead salmon are also eaten by gulls, ravens, eagles, otters and such, not to mention aquatic insects, which then go on to feed the salmon parr and smolts before they return to the sea, as well as the grayling, trout, char and such during those times when there are no salmon in the rivers. Then the young salmon themselves form part of the diet for other game fish. In the middle of all this, you can go to the places where rivers enter lakes and fish streamers for big char collected there to feed on migrating smolts. The schools of char are often under flocks of excited, hungry gulls and terns.

That's the obvious stuff you can see from a boat or while wading a river. There's also the plankton/salmon/seal/orca connection out at sea. In the grand scheme, that's what salmon do: They bring the nutrients from the ocean far up into the freshwater rivers, lakes and streams and there's no way I can convey the magnitude of it. It's just something you have to see.

And then there are the bears. Alaskan brown bears—along with rainbow trout—put on a large part of every year's growth gorging on salmon, and once you've stepped in a huge, steaming pile of bear crap you begin to see that their droppings are not an insignificant contribution to the fertilizer needed to grow the grasses that are fed upon by the caribou that are now and then eaten by the bears—and so on.

This is efficient, economical, messy, smelly, mystically circular and temperamental. It's especially temperamental if you count the commercial netting of salmon—the "nylon curtain," they call it—that can screw things up seriously when it's not properly regulated, as most people will tell you it, in fact, is not. Take away the salmon, as some would gladly do for a single year's profit, and the ecosystem would die.

They say that the silvers and, in some circumstances, the kings are the real fly rod salmon in Alaska. The sockeyes are loved as a food fish and for their overall contribution to the food chain, but in the circles we were traveling in—fly fishers and fly-fishing guides—they don't seem to be too highly rated.

One morning at Iliaska when the weather was too socked in for flying, some of the guides drove a crew of us over to the Newhalen River to join seventy-five or so other fishermen who were dredging for sockeyes. This is called "combat zone fishing," and one of the guides told me the Newhalen was nothing. "You should see the rivers you can drive to from Anchorage," he said.

I got into it after a while, even though I claim not to like fishing in a crowd or chunking lead. I mean, what the hell; these were big fish and this was Alaska, where things are sometimes done differently. In the true spirit of things, I got deeply interested in killing some fish to take home.

By the way, I believe that "chunking" is the proper, common term. It's onomatopoetic, coming from the distinctive "chunk" sound split shot makes when it hits the water.

When the ceiling lifted after a few hours, Ted and another pilot flew over to pick us up and take us to a secluded little river to catch big rainbow trout, possibly on dry flies. "You're about to go from the ridiculous to the sublime," Ted said.

Rainbows are what the guides and lodge owners brag about most—in terms of both numbers and size—and they're what many visiting fly fishers are looking for. After all, this is one of the few places on earth where, at the right time, with some skill, a little luck and maybe the right guide, you can bag your ten- or twelve- or (if the stories can be believed) even your fifteen-pound rainbow on a fly rod. The fish will be scavenging behind a run of salmon instead of sipping mayflies but, if you connect, it will be a by God, double-digit wallhanger.

Not far from Iliamna Lake by float plane, on a river the name of which I've been asked not to mention, I landed a six-pound rainbow on a dry fly. It was a nice fish, big enough to make the lodge book (volume III), in which, among other things, you can record for posterity any trout over four pounds caught on a dry fly.

It was a nice fish, but not a great one by Alaskan standards; memorable only because it was hooked on a floating caddis pattern instead of on a sunken salmon egg, flesh fly or streamer. On the other hand, it was probably the biggest trout I've ever caught on a dry fly.

People have written pages in that lodge book about a single, good fish—eloquent stories filled with keen observations and humor—but I couldn't think of anything more profound than, "Six-pound rainbow on a #14 olive Stimulator," dated and signed. It's not that I wasn't happy, I was just a little tongue-tied.

We caught salmon on wet flies and split shot, nice-sized arctic char on eggs and Woolly Bugger streamers, rainbows on streamers and eggs, and one day I got into some pretty Dolly Vardens, once again on eggs. Apparently you don't do a lot of dry fly fishing in Alaska and I understand some fishermen on their first trip there are a little disillusioned by that.

I won't say I was actually disappointed, but there were a few times when I got enough of lead and sink-tips and flies that looked less like bugs or fish and more like bangles from a stripper's costume. And, yes, those did happen to be the few times when we weren't catching fish. I've noticed that certain fishing tactics seem a lot more acceptable when they're working.

Still, that day on the river Ted Gerkin asked me not to write about—the one where the big rainbows would come up to a dry caddis fly—was a tremendous relief, and so was our first afternoon at Wood River Lodge on the Agulawok River.

There were fish rising right in front of the cabin as we lugged our gear from the plane, and when we rushed down there we found that they were rainbows and grayling, both up to eighteen or twenty inches, rising to a this-and-that hatch of caddis, mayflies and small stoneflies. The fish weren't *too* picky, but we did have to fish flies that at least approximated the appearance of the real bugs. I was already in the water with my five-weight rod strung up, DeWitt was playing a fish and Dan had just missed a strike, when I learned that I had to run back to the cabin and dig my dry fly boxes out of the bottom of the duffel bag. At that point in the trip I had caught countless big fish, but it almost killed me that, for five minutes, Dan and DeWitt were getting them while I was looking for those damned fly boxes.

The next day we could have flown out once again to catch great big something-or-others someplace else, but we unanimously voted to stay and fish the river right in front of the lodge. They gave us two guides with boats, and we fished from right after breakfast—say, 8:00 in the morning—until dusk, which would have been going on midnight. Sure, we broke for a shore lunch and dinner at the lodge, but that's still a long day. In fact, this has happened to me at least once every time I've gone north. I say, "Jeeze, I'm kind of tired for some reason," and the bright-eyed guide says, "Well, we *have* been fishing for about sixteen hours now . . ."

We caught rainbows, some nice big arctic char and my biggest sockeye of the trip (ten pounds) on streamers, but what I remember most clearly now are the grayling.

They were almost all good-sized, maybe fifteen to twenty inches, and throughout the day we'd find pods of them rising in the slack water beside faster currents. "That's because they're a lazy fish," Duncan said. That's Duncan Oswald, one of several guides at Wood River who specialize in fly fishing. He also ties the flies for the lodge and knows the river's hatches. That's significant because in Alaska you don't *have* to know the hatches to catch fish.

I fished for the grayling with a seven-foot, nine-inch Mike Clark bamboo rod and Dan broke out a sweet little Pezon & Michelle Parabolic. Neither rod raised any eyebrows and, in fact, I was surprised at how many cane rods I saw on that trip. Apparently, many Alaskan fly fishers have a darling little bamboo stashed away for just these kinds of occasions.

As I said, the hatches were scattered, but the best was a fall of size fourteen dark stoneflies. The grayling would execute a refusal rise to a #14 Royal Wulff, *sometimes* eat an Elk Hair Caddis, Irresistible or Stimulator, and absolutely hammer an elegantly simple deer hair and calf tail stonefly of Duncan's own design. I brought a few of these home with me to copy.

Some people will tell you that grayling are an easy fish— the bluegills of the north—but I've never found them to be like that. The few times I've fished for them in their native range, they've been catchable, but far from pushovers: easy enough that you can usually get some, but still hard enough that each fish is an event. And, of course, they're unbelievably, iridescently beautiful. The perfect game fish, in other words.

That night at the lodge over gin and tonics, one of the other guides said it was too bad we hadn't gone off with him to catch the pigs but, more for Duncan's benefit than ours, I think, he said he did realize that a salmon egg is "chunked," while a dry fly is *"presented."*

I'm sorry to say I don't remember that guide's name now. We met so many guides and bush pilots I don't remember half their names, and I don't have them written down anywhere. Since I claim to be a professional writer, I should probably keep better notes but, looking back on previous trips, I sometimes think I've missed what could have been pure moments because I was busy scribbling in a damned notebook, making sure I'd be able to spell the name of the river when I got back home.

Of the pilots, a man with Branch River Air Service was the most overtly professional. Before takeoff, shouting over the racket of the engine, he told us how the doors opened and the location of the life vests and first aid kit. There was even an abbreviated version of the notorious seat-back safety card: a silhouette of the plane with arrows pointing to each side labeled "door."

That was the first time we flew with him. The next morning he said, "All the safety stuff is the same as it was yesterday, okay?"

Then there was the guy flying for Iliaska who could give you a quick, appraising glance and guess your weight within a few pounds, and then do the same with your gear. Payload weights are constantly on the minds of bush pilots.

John, with Wood River Lodge, was the most acrobatic flier. Usually if you pointed out wildlife while in a plane, everyone would look and nod approvingly, but John would shout, "Yeah, cool!" and go into a diving spin to get a closer look. The first time he did that it took me by surprise. I was squashed down in the seat and my cheeks felt heavy from the increased gravity of the spin. The ground was wheeling directly off my right shoulder and coming up fast. John asked, "Anyone here get airsick?" I said, "Not until now," but I don't think he could hear me over the roaring of the engine.

Bernie had the crazy bush pilot act down pat. He turned the engine over and yelled, "Jeeze, it started!" Then he looked down at his instruments and said, loudly but apparently to himself, "Hell, I guess all these little switches are in the right place." Then, turning to me in the copilot's seat, he asked, "You ever fly one of these?"

Once in the air he launched into a fishing story. The motor was howling. We were both wearing headphones, but all I could hear through mine was static, which is kind of what Bernie's voice sounds like anyway. I could see his lips moving. He made casting motions with his right hand, line stripping motions with his left and then held his palms up in front of him to indicate a fish (salmon? rainbow?) about three feet long.

I shouted "Far out" into my microphone, which is all you ever have to say to a fish story.

Bernie yells on the ground, too, as do many Alaskans. It's a survival tactic. A ranger at Katmai National Park told me about a park employee who had recently been mauled by a bear. "She's a very quiet person," the ranger said. This wasn't an idle comment on the victim's personality; he meant she wasn't talking loudly and constantly to herself as she walked through the woods, so she had come upon the bear unannounced. Bears don't like that.

We saw lots of bears in Alaska. They were following the salmon runs, as we were—inadvertently or otherwise—so it was unavoidable. These animals are called Alaskan brown bears, although there's some disagreement among the scientists about whether they're a separate species from the grizzly. The main difference is size. A big brown bear looks just like a grizzly, but stands a foot taller and weighs as much as six hundred pounds more. When you're sharing a gravel bar with one, size does seem to be a defining factor.

A big sow and a yearling cub came down to the Newhalen River the first day we fished it. I was about fourth in the line of fishermen upstream from the spot the bears wanted. When one of the guides hooted, "Bear!" I looked, broke off the eight-pound salmon I was playing without a second thought and began wading slowly but deliberately upstream, as they tell you to do. Dan, who doesn't like bears much, was just ahead of me. He didn't say anything, but he was making a quiet noise deep in his throat that sounded like the cooing of a pigeon.

Later, DeWitt said it was interesting to see the "ripple of recognition" go through us when the bears waded out into the river.

We saw bears almost every day, and there are three things people tell you about them: that, nine times out of ten, the bear will decline a confrontation; that if he *doesn't* decline, it's probably your fault; and that a bear's personal space is no less than fifty yards. That seemed awfully close. I found that I had to be at about two hundred before it would occur to me that the adults were handsome and the cubs were actually pretty cute. Bears scare me badly, but I still like them a lot, which I take as evidence that I've negotiated something heavy.

We only had two bear encounters that seemed ticklish. One day we flew into the Morraine River, a beautiful but bleak tundra stream known for big rainbows. We were dropped off at a small lake with our guide and the light inflatable raft we'd use to float a few miles of river down to the pickup point.

It was an unsettled day with gray, scudding clouds and winds between thirty and forty knots. The last thing the pilot said was that the weather would "probably" allow him to pick us up that evening. To understand Alaskan weather, all you have to do is look at one of the weather maps they sell in souvenir shops up there where various parts of the state are labeled partly shitty, mostly shitty, moderately shitty and so on.

Of course the wind made for grueling fly-casting, but we were still picking up a few big rainbows on Woolly Buggers and a thing I think they were calling an Electric Egg Sucking Leech, although I might not be remembering that correctly.

We'd stopped for lunch on a little stretch of sandy beach and the guide was talking to me about some other writers he'd guided. "They all wanted something for nothing," he said. "They expected to spend a day with me and come home with all the secrets I've learned in ten years in the bush." I was just beginning to explain that all I wanted to know was what fly to tie on when a bear popped out of the brush about forty yards away.

He stood up on his hind feet and squinted at us. Bears

don't see well, but he knew there was something on this sand bar that wasn't there the last time he'd looked. The wind was blowing hard at right angles between us and the bear, so he couldn't get our scent.

When the bear dropped to all fours and came a little closer—cautious, but seized by curiosity—I asked the guide, "Should we launch the raft?" He said, "What good would that do?" and I remembered what someone had said a few days before: "You think you're safe in a boat until you see one of those guys trot across a deep, fast stream as if it wasn't even there." The Morraine was a small river, swift and deep here and there, but wadable by humans in most places.

Then the bear walked into the underbrush and we lost sight of him. Dan asked, "What should we do now?" and the guide said, "Finish your lunch."

Another day we flew into a spot where a small creek entered a lake. The plan was to wade up the creek a half mile or so to a place where, we'd been assured, there were huge rainbows and grayling, but there was a sow and two cubs around the first bend, so we had to turn back and work the inlet, where there didn't seem to be too many fish.

I won't try to describe the whole, grim dance in detail, but eventually a young male bear came down to the inlet and made it known that we had blundered into his personal space and that he wasn't pleased. Since he was on shore and we were already up to our armpits in the lake, we had a little trouble getting out of his way, although we tried. At one point the bear gave us some negative body language—lowered head, flattened ears. This doesn't sound like much on paper, but on site it's pretty damned impressive.

That bear herded us back and forth across the inlet a few times, and at one point Dan and DeWitt both lost their footing and went under while trying to move a little more deliberately than was possible in deep water and slippery rocks. At that point I was closest to the bear—I can't say how close, but far less than the prescribed fifty yards—and I kept my footing not because I'd remained calm exactly, but because I'd already come to terms with a horrible death and was wondering how badly I'd be missed back home.

Throughout the whole thing our guide, Nanci Morris, spoke in a calming voice, first to the bear, then to us, and she never unholstered her Smith and Wesson .44 magnum. She was the picture of composure, and said later she was more worried about that sow getting nervous because boars are known to attack cubs.

It turned out okay, but I was glad to hear the deep, unmistakable drone of the DeHavilland Beaver Nanci calls the Cream Puff coming to pick us up. It occurred to me that having an airplane come and save you from a bear is a great way to get over your fear of flying. When the plane taxied in, Dan waded out and kissed a pontoon, able to kid around now because it seemed we'd live.

Nanci is the head guide (excuse me, "Director of Sportfishing") at the Quinnat Landing Hotel in the town of King Salmon. Her specialty is trophy-sized kings, and in some magazine article or brochure she was once dubbed "the queen of the king salmon guides." Naturally, that stuck, as embarrassing publicity always does.

When I said something about getting to be head guide at a place like that at an obviously tender age, Nanci said, "Yeah, and, not to put too fine a point on it, try doing it as a woman."

I could see that. Competence is admired in a place like King Salmon, but men far outnumber women and at times the horniness is almost palpable. And it's a little rough—in a pleasant way for a tourist, but rough nonetheless. Over some beers in the hotel bar a pilot named Red told me, "We try to make a year's living here in five or six months, so we fight sleep deprivation half the year and depression the other half." He also said, gazing wistfully out at the Naknik River,

"Ah, Alaska. She seduces you every summer and then abandons you every winter."

Anyway, Nanci does seem to love that plane with something close to a passion. As head guide, she almost always manages to schedule it for her own trips and, although she talked about other things in the two days we all spent together, she kept coming back to the Cream Puff. When we walked down to the dock to board it or when it banked in to land and pick us up, she'd say, "Just look at it. God!"

It *is* a sweetheart. You see all kinds of other aircraft, but the Beaver is the classic, workhorse bush plane, the one everyone wants. They were discontinued in the 1960s, but they're still widely in use because, like only a handful of other things in life, they are absolutely perfect as is. This one is painted deep purple with a silver lightning bolt down each side, and it's a "cherry rebuilt"—might as well be brand new. A plane is everything in Alaska, and a great plane is sublime.

The first time I saw the Cream Puff it was sitting at a dock on the Naknik River and we were sitting in the bar at Quinnat Landing, near the big picture windows, eating thick steaks and talking about the fishing. During a lull in the conversation, Nanci gazed out at the Beaver and said, "See that plane out there? I love that plane. If that plane was a man, I just might say 'I do.' "

At which point every man in the joint looked out the window at the lovely old purple Beaver. Its big radial engine was idling. At that range it sounded like the purring of a large, happy cat.

13

Tying

GINGER
QUILL

*E*very winter—usually sometime in January—I resolve
to tie flies two or three nights a week so that, by spring, all
my fly boxes will be neat and well-stocked, like assault rifles with full clips, like sports cars with well-tuned engines,
like . . . well, there's no good analogy. Like fly boxes stuffed
with fresh, neat flies—enough to catch a thousand fish. Then,
every spring, I realize I only made a medium-sized dent and
I'm a little disappointed in myself.

Maybe I should stop doing that. In fact, I read somewhere
that traditional New Year's–style resolutions are going out of
style because we Americans are getting either lazier or more
realistic.

I wouldn't feel so bad if I'd spent the time rereading the great books I didn't fully appreciate in college, but the fact is I can't remember what happened to most of those long, cold nights except that I didn't tie flies. And that, I hate to admit, suggests an unhealthy amount of television.

But I do get the flies tied—usually in frantic sessions before trips, sometimes actually *on* those trips—and that's not all bad. Tying Green Drakes for an expedition that starts in two days, or whipping out some Pale Morning Duns on the tailgate of a pickup for a hatch that begins in an hour, adds a kind of immediacy to the job that I've come to like. And if the tailgate flies aren't exactly flawless, they still catch fish as often as not, which puts things into perspective.

Some fishermen actually prefer to tie their flies that way—through the season, as needed—but I liked it the few times I had at least the standard patterns pretty well-stocked. If nothing else, it kept that short notice tying time free. After all, you never know what's going to come up.

For example, around here some of the best mayfly hatches are the Blue-winged Olives. There are two sizes of fly—eighteens and twenty-twos—and they come off more or less predictably twice a year, spring and fall. To most of us these bugs are old, predictable friends, so we carry a variety of fly patterns to copy the nymphs, emergers and duns. We tend to neglect the spinners, though, because they're usually not "important," as they say.

But then last fall, for reasons I won't even guess at, the spinners (the adult, mating stage of these bugs) were at least as important as the more recognizable duns.

The trout did feed on the emerging duns, but the usually long, luxurious hatches tended to be sparse and short that season, and they were coming earlier in the day, too. Then the spinner falls would come on in late afternoon, especially on overcast days, and the bugs would be on the water for hours, with trout sipping them lazily and steadily. Often the spinners of both species would be on the water at the same time and the trout, in their typical, perverse way, always seemed to want the smaller one.

The first day A.K. and I hit this I did have a few tiny spinners in my fly box. They were old ones that I hadn't used in a long time, but I'd tied them because every now and then a dun hatch would be followed in the early evening by a light spinner fall, or early in the morning, before the hatch, you could find the odd fish rising in a backwater to a few leftover spinners from the night before. It was one of those flies that might get you into a few extra fish but that was not crucial to a good day's fishing. Many fishermen here don't carry any Blue-winged Olive spinners at all, and claim they don't miss them.

On that first day there was a smattering of large and small olive duns in the late morning, then a long lull, and then a glorious, blanket spinner fall in the afternoon. At first we didn't know what it was. Fish were rising all over the place in the glassy currents at the backs of the pools, and we thought it must be a midge hatch because of the casual porpoising way they were feeding. When we waded in and saw all the spinners on the water, we knew what they had to be, but it still took a minute to sink in. A.K. and I have fished Blue-winged Olive hatches together for a couple of decades now, and in all that time I don't think either of us had ever seen a full-blown spinner fall.

The #18 spinner (the one I had a few copies of) was a rusty red color, and the little #22, what we're told is a Paraleptophlebia, was a pale olive. I landed a few trout using a #22 Trike spinner—the wrong color (black body instead of olive) but the right size. I only had two of them, though, and I soon lost them to fish. There were some big trout rising, and I was fishing the kind of long, fine tippet that gives you a good, lifelike drift, but breaks easily.

So I ended up using a #18 Rusty Spinner. A few trout liked it well enough to eat it, but most didn't, and the few that did were little ones. This was one of those days when A.K. seriously outfished me. Not that either of us was counting, you understand, but one does notice.

Then A.K. somehow got down there without me for a day. He called the next morning and said he'd absolutely hammered trout on a spinner fly pattern of his own design: size twenty-two, sparse dun tails, body of dyed olive quill, black dubbed thorax and white hackle tip wings. (Right. Obvious. I'd have thought of it myself eventually.) He wanted to go back to the river the next day, so I sat down and tied a dozen of the flies he'd described.

This was a straightforward pattern, but it still took me a few tries to get a feel for the size and proportions. I tied a dozen (a nice, round, professional-sounding number) and except for the first two they were all trim and pretty.

Then Ed called and said he was going to meet us there. I told him I had *the* fly pattern and he said, "Good, I may have to borrow some from you."

So I went back and tied another half dozen so as to avoid being placed in a position I've been in more than once before: The fish are biting, I have the right fly, but there are only two left. One of my oldest and dearest friends wades over and says, "Can I bum one of those from you?" and I'm forced to say, "Look, man, life is hard."

The fly itself is a lovely thing and, as simple as it is, it's a surprisingly good copy of the natural insect. The fish liked it. I'd tied enough that I could have loaned some to Ed, but it turned out that he'd stayed up late tying a bunch of his own. Ed's like me in this regard, he has nothing against catching trout on other people's flies, but it's just noticeably better if you tied them yourself.

That was last fall, as I said. At this writing, the spring Olive hatches haven't started yet, but I can almost guarantee that they'll come in the old familiar mode: good hatches of duns followed by obscure spinner falls that surely happen sometime, somewhere, but that you never actually see.

Still, if I ever do see it again, I'll have the pattern. Sure, the little Trike spinner would probably work just as well, but it wouldn't be *exactly* the right fly, so trout caught on it—though better than no fish at all—would also fall short of being perfect. In fact, that seems to be where half the flies in my boxes came from in the first place. They represent something that happened once, and so will surely happen again eventually, given enough time. In that way, my fly selection makes sense in the same way my life does, that is, only to me.

There are some tiers, both amateur and professional, who produce perfect flies, and sometimes those fly patterns are startlingly accurate, right down to, as Dave Whitlock once said, "eyeballs, elbows and arseholes."

It's flies like these—incredibly detailed, every hair and feather in place—that tempt some of us, in emotional moments, to call fly-tying an "art." But if it *is* art, it's an unusual medium.

To tie a Ginger Quill dry fly—a simple, standard pattern—you start with a high-quality, light wire hook; tie in a few fibers from a ginger-colored spade hackle, cocked slightly upward for a tail; wrap on a pair of stripped ginger hackle stems for a trim, segmented, subtly tapered body; tie in a pair of dun-colored hen hackle tips for wings, with careful thread wraps between them so they're separated at the proper angle; wrap on a long ginger hackle so that the hackle collar extends just past the gap of the hook; wrap a small, neat head of tying thread and finish it off with a drop of clear lacquer.

It's a lovely fly that you'll admire for a few seconds before you drop it into your box and go on to the next one. Then, as soon as possible, you'll throw it in a river and let a bunch of trout chew on it until it comes apart or breaks off.

It's a matter of perception and presentation. If you put a frame around it, it's art; if you use it, it's craft. If you *could* use it but put a frame around it instead, I don't know what the hell it is.

True, flies by some famous tiers (especially dead ones)

can be worth a lot as collector's items, and you'll sometimes see exceptionally well-made trout and salmon flies mounted in shadow box frames. Still, a working fly, by its very nature, is a handsome but expendable item. So the second best thing you can say about a professional tier is that his flies are absolutely beautiful, but the *best* thing you can say is that they're just fine and he can tie two and a half dozen in an hour.

A.K. taught me most of what I know about fly-tying. It turned out to be a classic paradox—a simple job with endless complications—but the upshot is, tying flies is like splitting wood neatly or plowing a straight furrow: If there's an art to it, it's in the work itself rather than in the product.

I try to tie most of the flies I use myself, not as a matter of pride exactly, but just because there's a little more satisfaction to it. I do buy some occasionally, especially when there's some weird, regional pattern the local trout are insane for, and having tied professionally myself, I don't wince too much at the two dollars or so you can pay for a single fly now, even though I started tying my own when sixty-five cents apiece seemed too steep.

But of course money isn't the object. The object is to do as much of the work yourself as possible, thereby becoming self-sufficient and gaining the kind of nonlinear understanding that spreads in a circle around what seems, at first glance, to be the soul of the matter.

Eventually you may become like A.K., a professional tier who, except under the most dire circumstances and for reasons of his own, would rather not catch fish at all than catch them on someone else's flies.

Last summer A.K., Ed and I went to fish some private brook trout ponds not far from here. Ed had never fished the ponds before, so he called a few days early to ask what flies he needed to tie. "Small hoppers, damselfly nymphs and adult damsels," I said, because that's what the owner of the pond had told me.

We got on the water a little after noon on a warm, bright, breezy day—classic grasshopper weather. This little pond is set in an open foothills meadow that's covered with tall grass, and the few rises were all within a foot or two of the upwind bank, exactly where errant hoppers would be.

Yes, I know you're supposed to go into the scientific mode, check the water to see what bugs are there and then copy them, but sometimes it's too perfect, too obvious.

Ed and I tied on #14 hoppers because the owner had said to use small ones. A.K. didn't have any that size, so he tied on a big one, maybe a #8. "How much difference could it make?" he asked rhetorically.

I hooked a fish on my third or fourth cast, and by the time I'd released it, Ed had one on. They were both good brookies: maybe thirteen or fourteen inches, healthy, chunky and well-colored that far from spawning season.

We took a few more each along that east bank, and then we began to notice that A.K. wasn't getting them. We noticed this because it was quite odd. A.K. is an excellent fly fisher, and it's rare for him to be the one guy out of three who's not catching fish.

Of course you're not supposed to gloat at a time like that, but sometimes, in the glow of a few nice fish, your baser instincts get the best of you.

"I have a whole bunch of these little hoppers," I said to A.K. "I'd offer you one, but I know you refuse to fish with flies you didn't tie yourself."

"That's correct," he said.

It seemed as though the grasshopper action consisted of a handful of decent-sized brook trout working along that one bank. Ed and I either caught them all or we caught enough to spook the rest of them. We also found that they didn't care for the standard grasshopper twitch, they wanted the flies to lie absolutely still on the surface. Pretty picky for brook trout.

After the hopper fall was over, there was no clearly "right" fly pattern. We caught our fish on a variety of flies: damsel nymphs, floating beetles, the odd streamer, things like that. A.K. even made his big grasshopper work on one fish, which delighted him. Being a man of few words—at least while fishing—he held the trout up for us to see and said, "There!"

I've noticed that professional tiers, like artists, can sometimes get cranky. Or maybe it's the crankiness that comes first, giving them the predisposition to be meticulous and single-minded. For most of us, making our own flies is just a comfortable part of the process of fishing, a way to get inside of things in a nonscientific, somewhat intuitive and, okay, maybe even artistic way.

For the most part, fly-tying is a practical business. You want the flies to work, you want them to be as durable as the materials will allow, and you want to be able to tie them quickly and easily enough that you can use them up thoughtlessly.

Okay, fine, but then sooner or later the elements of style begin to creep in. You may begin to tie flies that are prettier than they'd have to be just to catch fish for reasons that aren't immediately evident. The bodies on your dry flies become trimmer, and not necessarily because trout like them better that way. There are hundreds of colors of commercial dubbing on the market, but none of them are quite right, so you begin to dye and blend your own. It's great when someone tells you you tie a pretty fly, but that's not precisely why you do it.

When you settle on one or two patterns to copy a bug you see often, you feel you've begun to gain some purchase on the hatch. Your Brown Drake is not just a brown *Green* Drake, because, although you can't put your finger on it, the former has quirks that the latter doesn't. There's a certain posture on the water, a way of holding the tail up a few extra degrees, maybe something you could only describe as the bug's attitude.

You feel as if you have some kind of understanding, and

catching a couple of fish seems like proof of that, so even on a strange river in a different state, you feel nicely at home.

There was a time when fly patterns were pretty much fixed and unassailable, but it's not like that anymore. Now it's perfectly okay if your patterns are a little different from anyone else's. Maybe it's even preferable, because the flies you tie are seen as a kind of self-expression.

Of course this isn't aimless. The practical end saves you from getting too self-indulgent and keeps you fundamentally engaged with the environment. As a fly tier, you can't get otherworldly because a beautiful fly that doesn't catch fish is *not* a beautiful fly. On the other hand, evaluating a fly solely on whether it catches fish is like saying a painting of Elvis on velvet is as good as a Picasso because both will cover the same crack in the plaster.

Not long ago I ran into a kid in West Yellowstone, Montana, who said he'd just come back from the Madison River. He was wearing a clean vest, new waders and a fluorescent orange hat. I'd say he was in his late teens or early twenties.

"How'd you do?" I asked.

"I caught my first trout on a fly I tied myself," the kid said proudly. This is a little like introducing a woman as your first wife: an admission that this is now, but more will surely happen.

I didn't ask how big the fish had been because that was clearly not the point, and I also stopped myself from putting a fatherly hand on his shoulder and saying something like, "You will remember this day for the rest of your life, my son," because some middle-aged guy pontificating wouldn't have added to the moment.

I said, "Congratulations," he said, "Thanks," and I walked over to my borrowed, bat-infested cabin to get some sleep. It was eleven o'clock and I'd been fishing all day myself.

And then it occurred to me that I didn't remember my first trout on my own fly. I stopped just outside the circle of the porch light and thought about it. The woods were dark. Off to the right I could hear the little spring creek gurgling.

It would have to have been sometime in the late 1960s. I'd guess it was a small brown trout from the St. Vrain River on an Adams dry fly, but that would only be a guess. I couldn't actually picture the fish, the river, the fly pattern or, oddly enough, even the feeling.

Oh, well, it must have really been something at the time.

CHAPTER

14

*A Few Days
Before Christmas*

A few days before Christmas last year, A.K. and I drove down to Pike National Forest and hiked into the Cheesman Canyon stretch of the South Platte River. The weather had been chilly for at least a week (meaning the water would be cold, even for trout), word was the flow was down to about thirty cubic feet per second (too low) and the grapevine hadn't had anything to say about the midge hatches in a while, which meant they were probably off. If there was any good news, it was that the river wasn't frozen bank to bank.

All the signs pointed to poor fishing or, as A.K. would say, in the tone of a schoolteacher correcting your grammar, "poor *catching*," since the fishing itself is always good. Now that I think about it, I guess that was the whole point.

I hadn't been out fishing—or doing much of anything else—in almost a month, and I was beginning to think all my friends were getting too old. All are at least in their forties now, and they seem so damn busy. No one had called to say, "Well, nothing much is happening, but let's at least go look at the Frying Pan River," or, "It's pretty cold, but let's see if we can shoot a couple of rabbits." When *I* made the calls, people were saying, "Oh, I don't know, this is happening, that's happening . . . I don't know . . ." God, I thought, I'm hanging out with a bunch of old men.

And for about that same month, A.K. had been back at his family home in Iowa. His father had died, and there were all those sad, final chores to be taken care of, including the selling of the farm where A.K. was born. In a typical example of understatement, he said it hadn't been much fun.

We talked about it a little when he got back, but I've noticed that in situations like this there's often surprisingly little to say. The late Mr. Best had lived a good, long, honest, largely uneventful life farming the land he was born on; hunting rabbits with the .22 rifle he'd bought used in the 1920s because it would have gone against his practical, Protestant upbringing to pay seven whole dollars for a new one. This kind of personal history is all but obsolete now and, aside from everything else, *that's* a damned shame.

I won't presume to speculate about what A.K. was feeling or what he had to "work through," as they say, but I knew he was not in a good mood. As for me, real trouble should show me that my own little problems are really nothing, but I'm more likely to see it as proof that a festering cloud of doom is settling on everything.

Anyway, when A.K. called and said he needed to go fishing, I said, "Yeah, I do, too," and I understood it wasn't going to matter much if the trout weren't biting.

• • •

We walked into the canyon at the fastest pace we could manage on the dangerously icy trail. On the drive down we had carefully established that there wasn't much chance of catching any fish, but once we were there a little of the old excitement began to kick in. We noted that there were no cars at the trailhead parking lot and no fresh tracks on the trail. That meant—for what it was worth—that we'd probably have the whole three miles of river to ourselves.

After looking at a few good pools, we settled on an old favorite spot. The day was chilly with a low, solid overcast and the water temperature on A.K.'s stream thermometer read thirty-six degrees, or four degrees below the trout's lower avoidance level. When the water temperature drops below forty, the trout become sluggish and so do the aquatic insects they feed on. It's a matter of predators evolving to match the habits of their prey, or at least that's how I like to see it.

And fishermen, bundled in three times the clothing they'd need for a hike on a cold day, can get a little sluggish themselves. You think of evolution because on a cold trout stream in midwinter, time seems numbingly huge. We stood there for a few minutes looking at the river. "This is going to be tough," I said, and A.K. replied, "Well, we knew that."

The fly to fish at a time like that is a String Thing. This is no more than a layer of white thread wrapped on a #20 hook, but it's almost an exact copy of the little wormlike midge larvae that are so numerous in that stretch of the Platte. Even on days when the food chain is turned down as low as it will go and the fish are sulking, you can sometimes get them to inhale a String Thing if you're persistent enough and your drifts are close to perfect.

This fly is so simple as to be offensive to A.K.—who's a professional fly tier, after all—but he sometimes has a few of them tucked into a corner of one of his fly boxes where maybe no one will notice them.

This is the kind of repetitive, meditational fishing that requires not so much skill as something I've heard called thoughtless, harmonious concentration. It's the kind of job that doesn't take all your wits; just enough of them to keep you from thinking very rigorously of anything else. On a cold day it also requires a twig fire and a pot of coffee on shore, which you repair to just *before* your feet actually go numb.

Wading out of the water to sit by the fire for a while is easy when the fishing is slow, and at those times the conversation wanders all over the place, from politics to fishing to sleeping bag design to the proper way to make boiled coffee. A.K. didn't say anything about his father that I can remember now, but, because it was in the air, I caught myself thinking about *my* dad a little when the talk petered out.

It occurred to me that I'm now a better fisherman than he was—maybe even a better outdoorsman in general—but that's only because I've had the time to put into it. I never did have the family or the regular job or his sense of "what a grown man's responsibilities in life ought to be." I still recall bits and pieces of the lectures, and I guess those memories aren't exactly fond ones.

Dad and I didn't see eye to eye about a lot of things, but that's only natural. When you grow up seeing one way in life, you're very likely to choose another for yourself, if only for some variety. But I think he'd have liked it that I moved out to Colorado where I fish a lot and make a decent living writing stories about it. He might even have come to understand why I didn't get all clobbered up with a lot of dependents and responsibilities. Dad liked to hunt and fish, but he never did as much of either as he'd have liked. He planned to make up for that after he retired, but he never made it that far. Many of the fathers of my generation did this same thing: They gave up what they thought of as childish things because they thought they were supposed to, and it killed a lot of them.

If Dad had lived, he might not have ended up sharing my

bohemian views on life, but when he saw that the result was a lot more fishing time, I'll bet he'd at least have stopped bitching at me.

So I didn't grow up to be my father (that's a kind of victory for most boys), but in some ways I may have become the man my father wanted to be, which is, I guess you'd say, interesting.

I did get one thing from him, though: the worst kind of workaholism. That's the kind where you're not always busy, but you always feel that you should be, so it can be hard to goof off effectively. One of the few times I can do nothing with a clear conscience is when I'm sitting next to a twig fire on the bank of a trout stream. And that, I suppose, is because nothing is all you can do when you're waiting for the fishing to pick up—even if it probably won't pick up for a month.

A.K. and I did well that day when you consider that, by rights, we shouldn't have caught anything at all. There was a period of less than an hour in midafternoon when the water temperature must have reached up into the low forties. I was fishing along on automatic pilot when a big trout bit my fly, bent the hook almost straight and got away before I could even think of giving it line. A few minutes later I hooked another one and got it almost to the net before it threw the hook. I really wanted to land that fish, but then when it got off I was glad I didn't have to freeze my hands releasing it. It was a nice rainbow. Maybe sixteen inches.

I switched to a little dry fly when I saw a single trout rise twice near the far bank, but by the time I got the knot tied the fish had stopped. I made a few casts anyway, notwithstanding the feeling that it was useless.

Fifty yards downstream, A.K. also had a few risers. He missed one and hooked and landed another on a dry fly. When he got that fish to the net, he gave a quiet little "whoop" so I'd notice. On a day when more fish were being caught, this wouldn't have been necessary.

After that the river went dead again and pretty much stayed that way until dark. We doused the fire and wandered around a little, doing more looking than fishing and making some tentative plans. In the coming year, aside from the fishing we'd naturally do around Colorado, there was the possibility of bass in Texas, trout in Montana, various game fish in Alaska and Atlantic salmon on a river somewhere in Canada.

Well, maybe these were just ideas instead of plans, but there comes a time when the former has to be bravely turned into the latter. Otherwise, you just talk and think and eventually they dissolve, either because other things pile up or because it just gets to be too late to do anything about them.

And there's another wrinkle to all this. The possible Alaska trip had to do with some friends who were moving there soon and who had already invited several of us to come up. "As soon as we get a line on something" (meaning good fishing), "we'll let you know," they said.

These folks are good planners, but they're also enthusiastic and quick to seize the moment. It wouldn't surprise me to get a phone call from them saying, "Be here in a week, the something-or-others are running."

This involves a fine point in the art of planning: maintaining the mental balance and self-confidence it takes to let you go at a moment's notice. Ed told me once that when he was younger he'd automatically say "yes" when some frantic fisherman called with little more than a rumor, while now he sees this creeping tendency to say "no" just as compulsively.

"It's something you need to pay attention to," he said, and I agree. Half of getting old is inexorable biology, but the other half is attitude.

My father liked to have things planned out in detail and I see that tendency in myself, but I've also learned to like the idea that I really don't know what's going to happen. I might as well like it because that's the way it is.

Ed again: "If you knew exactly what was gonna happen on a trip, you wouldn't even have to go."

So A.K. and I wandered the river like this, strolling, talking, making a few halfhearted casts here and there. The day had stayed that same, uniform damp gray, with the rock cliffs and the sky both looking like the undersides of old iron ships. If it had been warmer, it would have been great fishing weather.

We saw two ravens perched in a dead ponderosa pine tree. Every now and then one of them would turn to the other and poke it hard with its beak a few times. The bird getting poked didn't seem to respond in any way. I'm only an amateur bird watcher, which means I know what a raven is, but I have no idea why one would poke his partner like that.

There might have been another short flurry of feeding activity from the trout, but it was unlikely. It seemed as if it had gotten colder, although it may have only felt that way because we'd been out in it for so long. I do carry a little thermometer/compass gadget on my day pack, but I've found that I don't need an instrument to tell me when I'm cold.

We didn't stay until the light was almost gone out of desperation for more trout, but simply because that's what one does, probably in part because both our dads had that linear view of things. We're here to fish, so we fish. A equals B, period.

So in one way we were were just going through the motions. On the other hand, we ended up at a pool called the Ice Box because that was the most likely place to find feeding trout late on a cold December afternoon. You stay the whole day as a kind of observance, but you don't entirely blow off the fishing either.

On the way down to that last pool we had to cross a little

rip in the current, and A.K. pulled out ahead. He's thirteen years my senior, but he still wades better than I do in fast water, although both of us have gotten a little more careful in recent years. It's funny, but I didn't notice that a little of the spring had gone out of his step until it was back.

15

The Fishing Contest

*I*n September of 1991 I took part in the first annual Colorado Fly-casting Open tournament, a two-day event that was held in and around Lyons, Colorado. This was my first and only venture into competitive fishing, unless you count those arrangements where, for instance, the guy who catches the smallest fish of the day has to buy the beer.

I was talked into it. Bamboo rodmaker Mike Clark, an old friend of mine, was one of the organizers, and since this was a new and largely unknown event, they were trying to drum up contestants.

I walked into Mike's shop one afternoon to bum a cup of coffee and he said, "You're gonna fish in the tournament, aren't you?" I'd known this was coming, but I'd tried not to think about it. I guess I'd secretly hoped that if I just didn't volunteer it would slide by.

At first I said I disapproved of competitive fishing on philosophical grounds—the same terse answer I'd given the two or three other times I'd been asked to get into an official fishing contest of some kind. That had worked in the past and it was still true, but this time it sounded awfully self-righteous—the kind of crap you can sometimes lay on strangers, but not on friends. After all, who am I to approve or disapprove of anything?

"I don't mean to say it's the devil's work," I added, "I just don't think I'd like it."

"You ever do it?" Mike asked.

"No."

"So how do you know you wouldn't like it?"

My mother used to get me with that one.

I began to soften a little then. As I said, this was the first time this thing had ever been held, and there did seem to be some decent arguments for it: "It'll help build a constituency for conservation work on the stream," one guy said, and someone else pointed out that it could illustrate to the chamber of commerce types that a proper local industry is one that recognizes the value of a healthy natural environment. You know, fly-fishing instead of a paper mill.

And, too, I think the people behind the event—some friends of mine among them—were beginning to ask that inevitable question: What if we had a contest and nobody entered?

"How much is the entry fee?" I asked.

"A hundred dollars."

"Forget it," I said.

Mike glanced out through his shop window at the one-block, one-story main street and said, "Tell you what. I'll sponsor you."

"Oh, hell . . ."

Fly-fishing contests aren't exactly sweeping the country, thank God, but they have gotten more popular in the last

few years. The one everybody knows about is the Jackson
Hole One Fly in Jackson Hole, Wyoming. Jack Dennis started
this in the mid-eighties and, by most accounts, he's the one
who invented the idea of contestants being limited to one
fly for the whole event.

All the other fly-fishing contests I've heard of mimic this
one pretty closely. Teams or individuals fish for a day—accompanied by guides, sometimes called "judges"—and the
score is figured on either total trout or total *inches* of trout
fairly landed. When there are teams, sometimes the individual who catches the biggest or the most fish gets a little
something extra. I've never heard of the species of trout af-
fecting the scoring, but I understand that in the Colorado
Superfly Competition Kokanee salmon are somehow scored
differently.

Often specific beats on the river are assigned by drawing,
and they're usually rotated between morning and afternoon
sessions so no one can complain that the other team got the
honey hole.

And there's always that thing with the flies. You get one
or sometimes two flies, picked by you beforehand and then
approved by the judges, and that's it. Lose it (or them) and
you're done.

That naturally adds some artificial tactical aspects to it.
You fish more carefully than you normally would, passing
up good but tricky flies, and you use a cable of a leader that
ruins your drifts. And of course a bad choice of fly pattern
can't be corrected, so you pick a general attractor-style fly
and then hope against a hatch instead of for one.

The choice of fly can be agonizing. There are those who'll
fish a nymph in competition because, on a normal day on a
normal trout stream, more fish can be caught on nymphs
than on dry flies. Then there are those who'll fish a dry fly
because you're less likely to lose it and because, in a pinch,
it's easier to sink a dry fly than float a nymph.

You want a durable fly that won't fall apart with hard use.
The rules of some contests let you fix a fly on-stream, but

no actual fly-tying materials can be used. Repairs must be done with monofilament or "natural material commonly found on the stream." That would be grass and strips of tree bark rather than aluminum cans and plastic bags. I'm told that's usually a losing battle, so many fishermen tie up indestructible tournament flies using heavy thread, extra knots, wire and Super Glue.

Virtually all of these events are held for charity or, if you're like me and don't care for that word, let's say the proceeds go to fund a good, usually conservation-related cause.

The come-ons for these things usually talk about how much media exposure they'll get, as if media exposure in and of itself was a good thing, and about what the money that's raised will go for. Sometimes it's something specific, like habitat improvement on this or that stream, although sometimes it goes into some vague pot labeled "preservation of cold water fisheries," which could mean anything. A fair question to ask of any apparently good cause is, "How much of the money *actually goes to feed starving children in South America?*" or whatever.

Prizes are seldom if ever cash. Usually the top fisherman gets something like a good fly rod, maybe a little loving cup of the "World's Greatest Dad" variety for the mantel and the opportunity to bask briefly in whatever media glitz there might be. In other words, the prize is worth winning, but nowhere near enough to cheat for, which tends to keep things pretty laid back.

That's a saving grace. If anyone thinks we need a snazzier fly-fishing tournament with more industry sponsors and a bigger purse, all he should have to do is look at the horrors of competitive bass fishing: Top four anglers compete for seventy thousand dollars cash. And it's held at Disney World! And it's broadcast on The Nashville Network. That's not fishing, that's the kind of thing that has made the sports pages of most newspapers read like a cross between the business section and the police notes.

Jack Dennis's One Fly is still the undisputed big one in fly-fishing, and with luck it's as big as these things will ever get. It attracts celebrities and I'm told it's quite the scene, although there have been no scandals that I know of and I've yet to see a razzle-dazzle press release crowing about crowds and prize money both in the hundreds of thousands. I've talked to some people who have fished in the One Fly and they claim they actually had fun.

There can be as many as thirty-two four-person teams in the One Fly, plus guides, and it's popular enough that in recent years it's been by invitation only. There are several formal dinners involved and the entry fee is three thousand dollars per team. But from what I've seen of them, most of the fly-fishing tournaments are still small, local, funky, friendly and comparatively cheap to enter. The printed rules tend to be detailed, but brief and light on the legalese, except, of course, for the liability waiver.

The first Colorado Open was small and friendly enough and maybe even a little funkier than it was intended to be, but it was different from most in two ways. For one thing, it was for profit. Sure, there was an implication that the town of Lyons might well use the proceeds for stream improvement or research into minimum flows, but there were no promises. For another, at least part of it was an old-style *casting* tournament with courses for distance and accuracy based largely on the rules of the American Casting Association in Fenton, Missouri.

According to the organizers, the Colorado Open was designed to be a test of all-around fly-fishing skill under conditions that, as much as possible, resemble those of actual fishing. I wasn't on the planning committee, but I lobbied some people who were to bag the fishing event entirely and just make it a casting tournament. I said that the distance and accuracy courses might be a fair way to pick the best caster, but that one random day of fishing with only two flies wasn't a fair test of a fisherman's ability to catch trout. And anyway, fly-fishing, by nature, is a sport that doesn't—or shouldn't—involve rivalry. I quoted Jim Harrison: "Any spirit of competition in hunting or fishing dishonors the game," he said.

Someone asked, "Who's Jim Merriman?"

"*Harrison*," I said. "He's a poet and novelist."

"Oh."

The first day, Saturday, was the two-fly fishing contest. The night before I had gone to a Marcia Ball concert in Boulder. It was too loud (I seem to remember the blues being quieter), I stayed out too late and drank just enough gin and tonics to give me a mild hangover. The rules had specified "normal fishing conditions," right?

I chose a #14 Royal Wulff and a #14 Adams for my flies. Looking back on it, that was an odd choice. I knew the stream pretty well, and knew also that a better choice would have been a brace of #16 St. Vrain Caddis flies, or maybe a caddis for the morning and a small hopper for the afternoon. I think I picked the Adams and the Wulff because of the stance I'd decided to take on this. I was going to compete as a favor to Mike, but I wasn't going to take it seriously and I might just decide to look down on anyone who did.

When we presented our flies to the judges for inspection, everyone else's two flies looked better than mine. There were flawless Hares Ear nymphs (always a good choice), trim Blue-winged Olives (a hatch that could come off at that time of year) and one guy had a beautifully matched pair of #10 Coachman Trudes. I had grabbed my two flies out of a box at the last minute that morning. The Adams was new, but the Wulff looked used.

The actual fishing took place on an eighteen-mile stretch of the South Fork of the St. Vrain. A judge accompanied each fisherman to observe and keep score. There were no assigned beats, you picked your own spots and you could move as often as you wanted to. Scoring was simple: One trout was good for one point, size notwithstanding. Suckers didn't count. All fish had to be released immediately and a bad or clumsy release—one that might injure the fish—would cost you points.

You could fish any rod you wanted as long as it didn't exceed nine feet three-quarters of an inch in length—that is, a nine-foot rod allowing for slop—but you had to use the same rod for all the events, casting as well as fishing. I chose an eight-and-a-half-foot, six-weight bamboo that Mike made for me a few years ago fitted with a weight forward 7 line—a heavier rod than I care to fish on a small stream, but lighter than I'd choose to cast for distance. Either it was the right choice or it put me at a disadvantage in all three events.

I took my judge, Clint, to a stretch of pocket water not far from town, figuring my time would be better spent fishing than driving. I tied my Adams to a 2x, eight-pound-test leader so I wouldn't lose it and began casting. I wanted broken pocket water because the trout there tend to be a little less picky than they are in smoother currents. The heavy leader made the fly drift as if it were wired to a welding rod.

It was a bright, cool, early fall day. The cottonwoods and bigtooth maples along the stream were turning yellow and the dogwoods were red. I got in the water at the bottom of a good-looking pool. Clint found a flat rock in the sun, lay down with his hands behind his head and said, "If you get one, give me a yell."

I decided to work the stream quickly, covering the most water in the shortest possible time. That seemed like the best way to catch lots of fish (remember, size didn't count) and I wanted to keep Clint from taking a nap, which he seemed on the verge of doing. I was still a little hungover, and if I couldn't have a nap, then neither could he.

The Adams wasn't exactly the wrong fly—it never is—but it wasn't entirely right, either. That is, I was hooking a trout now and then, but not as many as I wanted to. I could remember better days on that stream, but that probably wasn't fair. A fisherman's memory is notoriously expansive, and we all know that if a guy says you can catch an average of fifty trout a day on some stream, he's talking about the most fish ever caught there in living memory, plus 10 percent.

More to the point, I figured at least some of the other contestants must be doing better. In the normal course of things I have sometimes wondered how other fishermen were doing, but actually worrying about it was a new experience.

I was happier than usual to see five- and six-inch trout because they were still worth one point, just like a big one, and they were quicker to land. But when I was hand-landing one and it wiggled off the hook (and I didn't get my point because I hadn't actually touched the fish) I started using the landing net. I used it on fish small enough to swim through the mesh.

Just before the scheduled lunch break, I found a little brown trout rising under some overhanging brush on the far bank. It was the kind of situation I'd been passing up, not wanting to snag my only fly, but that close to the break I figured what the hell, I can afford to lose the fly now because I'll get another one after lunch, and if I do this right I'll make another point.

After a few tries I got a nice cast over the fish and he made a classic refusal rise: came up, looked at the fly and turned away. He wanted the St. Vrain caddis pattern I should have picked instead of the stupid Adams. Clint was looking at his watch. The morning session would be over in five minutes.

I thought, Come on you little shit, time is money.

The casting events on Sunday were straightforward. For the distance competition we stood at a chalked line down in Meadow Park and cast as far as we could along a surveyor's tape lying on the grass. We got three casts and all the distances were added together for our score.

We helped each other stretch out our lines and then took some practice casts. There were about twenty people standing around watching. Half of them were asking the other half, "What's going on here?"

The accuracy course consisted of six stations set up in the pretty little stretch of trout stream that runs through the park. At each station the caster stood within three feet of a stake in the water and cast at a number of floating ring targets.

The scoring here was a little complex. You started with one hundred points and then gained points for hits and lost them for misses and ticks. (A "tick" is when your fly hits the water or a branch while you're false casting.) You could also decline a target and lose fewer points than if you tried it and missed a few times.

This was a difficult course set out by cruel judges who didn't have to compete themselves, although I have to say it was realistic. Most of the targets were in places where you might catch a trout in a small stream like this, and there were plenty of overhanging branches and snags to grab your hookless tournament fly, just like in the real world. Other accuracy courses are sometimes laid out on lawns or open casting pools. This one was a lot more interesting.

And, naturally, there was pressure. A judge stood near each ring, one or two were behind you to watch your back cast and one was on the bank with a clipboard, keeping score. With each cast voices would come from different directions saying "Tick" or "Miss" or occasionally "Hit," while comments drifted over from the small crowd of spectators: things like, "He's not as good as that guy in the blue hat, is he?"

A tournament that accurately represented all the subtleties of fly-fishing doesn't exist and probably never will. It would have to have not only casting and fish-catching competitions, but also categories for fashion (Old World, punk, neon, blue-collar), not to mention lunch and wine selection, the invention and naming of fly patterns, bird and edible plant identification, good-heartedness, humor, lying, trespassing, philosophical detachment, creative misdirection of fellow anglers and so on.

Scoring on anything as obvious as number of fish or total

inches would be ridiculously simple-minded. A big, dumb fish would have to be worth fewer points than a little, smart one, and trout not caught would have to be worth something, too. If you got a large brown in a difficult spot to inspect and refuse five different fly patterns without putting him down, you'd get, say, ten points. If you called him a bastard, your score would remain the same, but if you *meant* it, you'd lose five points.

If the event was scheduled for a day that happened to be bright and sunny, you'd have to get at least one hundred points for declaring that you were going to stay home, patch the canoe and wait for a cloudy day to fish.

It would also have to be possible for a guy who caught no fish to beat a guy who caught twenty. He could do it by getting skunked with good humor while fishing a hundred-year-old bamboo rod, wearing creatively patched waders and having elk paté on melba toast and Thunderbird wine for lunch. Or maybe he could make up enough points in the Zen category by honestly not caring or, better yet, fishing without a fly as an exercise in meditation and then saying to the judges afterward, "Well, catching trout and not catching trout really amount to the same thing, right?"

All fish would have to be released immediately, unless you had a really neat recipe and found some wild mushrooms along the stream to go with it. Extra points would be awarded if you cooked the fish on site, but if the mushrooms turned out to be poisonous, you'd be disqualified.

If you won the tournament and the check for your entry fee bounced a day later, you would also receive the special Board of Governors' No Visible Means of Support Award. A small trophy would also go to the judge who was the least judgmental.

For a long time now I've said I didn't like fly-fishing contests because they seem unnatural, and now that I've fished in one, I can say that with even more conviction. That is, *I* don't like them. You, of course, can make up your own mind.

For the record, I came in dead third in all three events in a very small field of competitors. Afterward Mike said, "Well, I guess that makes you the third best fly fisherman in Colorado," which he and I both know is pretty damned far from the truth.

On a personal level, I came very close to wishing ill on a friend. At lunch on Saturday, I learned that Dale Darling was several fish (points, that is) ahead of me. Dale is a good fisherman and he knows that stream as well as anyone, so it was unlikely that he'd use the wrong fly in the afternoon session or be unable to locate trout. I didn't exactly hope he'd slip on a wet rock and break his casting arm, but I allowed as how that would be to my advantage.

So what does that mean? If there was a quarter-million-dollar purse at stake, would I have had a crew of hired henchmen out there greasing all the rocks?

The prize here was the custom bamboo fly rod of your choice from Mike Clark and a little bit of glory—both worth having, although the former is probably worth more and will certainly last longer than the latter. Having decided not to take this contest seriously, I guess I failed when it occurred to me that it would actually be kind of neat to win.

Okay, so there's a kind of openheartedness about these things that I never learned. That's why I fish instead of playing on a local softball team. Sports that require two teams or two players for a match or where the participants gamble with their own money are *about* competition, but fly-fishing is solitary, contemplative, misanthropic, scientific in some hands, poetic in others and laced with conflicting aesthetic considerations. It's not even clear if catching fish is actually the point. I just don't think you can shoehorn all that into the great American misconception that life consists of a few champions and a whole bunch of losers.

And then there's the cuteness factor. In a sense, the one

or two fly business is as necessary as the sack in a sack race, but in fact one of the keys to catching trout is the ability to assess the situation and change from the fly that was right five minutes ago to the fly that's right now, not to mention the knowledge and forethought it takes to have those flies with you.

If competition dishonors the game, what does engineered silliness do to the competitors? On the other hand, if you're worried about your dignity, are you taking yourself too seriously? Does competition trivialize fly-fishing? Is it possible to trivialize something that, at its best, shouldn't be that important? I'd say a *real* fly fisherman would never stoop so low as to compete with his colleagues, except that that would be the most sanctimonious statement I've ever made.

Not long ago a man called and asked me to enter a contest they were having over on the West Slope. They were going to field a bunch of two-person teams composed of a fly fisherman and a golfer. One day you fished, the next day you played eighteen holes. It was all for an unspecified good cause and there was supposed to be lots of press coverage.

"I don't golf," I said.

"No, see, that's the point," the guy said. "You don't golf, and you'll be paired with a golfer who doesn't fish, so you'll both have the opportunity to make fools of yourselves. They're gonna videotape it. It'll be a hoot!"

"You don't understand," I said, "I am philosophically *opposed* to golf."

16

West

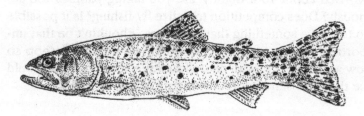

Not long ago A.K. Best and I found ourselves in West Yellowstone, Montana, on what we'll call, for official purposes, a business trip.

The Federation of Fly Fishers Conclave was in town, and Jim Criner, now owner of Bud Lilly's Trout Shop, asked us to come up and sign copies of our books in the store for a couple of mornings. Mornings, that is, so we could sneak out and fish in the afternoons. He also said he'd put us up and we could stay as long as we liked. Jim had thought this through. He understood we weren't going to be on expense accounts from our publishers, so he felt we might need a little incentive to make the thirteen-hour drive from Colorado.

The book signings were actually very successful, but there were still some of those inevitable doldrums to get through. A good way to stay humble about being a writer is to sit at a table with your life's work in front of you and wait for, say, an hour and a half for an adoring fan to show up. Finally a guy does walk over. He smiles and says, "Hi, you got a public toilet here?"

Some years ago A.K. and I both spent time working in fly shops, so when there didn't happen to be anyone wanting an autograph, our tendency was to go on automatic: helping people try on waders and select flies, which beats sitting around trying to be famous when things are slow.

I also bought a new hat from the shop. A few weeks before, while we were camped at Roy Palm's place on the Frying Pan River in Colorado, Roy's sweet little bird dog pup had eaten my old one.

I wouldn't have kicked the dog even if she wasn't worth a reported four thousand dollars and even if Roy hadn't been very good to me over the years. Puppies will be puppies and fishing hats, even old favorite ones, are expendable. The only thing that bothered me was, a new fishing hat cost almost forty dollars. I must be getting old. I remember when you could buy a Hardy reel for forty dollars.

In fact, that's about what a good fly reel went for the first time I came to West Yellowstone in the 1970s, back when Bud Lilly still owned Bud Lilly's Trout Shop. There's a gentrified covered mall in town now (at least it's small) and at a neat little bookstore called the Book Peddler you can actually get a cup of cappuccino, but aside from a few things like that, the place hasn't changed much. It's still a small, funky, honestly rustic, somewhat touristy, largely one-story western town that grew up haphazardly at the west entrance to Yellowstone National Park.

When mail first started arriving there in 1908, the town— or at least the post office—was called Riverside. The following year it was changed to Yellowstone and then, in 1920, it became *West* Yellowstone. Now, in regional anglers' shorthand, it's often referred to simply as "West."

West Yellowstone is arguably the capital city of American fly-fishing. It's a town with 924 year-round residents that supports five fly shops, countless guides and fly tiers and the

Federation of Fly Fishers international headquarters. Not every business in town has stuffed trout on the walls, but those that don't seem oddly stark. World famous western trout rivers like the Madison, Yellowstone, Gibbon, Firehole and Henry's Fork, not to mention many lesser-known streams and lakes, are within easy day-trip range.

The trout-fishing in the area is wonderful, or, fishing being what it is, let's say it *can* be when the conditions are right. Whether it's as fabulous as it once was is a matter of some debate. There's always the suspicion that it was better in the good old days and Al McClane, one of the early jet set angling writers and an undisputed expert in such matters, has said, "Montana fishing has survived as well as can be expected against the onslaught of civilization."

Then again, Bud Lilly, who was born in that country and should know, said, "When the fishing around West Yellowstone started to get a lot of attention from the fishing writers in the late 1960s and early 1970s, those of us who lived there noticed a surprising increase in the size of fish being reported (but not seen or photographed) from some rivers."

It's a scandalous implication, but then fishermen—let alone writers—*have* been known to exaggerate.

So let's just say that the fishing is better than average at the very least and, more important, it is legendary. Even if the trout you catch are only a few inches longer than the ones you get back home, they are nonetheless from rivers that are, as they say, part of the literature of the sport. That's important. In certain circles, the names of famous rivers can be dropped as impressively as those of movie stars.

So fly-fishing in the West Yellowstone area amounts to a kind of pilgrimage. An unofficial survey of license plates reveals that most of the visitors are from states west of the Mississippi, but you see plates from all over—Florida, Kentucky, Maine, pick a place—and in years past I've run into anglers from England, Australia, Germany, Japan and New Zealand.

One of the New Zealanders, with a deadpan delivery worthy of a native Montanan, said he was having a nice time, even though, compared to back home, the beer was watery and the trout were small.

When I asked Vicki Eggers at the West Yellowstone Chamber of Commerce how many fishermen the town saw in a season, she said she couldn't say, but it was "a sizable number." To the same question, a fly shop owner or a guide will say, "Plenty," and a fisherman may say, "Too many."

Even if you didn't know beforehand, you'd spot this as a fishing town before you'd driven two blocks. Maybe it's the businesses that cater to anglers in one way or another or all the obvious fishing vehicles, ranging from official-looking pickups towing Mackenzie boats to decrepit Volkswagens with float tubes strapped on top.

Or maybe it's the fishermen themselves. As you walk or drive down the main drag, you keep thinking you see people you know, but before you can turn to whomever you're with and say, "Isn't that. . . ?" you realize it's not the specific person you recognize, but the type: ageless—say, forty on up—male or female, fit, tanned, dressed in a practical, sporting sort of way, often wearing the expression Ed Engle calls the hundred-mile stare. Fly fishers. It's hard to explain, but they don't have to be wearing hip boots. You pick them out the way members of any subculture can spot each other pretty much at a glance.

And it works the other way around, too. I can't remember ever buying gas, coffee or anything else in West without being asked, "How's the fishing?" I don't know how they can tell I'm not there to look at the geysers; it's just obvious somehow.

Of course, sometimes you do recognize someone, either a friend from somewhere or one of the many angling celebrities who show up in town on a fairly regular basis. On any street corner or in any bar, café or fly shop you might spot Ernest Schweibert, Doug Swisher, Gary LaFontaine, Nick Lyons, Dave Whitlock or almost any other face you've seen on the dust jacket of a fly-fishing book. In years past it might have been Lee Wulff or Arnold Gingrich. Everyone shows up there sooner or later.

I've been told that angling notoriety is the best kind in that, although certain people may know who you are, you can still walk down any street in any town in the country without being recognized—except maybe in West.

A.K. and I did slip out those first two afternoons. We drove the ninety-mile round trip to a place we know on the Yellowstone River in the park and dragged back into West between 10:30 and 11:00 at night, just in time to get supper at Thiem's Café.

When we arrived in town we'd asked a couple of local contacts the two questions one must have answered immediately, namely, where are the fish biting and what is the current fisherman's café? Both things change from time to time. The consensus was, the Madison and Yellowstone rivers, and Thiem's.

The right café must be casual and cozy (pine paneling is nice, but optional), have good food served in generous portions, have quick service (at least in the morning when you're in a hurry), have waiters and waitresses who can stand up to the endless, corny wisecracks, and keep fishermen's hours.

It also helps if the place has the proper history. Thiem's, like many other establishments in West, displays the obligatory collection of snapshots dating back at least to the 1950s showing the building in winter. On the wall near the bathroom door there are shots of Thiem's—formerly Chat's, formerly Huck's—buried in snow up to the eaves, with just the sign visible at the top of the drift. If no one gets married or catches a huge trout, this might be the only photograph a West Yellowstonian takes in a year. It's a way locals have of reminding us summer tourists that we're dilettantes compared to those who spend their winters there.

The right café provides not only food, but gossip. It's rare for a fisherman you don't know well to tell you precisely where he caught a lot of big trout and what fly he was using, but it's just as rare for him to be able to entirely contain himself if he's done well. Consequently, if you pay attention and read between the lines, you can deduce that certain insect hatches are on and that people are generally "doing okay" on a stretch of a certain river roughly between this bridge and that roadhouse. This is B-list stuff, but valuable just the same.

You can also learn who's staying in whose spare cabin, guest room or back porch, borrowing whose drift boat or guiding for which shop, although trying to look anyone up is usually a waste of time. Someone you know may be "in town," but of course that's a euphemism. They're actually out fishing, dawn till dusk, and if they're into something good, they probably didn't tell anyone where they were going. You learn to say, "Well, maybe we'll run into him."

And you really do want to run into him because it's the people you know who give you the best tips about where there are big fish that are currently biting and that everyone isn't onto: the *A*-list material. There can be mobs of fishermen in and around West in the summer, but there are also countless miles of good water in the immediate area, which, depending on how hard you want to drive, includes the park (which is in Wyoming), a good chunk of Montana and a sizable corner of Idaho. There are always secrets to be learned.

Around West, the best fishing tips often come with the standard boilerplate grizzly disclaimer: "You park at the bridge, cross the river, hike downstream until the trail peters out, then go on for another two miles and start fishing at the big bend in the river. Now, there *are* some bears down there . . ."

This is done for a number of reasons. First, there really are a few grizzlies around, although they're hardly ever seen. Statistically, your chances of getting stomped by a bison or hit by a car are far greater than those of being attacked by a bear, but it does happen, and a bear attack can be extremely definitive. If you sent some tenderfoot to a fishing spot where grizzlies had been seen a time or two over the last few seasons and a week later the search party turned up a broken fly rod and a single, bloody hiking boot, you might feel a little funny about it if you hadn't issued the usual warning. So local etiquette demands that you say, "Now, there *are* some bears down there . . ." so if anything happens it won't be your fault.

And I think there's also a subtle character check involved. When a guy gives up a great spot, he wants to think you're worthy of it. If a little thing like a grizzly bear is going to scare you off, it's probably just as well.

In some hands this whole bear business can be yet another one of those subtle digs that locals really do have a right to. Sure, you had a good trip and caught lots of trout, but a competent local smart-ass can send you home thinking you probably could have gotten into even bigger fish if you'd only had more guts.

I guess you just have to understand the relationship between the residents of a tourist town and the tourists themselves. Locals can be like cowboys: They may love the life and the region, but they can eventually get tired of the cows.

People who like trout have the same kind of affection for West that other people have for, say, Paris. That is, it begins as a kind of cultural conditioning before we've even seen the place, and then once we've been there a few times we begin to feel like honorary citizens, strolling its sidewalks with a proprietary air. After all, we're fly fishermen, and this is a fly-fishing town.

To be honest, we tend to look down a little on the regular tourists who only come to view the wildlife from the car and maybe do some shopping in town because they are there as spectators, while we're there to participate. Granted, fly fishers are an arrogant bunch as a rule, but when people stop their cars, run down to take your picture while you're fishing, and then ask you things like, "Where do they keep the buffalo in the winter?" it's hard not to feel a little superior.

On the other hand, I can't say I know the town itself well. Over the past fifteen years or so, I've been in all the fly shops, some of the gas stations and cafés, the Laundromat, a book store and the post office. Once, years ago, a bunch of us rented a room in the Alpine Motel for an afternoon so we could take showers, but we didn't stay the night, and I have now had a cup of authentic West Yellowstone cappuccino, which was real good.

I'm told there are one or two decent restaurants, but I've never eaten in them because they don't stay open late enough. On this last trip, one of our publishers told A.K. and me that, although he wouldn't spring for the trip, he would reimburse us for a dinner. We wanted to stick him good—and he fully expected that—but the best we could do was a couple of chicken fried steak specials at Thiem's.

I can't remember offhand the numbers of the highways leading out of town in three directions, but I know where they go. To the east is the road into the park that takes you to the Firehole, upper Madison, Yellowstone and such. The road north goes to Bozeman and the Gallatin River, crossing the Madison, Cougar Creek, Duck Creek and so on. (Duck Creek is pretty good, but there *are* some bears.) The Idaho Road goes south, toward the Henry's Fork and beyond.

Like most fishermen who show up in West on a more or less regular basis to eat, sleep, buy trout flies and ask directions, I know the surrounding rivers better than the town. That's not to say I'm anything but a normal duffer, but I've been there often enough—and been out with enough good guides—that I do have some spots.

A "spot" doesn't have to be remote (some good ones are within sight of roads) and it doesn't have to be completely unknown. It just has to be a good place to fish that isn't a regular stop for half the guides and fly fishers in three states; a place you stand a fair chance of having all to yourself and that you wouldn't tell just anyone about.

Like that stretch of the Yellowstone A.K. and I know about. It's miles from the famous spots on that river that everyone fishes. There are fewer cutthroat trout there, but they are bigger and healthier. A friend who spends his summers in West took us there years ago, but we now think of it as our spot. In all the time we've been fishing it we've seen two other anglers and a bull moose.

That's not to say we always catch fish there. Once a guide asked me if catching those big, dumb cutthroats in the Yellowstone wasn't a little like shooting fish in a barrel. I had to say, "Not to me."

We fished that spot those first two afternoons after the book signings and we caught some nice big trout. Then on the second night, over buffalo burgers at Thiem's, we ran into an East Coast guide that A.K. knows. A.K. is a professional fly tier and by now he knows half the people in the business.

This guy knew we'd been fishing the area off and on for quite a few years, so he naturally assumed we knew what we were doing. After all, fly-fishing is one small part of American culture where it's still assumed that experience and a little age naturally bring wisdom. After the usual pleasantries, the guy asked how we'd been doing—the standard opening move.

"Oh," I said, "we've been getting into some fish," trying to sound as if, you know, we'd been holding up our end, but it was nothing really fabulous or anything, while at the same time leaving open the possibility that it *had* been fabulous and I was just being cagey.

"Where?" the guy asked casually, and A.K. answered, "On the Yellowstone," glancing at me now because we were getting into a sensitive area.

"Oh," the guide said, "where exactly on the Yellowstone?"

At this point in these classic, ticklish conversations, the

questioner usually gives up on innocence (he knows he's just asked an impertinent question) and tries for just the right note of brazenness. The interviewee is then faced with either telling him or ending it right there without being too rude.

A.K. looked up from his buffalo burger and said, with finality, "Not where you think."

By now we have a handful of places like this between us. Most were gifts from friends, a precious few are ours alone and were hard won. We don't tell other visitors about them because we don't want the word to get around, and we don't tell locals for fear these spots aren't as secret as we think they are. In this town you want to feel plugged into the local fly-fishing mystique, if only for a week or so out of every summer, and nothing will deflate you quicker than hearing someone say, "Oh, hell, everyone knows about *that.*"

So we assume that recognizable West Yellowstone pose: modest, seasoned and ever so slightly self-satisfied. The implication being, yes, I guess we do know a thing or two about the fishing around here, and, no, we don't really care to go into it. If nothing else, we know how to fit in here. We understand that the less you say about fly-fishing, the more people will assume you know.

I'm like most fishermen when it comes to night fishing: I know something about it (or at least I'm familiar with the mythology) but I don't actually go out and do it much, if only because it takes a sharpness that's hard for me to muster up at the end of the day.

I'm essentially diurnal, like most modern humans, and too often I feel as if night is a different, unfamiliar place where I don't feel at home. But then that's a thought I have coming off the river at dusk or maybe in camp in the evening, enclosed in my little dome of firelight; the idea that by dark you should *be* somewhere. Once you get out in it, night isn't really that foreign. It's more like a large room in your own house where, for reasons of habit, you seldom go.

I'm talking about real night now, not illuminated city or suburban, controlled-environment, flick-of-a-switch night. You know, the kind where it actually gets dark and things are different.

One of the best reasons I can think of for being active at night is that many of the fish we like to chase in the daytime are at least partly nocturnal, and some of them, like largemouth bass and brown trout, are notorious for it. In some places, the really big fish can take to feeding exclusively under cover of darkness and they'll be seen in daylight only when spawning or, rarely, when there's some fabulous feeding opportunity like a salmon fly or Green Drake hatch.

When you see these big fish where you never saw them before, your first thought is, Where did they come from? But deep down you know they're just shy; you know they're really always there to be caught every night. It's *you* who've been missing.

Like most common wisdom, this is correct often enough, but an honest night fisher will be the first to tell you it doesn't always work. The fish don't always bite, and when they do it's not always the big ones. Good fishing depends on so many things: water temperature, stream flow, turbidity, insect lifecycles, time of year, the phase of the moon (both for the light it sheds and, perhaps, for more mysterious reasons). In actual fact, night fishing is a lot like day fishing, except you can't see what you're doing.

I'm always tantalized by the idea of big fish, but what I really enjoy about night fishing is being out with the owls, bats, rabbits, deer, raccoons and such. Half the natural world is nocturnal, and sometimes I get to thinking about how much I miss by sleeping when it's dark. And there's also a pleasant surreptitious feeling to it—"under cover of darkness" and all that. It's almost like poaching but without the moral dilemma or the possibility of getting caught.

I'm a typical, more or less civilized, late-twentieth-century light junkie, so I'm naturally a little apprehensive about being out at night, but I know it's not the actual darkness that's dangerous, only the possible results of it. I could bump into something, fall down, walk off a high bank, wade into barbed wire or get lost. This is a subtle but important distinction: I know the darkness itself is not going to swallow me up.

The last time I went night fishing was in August on the Roaring Fork River in Colorado. A few of us had been fishing the Green Drake and Pale Morning Dun mayfly hatches on the nearby Frying Pan: pretty, daytime, highly visual stuff. After a few good days of this, Roy Palm—whose land we were camping on—said he and one of his guides were going to go night fish a spot they have on the Fork and asked if we wanted to come along.

I, for one, almost always accept invitations like that. Roy has lived for many years now within sight of one great trout river and very near another. He's a guide and he owns the Frying Pan Angler fly shop in Basalt. At least half of the hot local fly patterns for the area originally came from Roy's vise. He may not know everything about the fishing thereabouts, but I doubt anyone knows more.

And it's also just a general principle that when the boys at the fly shop ask you to join them after hours at an unspecified place they know of, the only proper response is, "Okay, where and when?" Good guides will always go the full distance to put their clients into the best fishing, with just one footnote: If only to keep themselves interested, they'll hold a little something back for themselves. Night fishing is custom made for that because it's something most sports wouldn't want to do anyway.

We slogged down to the river through an overgrown stretch of swampy wetland that was hard going even with a little light left in the sky. The faint trail we were on wound around several odd-shaped ponds, and I could see that on the way back I'd come on a couple of forks that went off in different directions. I tried to think, okay, left, right, and then left again, reversed, of course, because I'll be going the other way coming out, but I knew I'd forget that too soon. There'd be the beam of a pocket flashlight to help, but that doesn't do as much for you as you'd think. That small, lit-up piece of trail could be anywhere. It's like having someone quote a random passage from a book you read once and trying to guess what page it's on. I decided to locate one of the people I was with when it was time to leave. Two of these guys were locals who would, presumably, know the way out.

That particular stretch of river was wide and fast, with the kind of slick, cobbled bottom fishermen like to call "greased cannon balls"—tricky to wade even when you can see what you're doing. But the stream bed dropped off quickly where I was, so I figured at least some fish would be working close to shore and I wouldn't have to wade too far out.

In fact, isn't that what's supposed to happen at night? Aren't the big fish supposed to move out of the mysterious depths and into the shallows just a roll cast away? That's the theory, but I've seen fishing theories come up short. I remember thinking I should either do more of this or not mess with it at all.

There were about twenty yards of slower current between the bank and the river's main channel that I figured to be the fishable water. I tried to get a picture of that in my mind, as well as one of the thick stand of willows behind me. I'd have to remember to keep my back cast high.

These are the logistical matters you think about at dusk, when you can still see.

The word was there might be a good night caddis hatch here, but that had been carefully offered without a guarantee. Caddis hatches can be spooky and guides like to hedge their bets, even when they're off duty.

There were a few small caddis flies swarming over the water in the last light—not a proper hatch, but a good sign— so I began with a #14 Elk Hair Caddis dry fly. That was a size or two larger than the naturals, but this is acceptable. There's something about night fishing that changes the scale of things and lets you fish larger flies. In fact, there's one school of thought that says if the trout are feeding on a #16 caddis, you should tie on a #2 Muddler Minnow.

This was a pretty spot. The Roaring Fork is a big, wide river for Colorado, and it seems to get bigger, not to mention louder, at night. Behind me was the swamp and the thick little grove of willows. To the west, where the river turned sharply, was a high cliff above a bend pool that looked bottomless. To the east was a line of rocky hills that I knew to be bright red with scattered green juniper and pine, but by then the colors were quickly bleeding out of things and it was all becoming shades of gray.

Across the river—maybe seventy-five yards wide there—were the sloping, rocky pastures, barbed-wire fences and crooked, unpainted outbuildings of a sheep ranch. I could hear sheep bleating peacefully—a sound that's been called the coyote's dinner bell—and I thought I could just make some of them out over there, although the gray bumps I saw could have been rocks.

When one of the bumps began to move I thought, Sheep. Then, when I saw the ambling way it walked, I revised that to sheep*dog*.

I began casting upstream, working the water in a fan pattern starting parallel to the bank and working out into the main current. Operating on some vision of thoroughness, I'd do this twice before taking a few steps and doing the same thing again. Thinking of that grayish-olive wall of willows, I was trying to approximate a steeple cast, keeping the line high behind me. I thought I could hear trout rising, but I couldn't be sure. A big river makes a lot of noise: a large overall rush with scattered plops and gurgles. When you're fishing a dry fly on a dead drift, you set the hook on any plop that sounds unusually definitive. Sometimes there's a fish there, but usually all you feel is the loose tug and slide of your line against the water.

After an indeterminate amount of time (time changes in

the dark, too) I reeled in and, with the help of a small flash-light, clipped off the little caddis pattern and tied on the biggest dry fly I could find, a #8 or #10 Royal Trude with an inch-long white calf tail wing. I turned my back to the river to keep the flashlight beam off the water. I don't know if this is really necessary or not, but several night fishers have told me it is. If nothing else, it probably doesn't hurt.

The logic for big flies at night has always seemed shaky to me. Are there larger bugs on the water at night than there are in the daytime? Not usually, and when there are, this is typi-cally well-known among the local anglers. Still, it works, the theory being that fish can see a big fly well at night and, un-der the cover of darkness, they become greedy and reckless.

Ideally, a night fly should be black because after dark color means little or nothing. The trout are looking upward through whorly currents into faint starlight, so what you want is the darkest, sharpest silhouette possible: black. And when you think of it that way, sure, big too.

Another theory calls for a black body with a big white wing for visibility, but that can't be right. Your eyes become ac-customed to the darkness, and starlight does faintly outline the top halves of certain objects with a dull, colorless glow, but I defy anyone to say he can actually see the white wing of a fly thirty yards out on a mostly black river filled with the shifting dull silver bumps of the current.

I have tied night flies—big, bushy, all-black hair-wing jobs, often with a thin silver tinsel rib on the body because I think that looks elegant—but I never make very many and they're the last ones I replace when the fly boxes are getting low, so I'm often caught without them. I tied on the big Trude be-cause it was the closest thing I had to what I wanted. Then I turned off the little flashlight and stood for a few minutes to let my eyes get accustomed to the darkness again. I felt the wings of a bug tickle my cheek just above the beard and tried to picture the air filled with caddis flies and the water boiling with trout.

I listened for it, but all I could make out was water moving. I did once hear a caddis hatch at night. The flies were large, the night was still and the river was slow and quiet. There was a soft hum with liquid blips in it and the slicing of bats' wings. It was very much like the sound I once heard, years ago, after being hit very hard in the face by a guy with whom I had a small misunderstanding.

A few minutes later I hooked and landed one modest-sized trout. I think it was a brown and I think it was about a foot long, although I can't be sure on either count because I hand-landed it and released it by feel. You don't want to use the flashlight unless you have to because every time you turn it off again you are lost and blinded for a while.

I couldn't remember why I'd set the hook on that fish. It wasn't dumb luck, though, because I could recall hearing that internal command: "Set now." I could fish for another fifty years and never get used to the surprise of guessing right.

I thought surely the caddis hatch was going good. Now and then other flies brushed my face or the backs of my hands or bopped my canvas hat, and when you extrapolate that to thousands of cubic feet of cool, summer air over one of the best trout rivers in the state, you have to imagine the hatch of a lifetime. But you do have to imagine it.

Sometime later I made a short cast upstream and heard a splash more or less in that direction. It was not a sound the current had made in the last couple of hours. I raised the rod tip and, sure enough, there was the weight of a fish. At a time like that you naturally wonder how many strikes you didn't hear.

This seemed like a heavy trout, but it was hard to tell for sure because he immediately bored out into the fast water and took off downstream, peeling line from the reel. I may have shouted something because the sheepdog across the river started to bark.

I was using an eight-and-a-half-foot, six-weight rod with

a weight forward 7 line, something stout for the possible large trout, and the kind of rod you can get away with at night when delicacy isn't an issue. This is an old favorite rod and I thought I could judge the weight of the trout by the heft of it, but in fast current like that you usually feel more water than fish.

Moments like this have a familiar resonance that seems to go beyond what's happening right then, and I wish I could hand the rod to one of those people who ask, "What *is* it that gets you guys so cranked up about fishing, anyway?"

The fish is out there somewhere, one of many, but this one is now potentially yours. It has a mind of its own, but, although you haven't captured it yet, you have a tentative grip on it. You know what it is, but there's still a lot you don't know. It's *probably* a trout, although it could be a whitefish, in which case there will be some disappointment. At this point you can only guess at its size and weight.

Here is a thing you want—at the moment, it's a fish, but this exact same feeling could be about love, success, long life or whatever. You have hold of it with a good rod and a big enough hook, but you can't see what you're doing and you know it's not going to come to you like a puppy.

I let the fish run downstream and carefully eased him out of the current into the quieter water near the bank. When the weight of the river went off the line, there still seemed to be a lot left. Then, trying to keep the line tight, I stumbled and felt my way down to him.

When I got close he shot out into the current again and made another wide loop downstream. I tried to stay out of the water to make better time, but feeling along in the dark puts you at about the same pace as wading, so it didn't make much difference. My right foot would splash shallow water, and then five steps farther on my left shoulder would be brushed by willow leaves, so I knew I was weaving.

I thought I was getting close to the big pool at the bottom

of that cliff, and I knew that if the fish ran downstream from
there I wouldn't be able to follow and probably couldn't
winch him back up through the current. I tried to feel the
shape of the bank curving out, but I didn't know exactly
where the bank was. There was a riffle at the head of that
bend pool that I thought I should hear when I got close. I
didn't hear it, so maybe it was still okay. Then again, I didn't
know how far out the fish was.

I felt my reel to try to see how much line was left on it,
but it was hard to picture. Some, maybe lots.

The fish let himself be played back against the bank again.
I couldn't hear the riffle and I hadn't felt the rush of it in the
line, so I knew he was in slack water where I could get at
him. I waded down—I was in the water, although I didn't remember getting in—and fumbled for the net when the angle of the line seemed to indicate the fish was more or less
at my feet.

I made a mess of netting him, thinking I knew where he
was, only to come up two or three times with a dripping but
empty landing net. I finally managed it with the rod in my
left hand, net in my right and the flashlight in my teeth.

It was a brown trout, not a bright, golden yellow one, but
a washed-out, older fish; brownish ochre on the back shading to an almost bluish silver with big black spots. He'd
fought like a five-pounder, but in the net he looked and felt
more like four. And, yes, weight and length change at night,
too. Maybe he was more like twenty inches and a fat three
pounds, but he was my fish and it hurt a little to let him go.

I was stumbling back upstream, thinking I could keep fishing the dry fly, switch to the biggest black Woolly Bugger
streamer I had or quit while I was ahead. A nice big fish can
seem like a proper end to things, especially when it's well
past midnight and you've been fishing since seven o'clock
on what would now be *yesterday* morning.

Then I ran into one of my hosts, who was wading downstream looking for me. He was a big shape with a hat and I

couldn't tell who it was until he spoke. He asked how I'd done.

"I got a nice one," I said, and he didn't ask how nice, knowing that this isn't always easy to explain. Instead he said, "Do you remember where the trail back to the car is?"

18

One Fish

I want to tell you about one fish I caught recently. I'll be bragging here, but I feel I deserve that. It's so seldom I get everything right.

This happened on a river in Colorado during a great Pale Morning Dun mayfly hatch. There's a stretch of braided

pocket water a few miles downstream from a catch and release area that's known to guides and locals as Old Faithful,
not so much because the fishing is easy, but because the
hatches are good there and trout rise dependably.

I was on the river with Steve Binder and Ed Engle, and the
first day we fished the Old Faithful stretch I spent an hour
or so in a spot I knew to be especially difficult. I guess I
could say I took the hard spot and left the easier stretches
for my two friends, but that would be misleading.

The thing is, there's a secret hidden in difficult water. It's
hard to fish, but because of that a lot of people pass it up
and a lot of other people fish it poorly and catch nothing.
Consequently, if you can get a good cast in there and a reasonable drift, the fish are actually—in a convoluted sort of
way—pretty easy to hook. And there's also a fair chance
they'll be big, strong, healthy and unscarred.

This spot has a wide, dangerously fast, thigh-deep rip on
the near side, a long, narrow tongue of slower current beyond that where the flow is broken by a big, red rock, then
another rip and then a complicated plunge pool where three
separate currents spill in, one fast and deep, the others
smaller and slower.

I'd learned in past years that if you could wade out far
enough in the rip, you could throw a slack cast with an upstream mend into that first narrow glide and get a good dry
fly drift. I'd also learned that this was worth doing because
lots of trout would stack up in there during a hatch.

So I did that, caught four or five trout and missed or
spooked twice that many more. Then I got to looking at the
plunge pool on the far side of the river that, for some reason, I'd never paid much attention to before. There were
some mayflies floating on the surface over there and every
now and then—if you stood and watched long enough—a
large head would show in one place or another as what
looked like a pod of several large trout ate the flies.

It was the kind of spot that looked impossible, calling for
a long cast that would have to loop the line upstream and

then down in half a dozen places and then pile two feet of leader to allow a dry fly to dead-drift six inches or so. You've seen places like that on trout streams before. The currents are so complex and confused that the water sometimes seems to stand still and tremble, not knowing where to go next, but in fact it's moving very fast.

I could see that if I got over to the far side of the rip it would be a little easier, but I'd already waded out as far as I could get without being washed downstream, and even where I was, the footing was a little unsure.

I made the cast anyway, out of curiosity. It was the best snake-curve, multiple up-and-downstream hook, pile cast I could muster, but the fly ripped through the pool, leaving a wide wake and apparently spooking the fish. I stood there watching for a long time but, although the flies kept coming, there were no more rises.

The next day we got in the river a little farther upstream and, when the hatch began to come off, I headed down to my spot. The night before in camp—somewhere in the middle of a loud discussion about money, politics and the media—I'd told Ed and Steve about the fish and said I was going to get over there for a better cast even at the risk of drowning. (By the next morning, having developed a more rested, calculating kind of excitement about it, I thought maybe I'd find an easier place to cross.)

This, by the way, is the main difference between the guys you're with and strangers: You don't describe a place like this to someone you meet in a bar for fear that the next day you'll find him standing in your spot, but your friends will leave it for you—at least this one time.

While I was looking for a place to wade across and not locating an easy one, I found an old broom handle on the bank that someone had been using as a wading staff. Whoever had had this thing last had carved a crude notch around one end to hold a cord, and the other end was mashed where it had been pushed against wet rocks. No telling if they'd lost it or just thrown it away. I picked it up and showed it to Ed, who was just wading by at the time. He said matter-of-factly, "That is a gift from the gods."

So with the help of the stick I got over to the other side of the rip. It wasn't really that hard and I might have made it even without a staff. Then again, I might not have. I have this old bad knee that has made me a careful wader. It's kept me from some fish, but it's probably also saved my ass more than once.

When I got where I wanted to be, I saw that I'd been wrong about the pod of big trout. There was actually only one large, fat rainbow, and he was cruising around in what appreared to be random patterns in a pool roughly four or five yards square. The currents were even more conflicting and braided than they'd seemed from the other side of the river, but up close like that I could make shorter casts, keep more line off the water and stand a much better chance.

By this time the mayflies were roaring out of the current in the main channel and at least a dozen trout were rising steadily, but back in the plunge pool there were only a few of them at any one time, so this big trout was cruising widely. He'd take a fly and then noodle around the pool looking for another one. You could tell when he saw a bug because he'd straighten out purposefully and glide over to take it. He seemed to be able to spot them from as far away as two feet.

All I could do was keep my fly in the air by false casting, wait for the fish to rise, see which direction he headed in next and then try to put the fly in front of him. I knew he'd spook if the fly started to drag, so just before the currents grabbed my leader on every cast, I'd have to pick it up, even if the fish was heading right for it.

The trout was wandering all around the pool, and as often as not he'd be in a spot where I didn't think I could get a fair drift. When he worked his way into a relatively easy spot, I'd put the fly down for a few seconds. The rest of the time I just stood there false casting and remembering my uncle Leonard saying, "If you wanna catch fish, you gotta have your hook in the water."

Without going into even more detail, I'll just say that after I don't know how long it all came together, the fish ate the fly and I hooked him. He fought beautifully, jumping once and making a couple of what would have been reel-screaming runs except that I was fishing with a Peerless fly reel that doesn't scream so much as it purrs.

I didn't measure the fish, but I'll guess him at a heavy nineteen or maybe even twenty inches. I took a quick snapshot and released him. He seemed tired, but okay. Then I waded over to a convenient rock and sat down for a while. Catching a big, difficult trout after two days is the kind of thing you have to get straight about.

At first it's a glorious rush of egotism and you begin to feel like death from above. Then you allow that, although you *are* getting to be a pretty damned good fisherman, there was still that element of dumb luck about it. A dozen things could have conspired against getting the right drift at the moment the fish was there to see it, and even then he might have decided he didn't like the fly or he might have taken a natural right next to it. In other words, the spiritually profitable attitude here is not pride but humility.

Of course, wondering how you should feel about this gets you into the area of why you fish in the first place. That's always been an interesting question to me, but I'm beginning to think the only people who really care are a handful of writers and some idly curious nonanglers. The fishermen who don't worry about it are the ones who seem to be having the most fun.

Maybe fishermen are more like cowboys than they appear to be. I've just been reading *The Muddy Fork & Other Things*, in which author James Crumly says that a cowboy is just someone who got up on a horse and never learned how to get down. In this case, it would be a guy who caught a fish one day, thought it was pretty neat, and that was that: no mystique, no real reason.

Or maybe it's some kind of stubborn, unreasoning pride. Fishermen certainly have that, and Crumly says that the cow-

boys he knows eventually ended up with skin cancer, crip-
pling arthritis, broken bones and no money, but, "They pitied
everybody who couldn't live the cowboy life."

It's tempting to launch a psycho-sociological theory here
about the fly fisher as cowboy in modern American sporting
mythology, but then my old friend A.K. says the proper response to hooking a big, difficult trout is the most primitive
one you're capable of, or, as he puts it, "Me fool fish."

So maybe what you should do when you catch a great
trout is go back to camp and make a pot of coffee because
there will not be a bigger or better fish today. Sooner or later
your partners will wander in and you can tell them all about
it. That's your reward: a potentially great story that you may
be able to tell well.